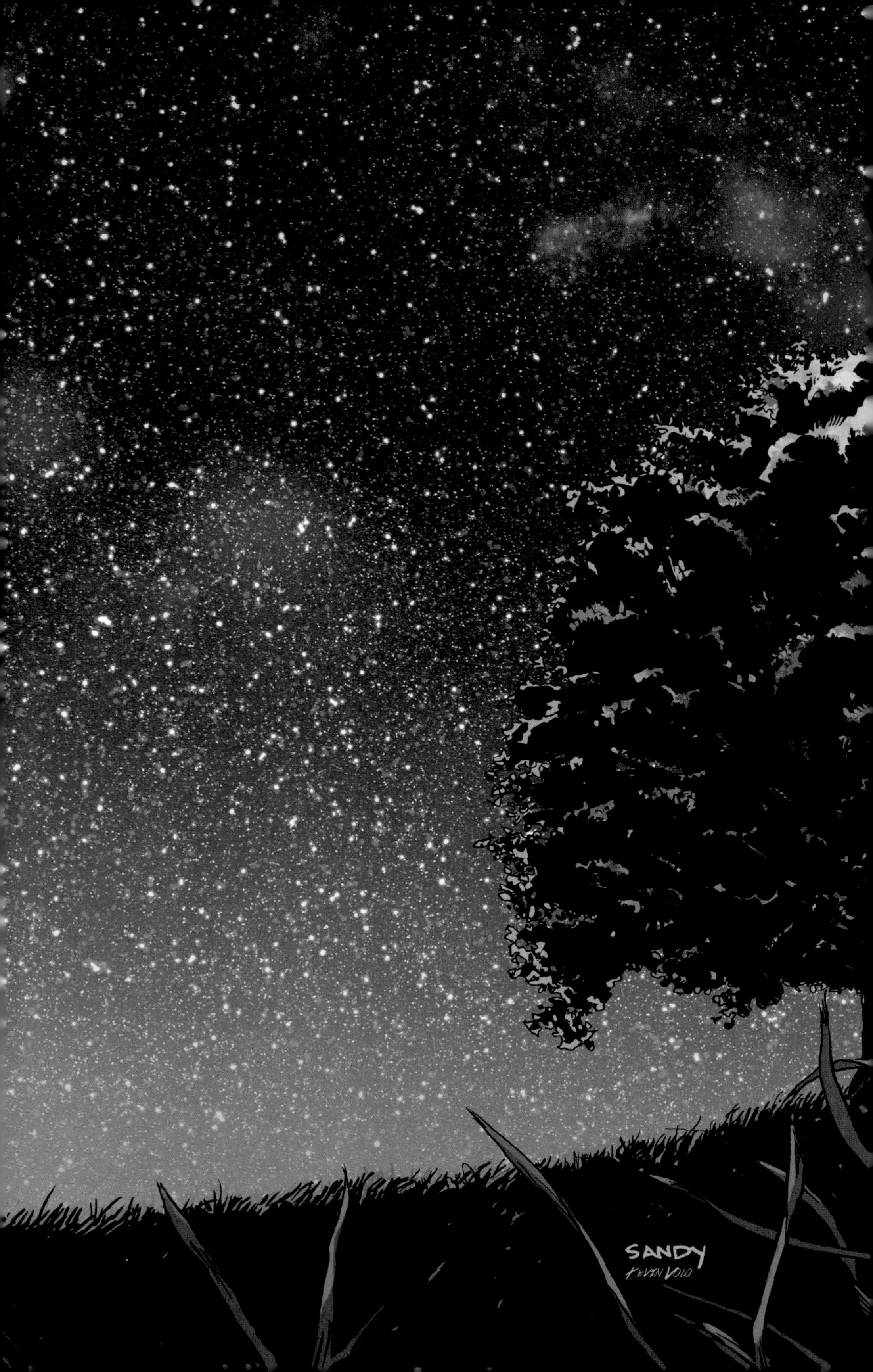

SANDY
Kevin Volo

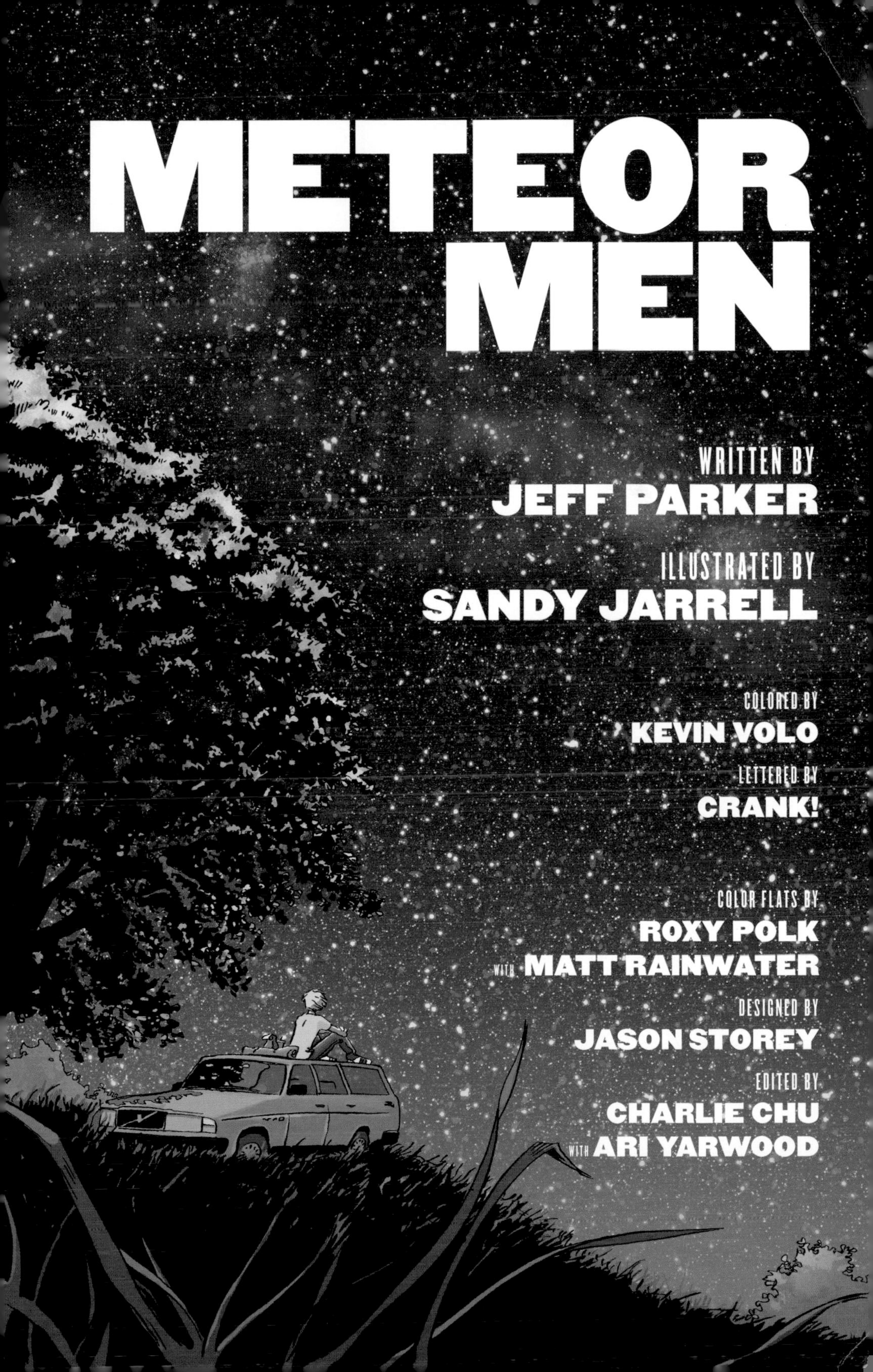

METEOR MEN

WRITTEN BY
JEFF PARKER

ILLUSTRATED BY
SANDY JARRELL

COLORED BY
KEVIN VOLO

LETTERED BY
CRANK!

COLOR FLATS BY
ROXY POLK
WITH **MATT RAINWATER**

DESIGNED BY
JASON STOREY

EDITED BY
CHARLIE CHU
WITH **ARI YARWOOD**

METEOR MEN

PUBLISHED BY ONI PRESS, INC.

JOE NOZEMACK, PUBLISHER

JAMES LUCAS JONES, EDITOR IN CHIEF

CHEYENNE ALLOTT, DIRECTOR OF SALES

JOHN SCHORK, DIRECTOR OR MARKETING

TROY LOOK, PRODUCTION MANAGER

JASON STOREY, SENIOR DESIGNER

CHARLIE CHU, EDITOR

ROBIN HERRERA, ASSOCIATE EDITOR

BRAD ROOKS, INVENTORY COORDINATOR

ARI YARWOOD, ADMINISTRATIVE ASSISTANT

JUNG LEE, OFFICE ASSISTANT

JARED JONES, PRODUCTION ASSISTANT

ONI PRESS, INC.
1305 SE MARTIN LUTHER KING JR. BLVD
SUITE A
PORTLAND, OR 97214

ONIPRESS.COM
FACEBOOK.COM/ONIPRESS • TWITTER.COM/ONIPRESS
ONIPRESS.TUMBLR.COM • INSTAGRAM.COM/ONIPRESS

PARKERSPACE.COM • @JEFFPARKER
SANDYJARRELL.COM • @SANDY_JARRELL
ENIGMAMEDIAGROUP • @KEVINVOLO

FIRST EDITION: OCTOBER 2014

ISBN: 978-1-62010-151-3 • eISBN: 978-1-62010-152-0

LIBRARY OF CONGRESS CONTROL NUMBER: 2014934910

2 3 4 5 6 7 8 9 10

PRINTED IN CHINA.

TO MY OWN STELLAR EVENT
JILL, WHO WOULD NEVER BRING
ABOUT THE END OF MANKIND.

-JEFF PARKER

TO KAREN FOR HER ENDLESS
ENCOURAGEMENT AND SUPPORT,
TO VALERIE FOR HUGS AND STUFF,
TO RAYMOND FOR LOANING ALDEN
HIS HAIR, TO VANCE FOR MAKING ME
BETTER AT COMICS, AND TO PARKER
FOR BEING A TOTAL U.F.BRO.

-SANDY JARRELL

TO MY AMAZING SON MAX AND
EQUALLY AMAZING WIFE JUDY.

-KEVIN VOLO

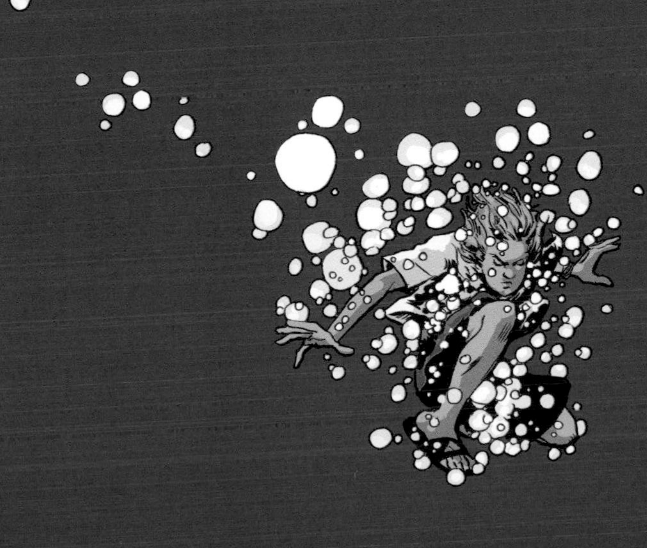

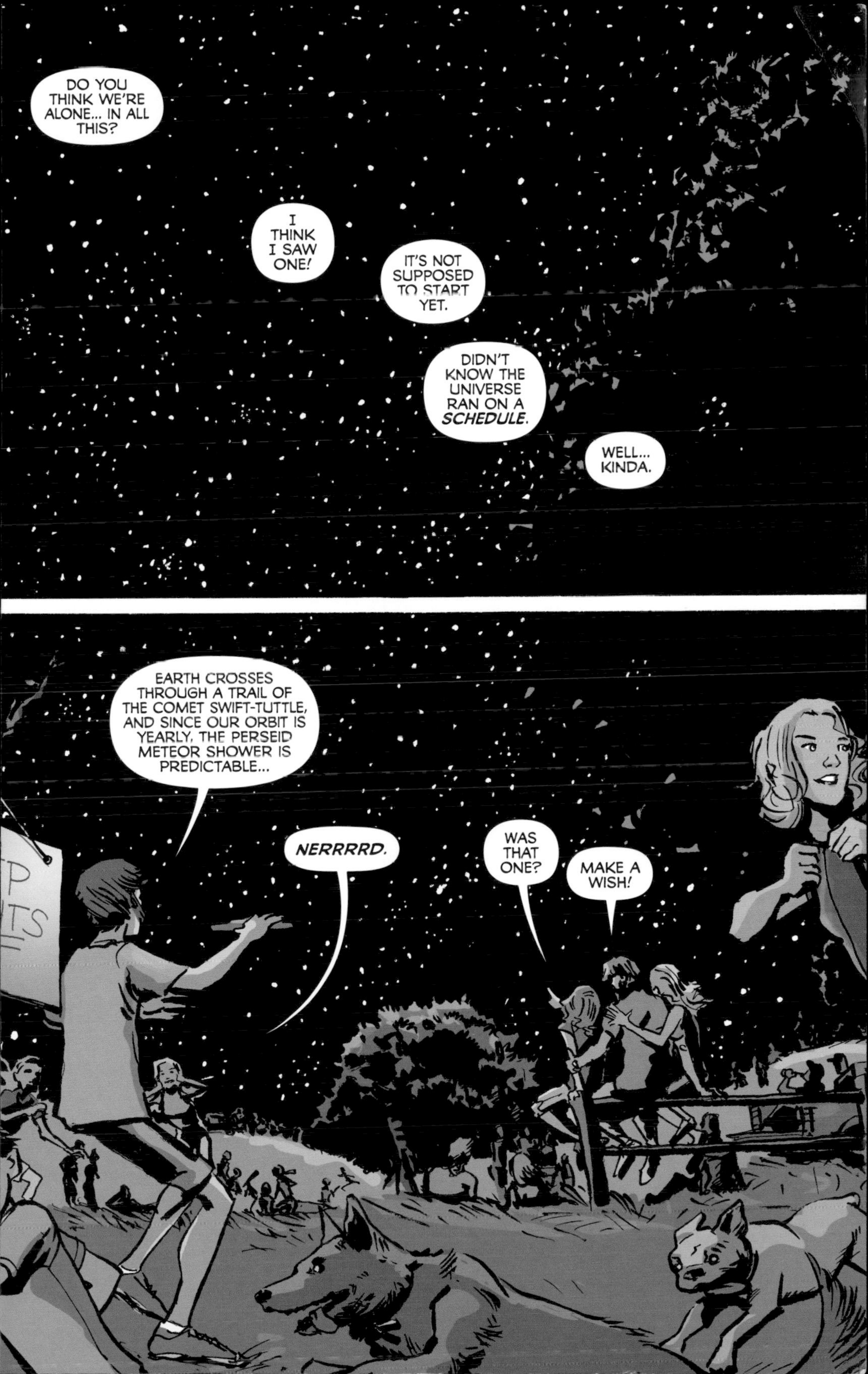
DO YOU THINK WE'RE ALONE... IN ALL THIS?
I THINK I SAW ONE!
IT'S NOT SUPPOSED TO START YET.
DIDN'T KNOW THE UNIVERSE RAN ON A *SCHEDULE*.
WELL... KINDA.
EARTH CROSSES THROUGH A TRAIL OF THE COMET SWIFT-TUTTLE, AND SINCE OUR ORBIT IS YEARLY, THE PERSEID METEOR SHOWER IS PREDICTABLE...
NERRRRD.
WAS THAT ONE?
MAKE A WISH!

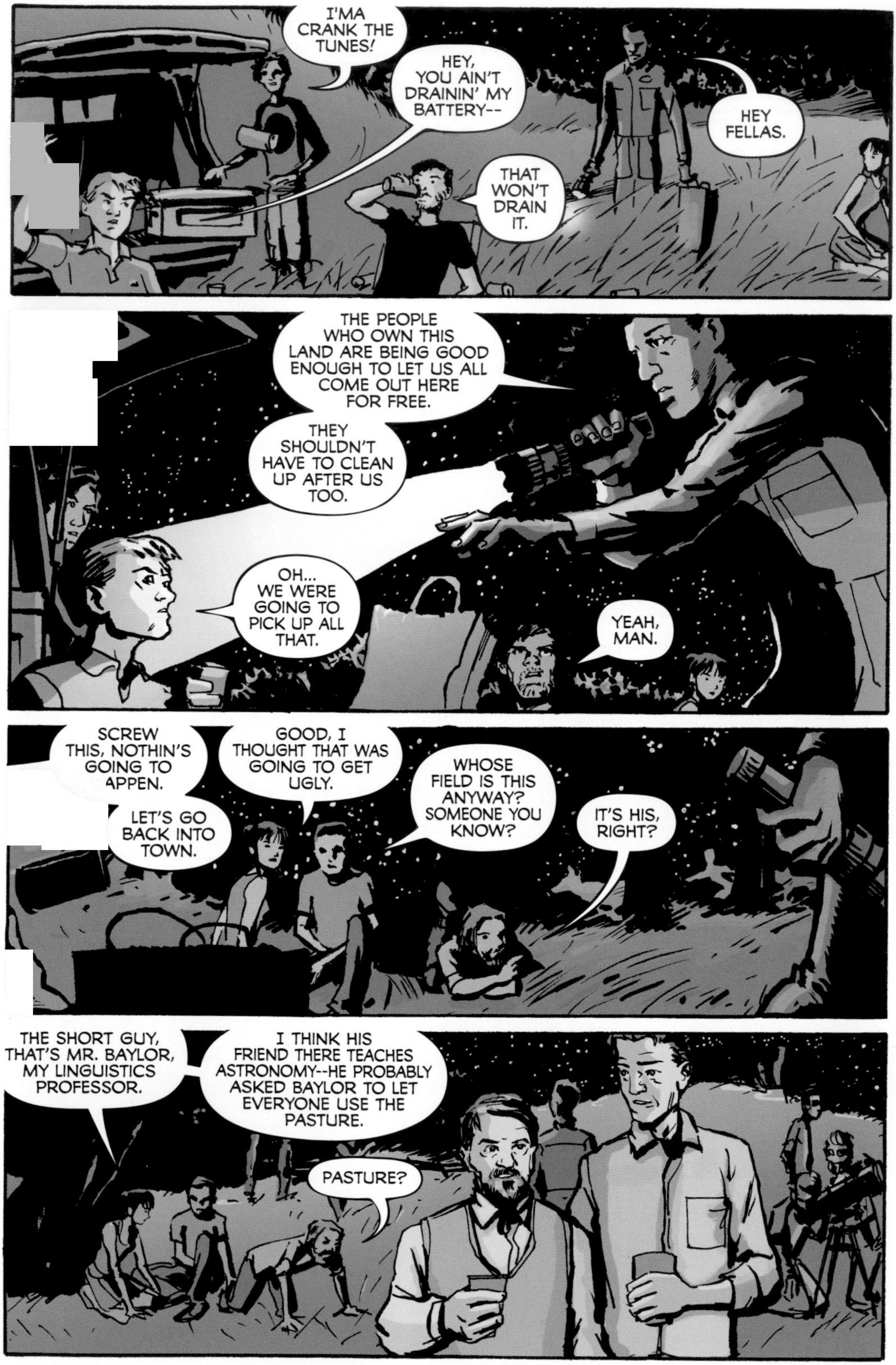
I'MA CRANK THE TUNES!
HEY, YOU AIN'T DRAININ' MY BATTERY--
THAT WON'T DRAIN IT.
HEY FELLAS.
THE PEOPLE WHO OWN THIS LAND ARE BEING GOOD ENOUGH TO LET US ALL COME OUT HERE FOR FREE.
THEY SHOULDN'T HAVE TO CLEAN UP AFTER US TOO.
OH... WE WERE GOING TO PICK UP ALL THAT.
YEAH, MAN.
SCREW THIS, NOTHIN'S GOING TO APPEN.
LET'S GO BACK INTO TOWN.
GOOD, I THOUGHT THAT WAS GOING TO GET UGLY.
WHOSE FIELD IS THIS ANYWAY? SOMEONE YOU KNOW?
IT'S HIS, RIGHT?
THE SHORT GUY, THAT'S MR. BAYLOR, MY LINGUISTICS PROFESSOR.
I THINK HIS FRIEND THERE TEACHES ASTRONOMY--HE PROBABLY ASKED BAYLOR TO LET EVERYONE USE THE PASTURE.
PASTURE?

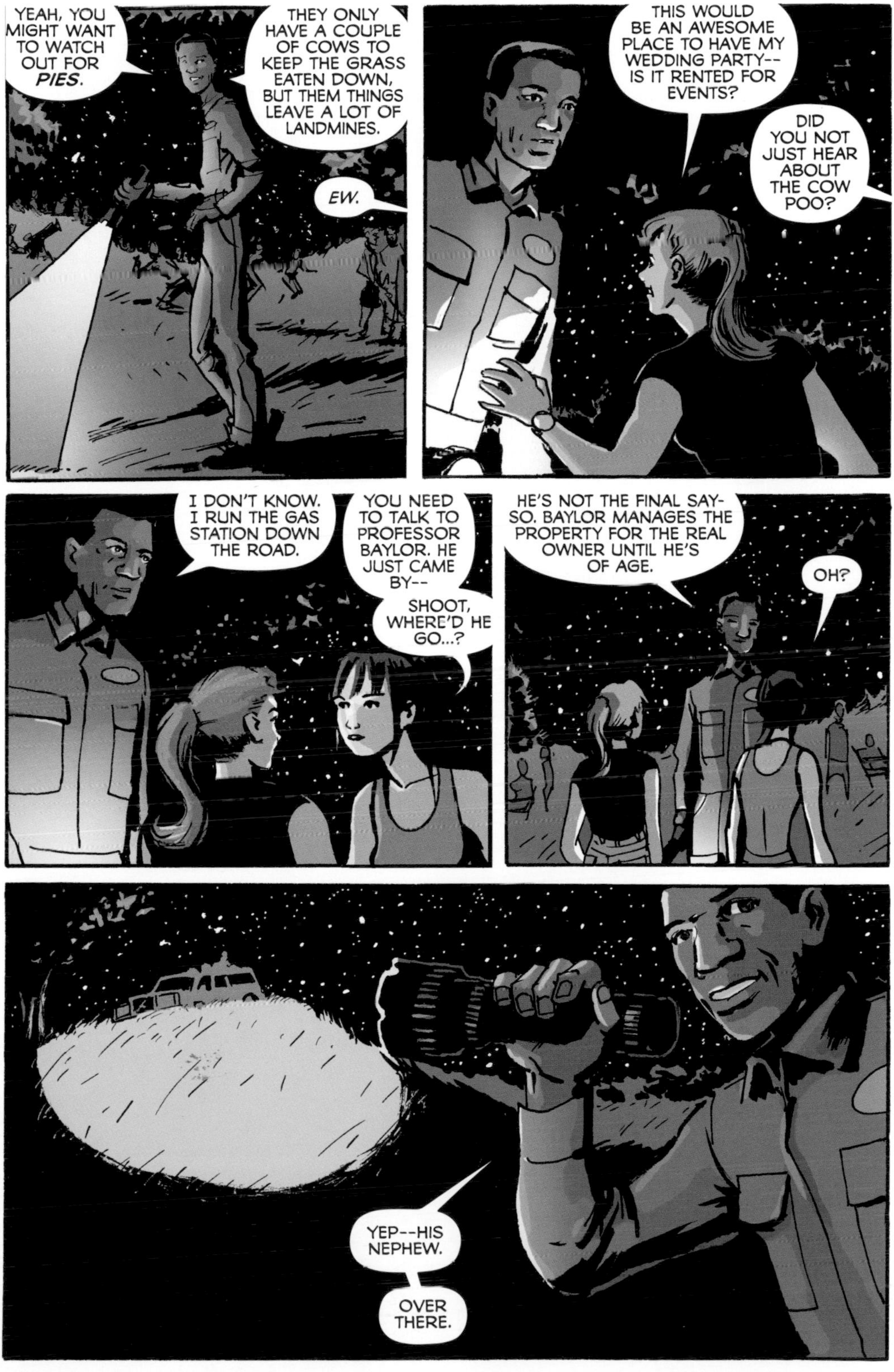
YEAH, YOU MIGHT WANT TO WATCH OUT FOR *PIES*.
THEY ONLY HAVE A COUPLE OF COWS TO KEEP THE GRASS EATEN DOWN, BUT THEM THINGS LEAVE A LOT OF LANDMINES.
EW.
THIS WOULD BE AN AWESOME PLACE TO HAVE MY WEDDING PARTY-- IS IT RENTED FOR EVENTS?
DID YOU NOT JUST HEAR ABOUT THE COW POO?
I DON'T KNOW. I RUN THE GAS STATION DOWN THE ROAD.
YOU NEED TO TALK TO PROFESSOR BAYLOR. HE JUST CAME BY--
SHOOT, WHERE'D HE GO...?
HE'S NOT THE FINAL SAY-SO. BAYLOR MANAGES THE PROPERTY FOR THE REAL OWNER UNTIL HE'S OF AGE.
OH?
YEP--HIS NEPHEW.
OVER THERE.

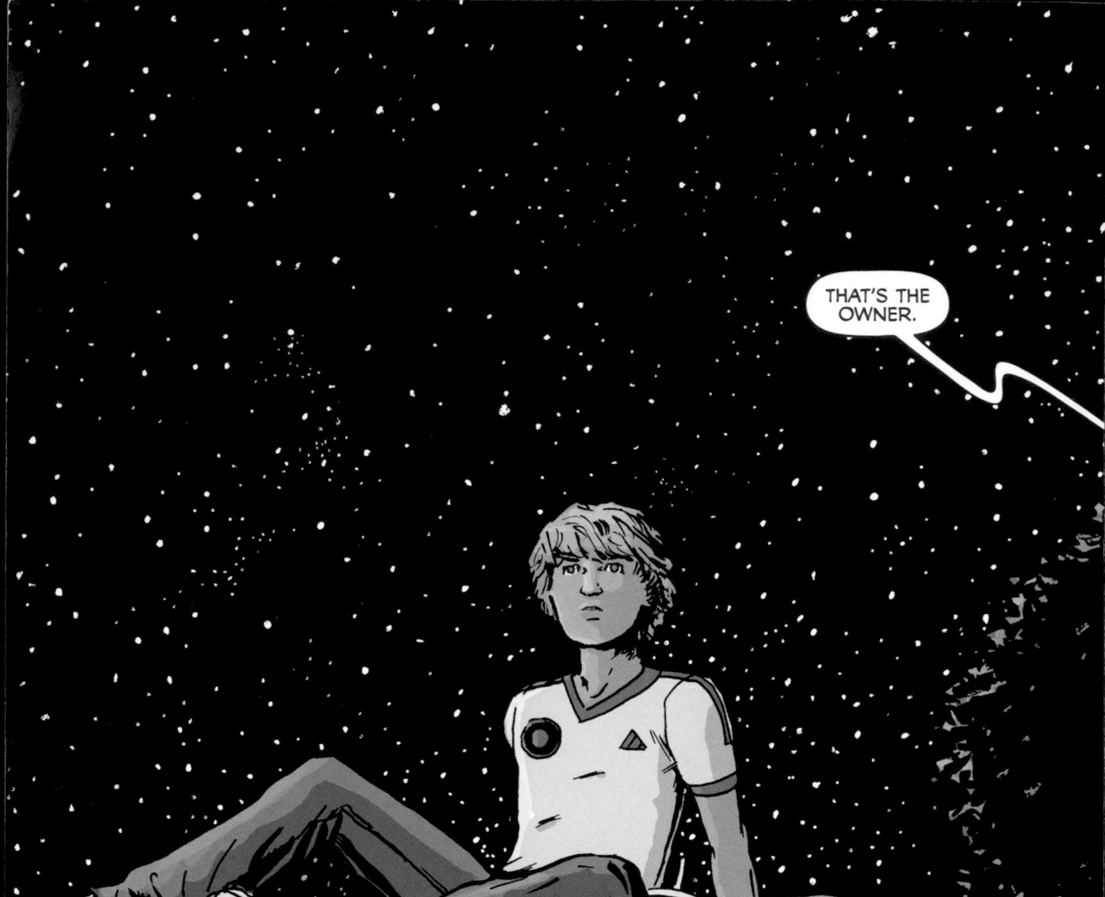
THAT'S THE OWNER.

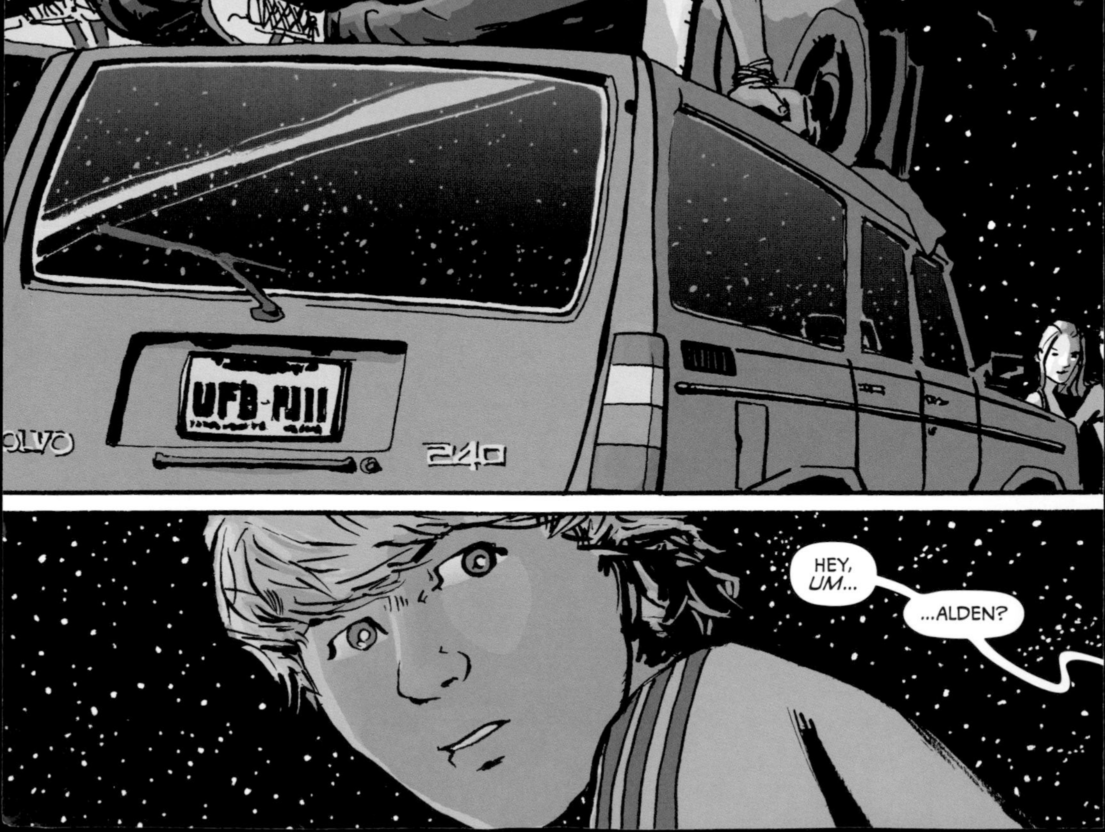
HEY, *UM*...
...ALDEN?

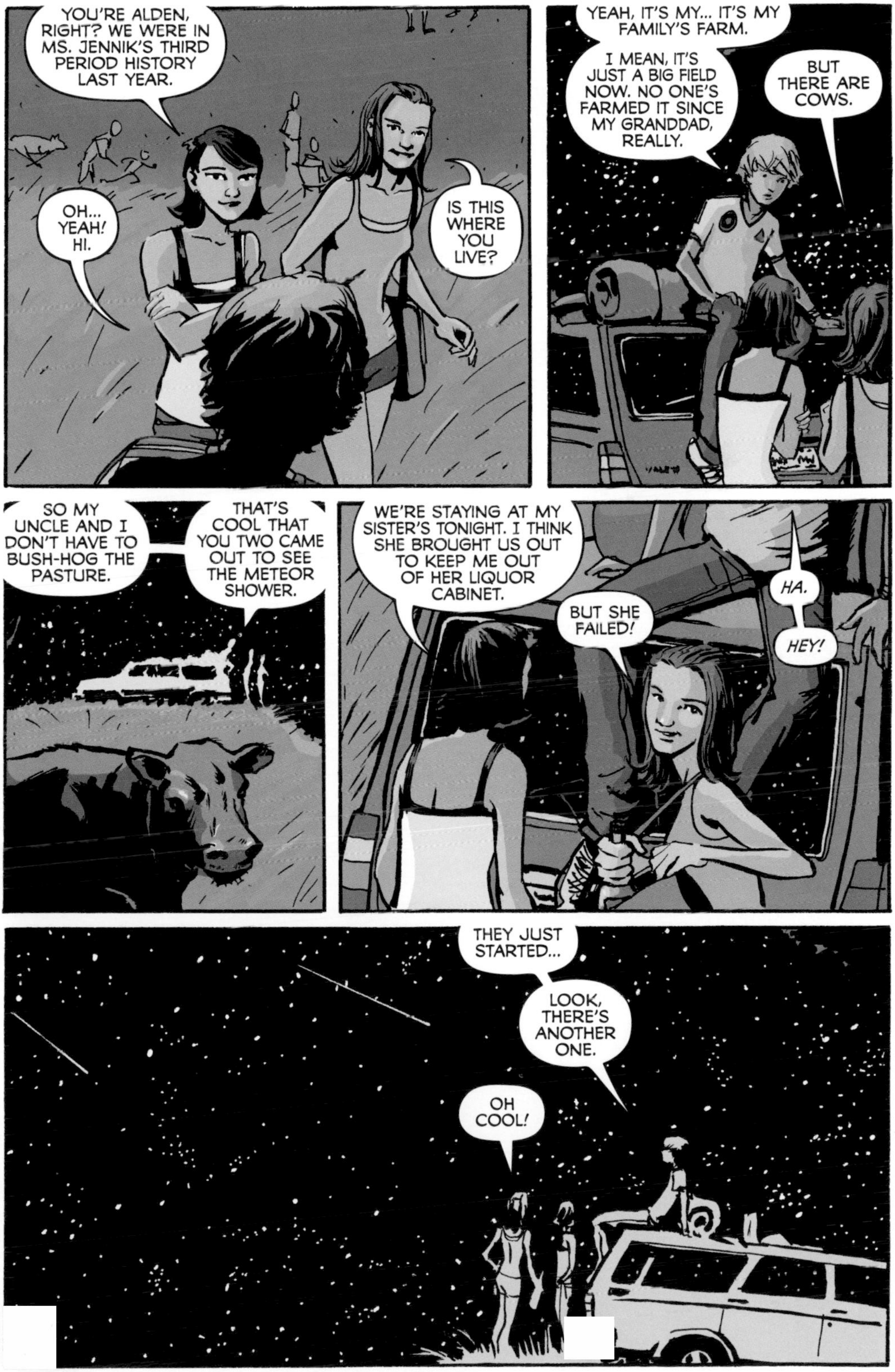
YOU'RE ALDEN, RIGHT? WE WERE IN MS. JENNIK'S THIRD PERIOD HISTORY LAST YEAR.
OH... YEAH! HI.
IS THIS WHERE YOU LIVE?
YEAH, IT'S MY... IT'S MY FAMILY'S FARM.
I MEAN, IT'S JUST A BIG FIELD NOW. NO ONE'S FARMED IT SINCE MY GRANDDAD, REALLY.
BUT THERE ARE COWS.
SO MY UNCLE AND I DON'T HAVE TO BUSH-HOG THE PASTURE.
THAT'S COOL THAT YOU TWO CAME OUT TO SEE THE METEOR SHOWER.
WE'RE STAYING AT MY SISTER'S TONIGHT. I THINK SHE BROUGHT US OUT TO KEEP ME OUT OF HER LIQUOR CABINET.
BUT SHE FAILED!
HA.
HEY!
THEY JUST STARTED...
LOOK, THERE'S ANOTHER ONE.
OH COOL!

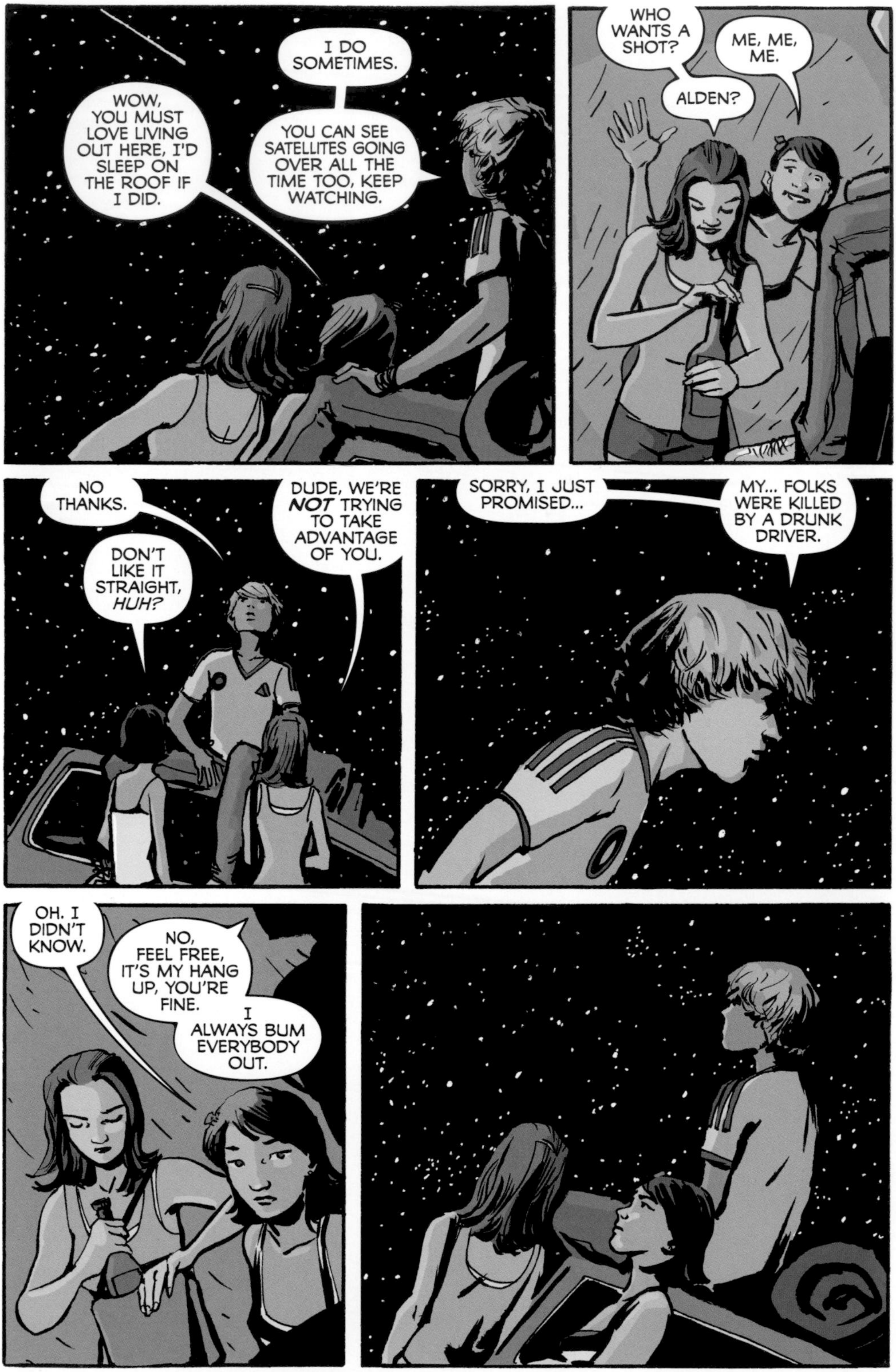
WOW, YOU MUST LOVE LIVING OUT HERE, I'D SLEEP ON THE ROOF IF I DID.
I DO SOMETIMES.
YOU CAN SEE SATELLITES GOING OVER ALL THE TIME TOO, KEEP WATCHING.
WHO WANTS A SHOT?
ME, ME, ME.
ALDEN?
NO THANKS.
DON'T LIKE IT STRAIGHT, *HUH?*
DUDE, WE'RE ***NOT*** TRYING TO TAKE ADVANTAGE OF YOU.
SORRY, I JUST PROMISED...
MY... FOLKS WERE KILLED BY A DRUNK DRIVER.
OH. I DIDN'T KNOW.
NO, FEEL FREE, IT'S MY HANG UP, YOU'RE FINE.
I ALWAYS BUM EVERYBODY OUT.

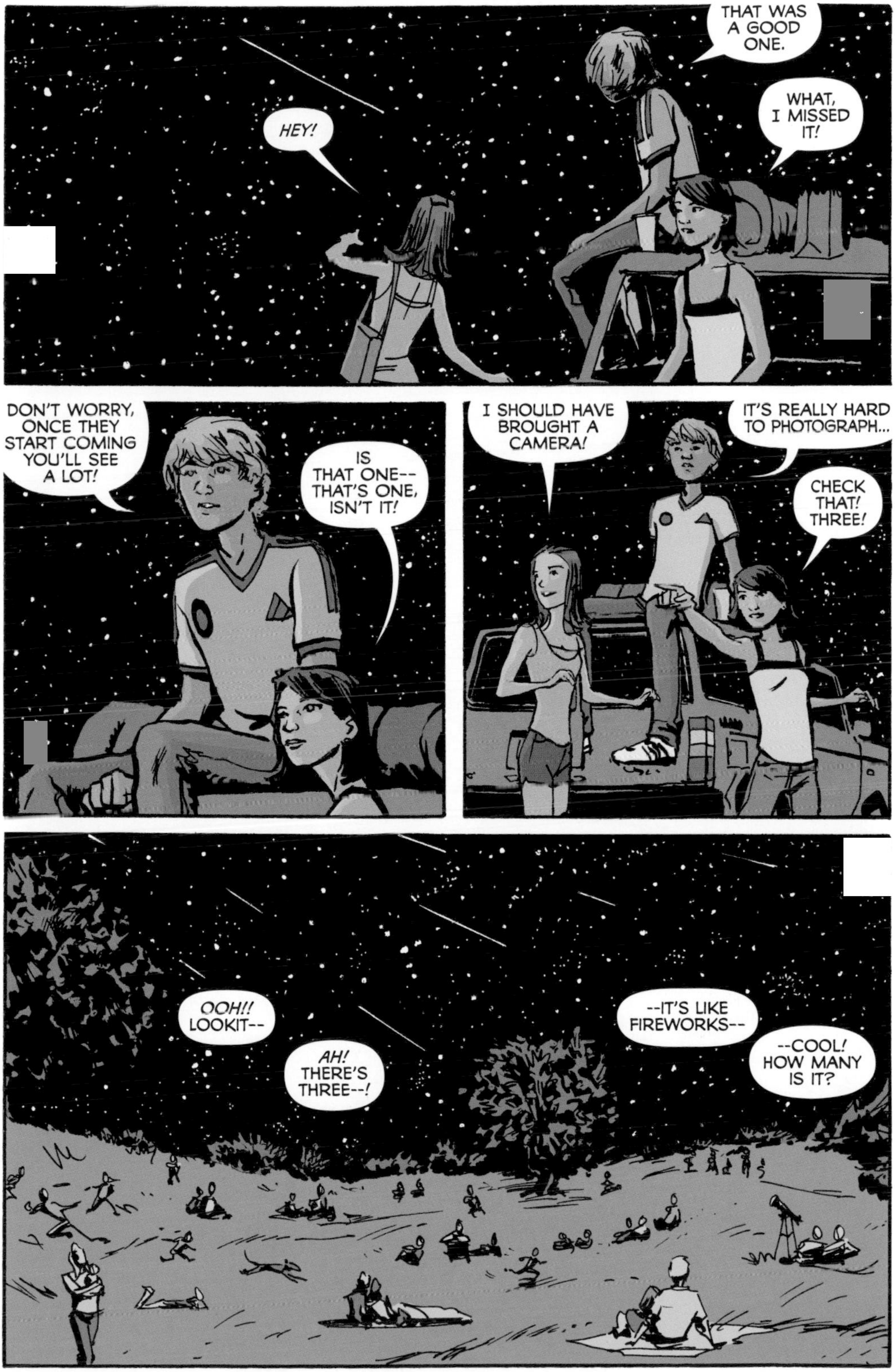
HEY!
THAT WAS A GOOD ONE.
WHAT, I MISSED IT!
DON'T WORRY, ONCE THEY START COMING YOU'LL SEE A LOT!
IS THAT ONE-- THAT'S ONE, ISN'T IT!
I SHOULD HAVE BROUGHT A CAMERA!
IT'S REALLY HARD TO PHOTOGRAPH...
CHECK THAT! THREE!
OOH!! LOOKIT--
AH! THERE'S THREE--!
--IT'S LIKE FIREWORKS--
--COOL! HOW MANY IS IT?

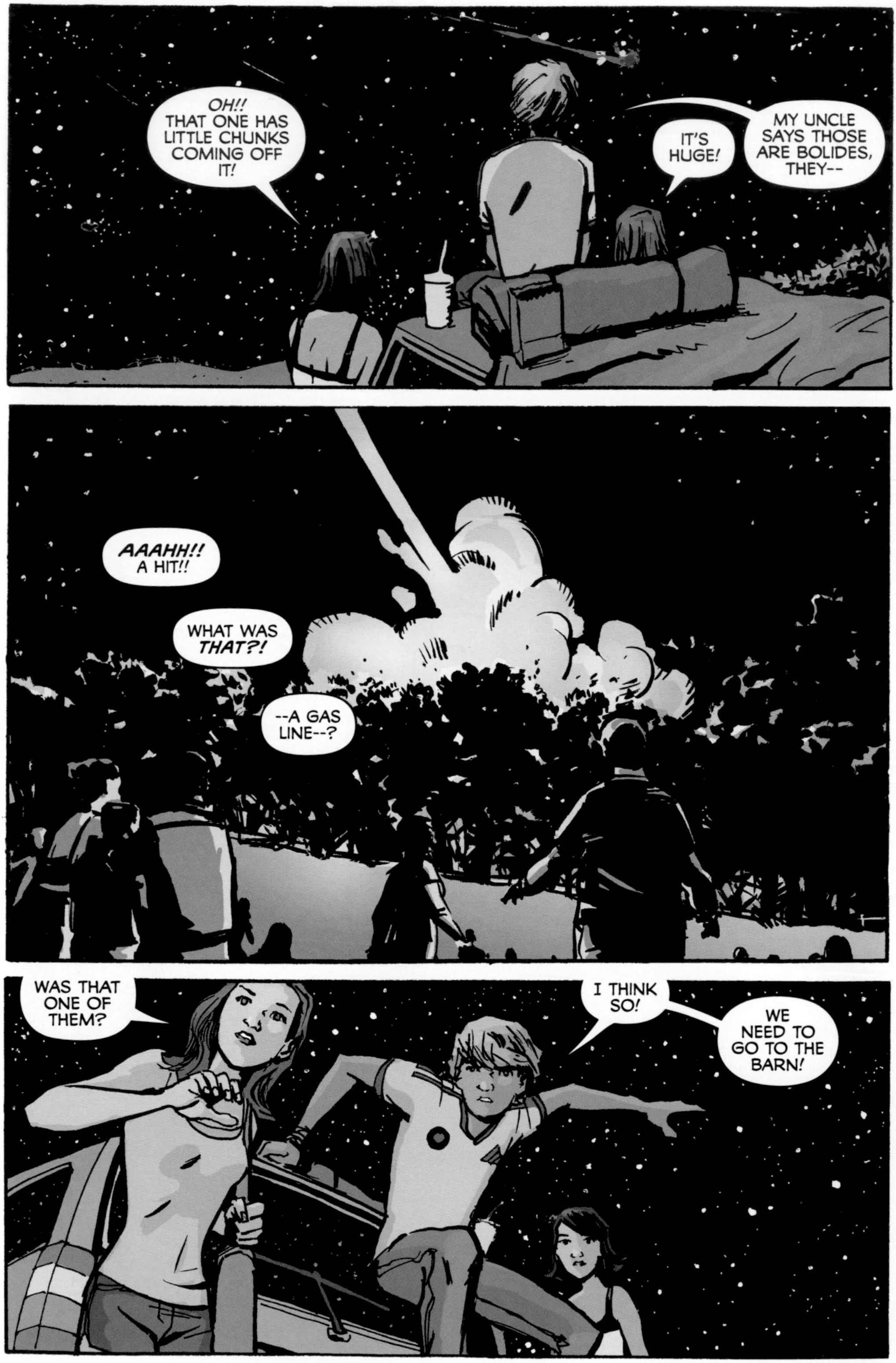
OH!! THAT ONE HAS LITTLE CHUNKS COMING OFF IT!
IT'S HUGE!
MY UNCLE SAYS THOSE ARE BOLIDES, THEY--
AAAHH!! A HIT!!
WHAT WAS THAT?!
--A GAS LINE--?
WAS THAT ONE OF THEM?
I THINK SO!
WE NEED TO GO TO THE BARN!

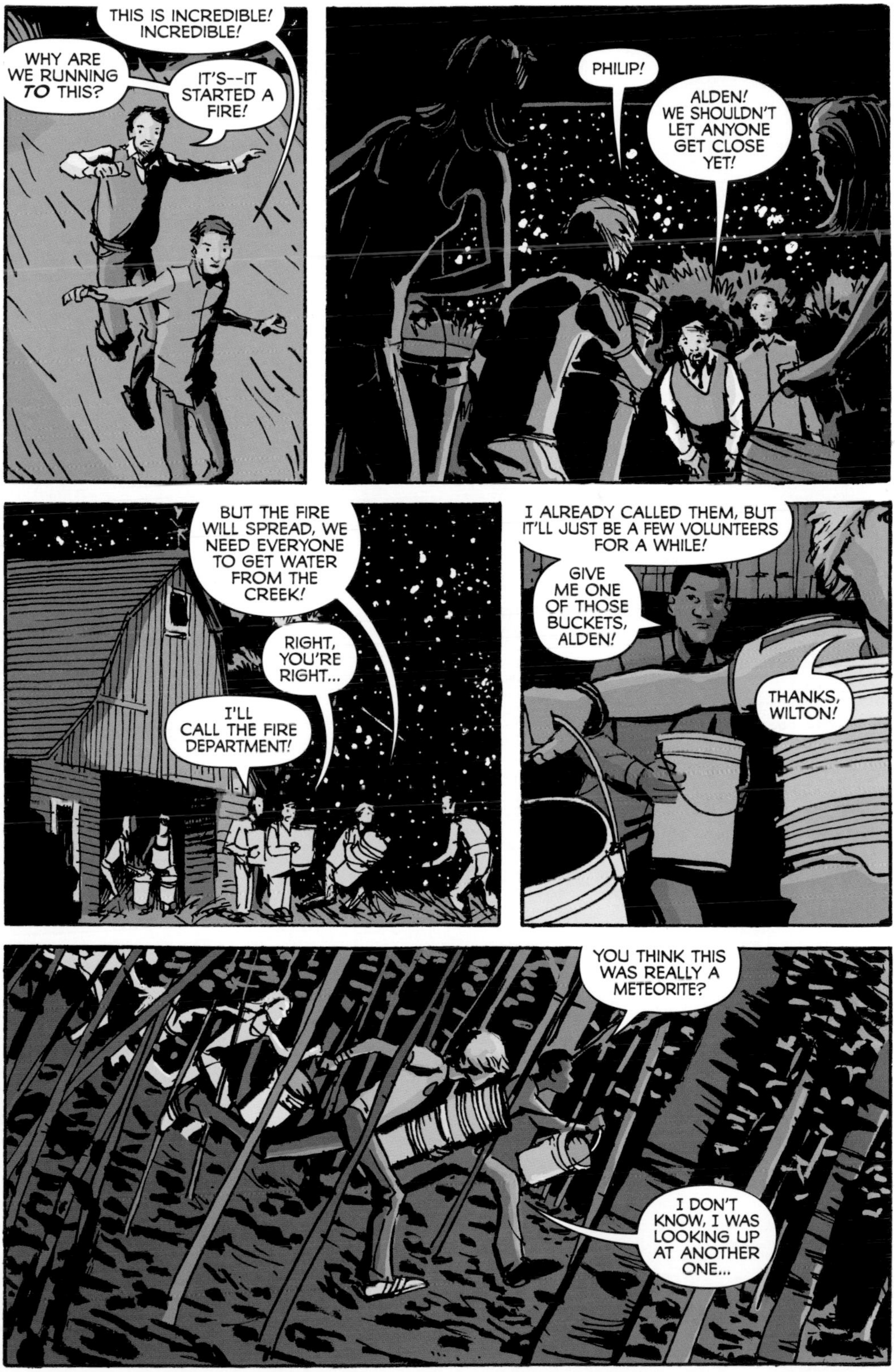
THIS IS INCREDIBLE! INCREDIBLE!
WHY ARE WE RUNNING *TO* THIS?
IT'S--IT STARTED A FIRE!
PHILIP!
ALDEN! WE SHOULDN'T LET ANYONE GET CLOSE YET!
BUT THE FIRE WILL SPREAD, WE NEED EVERYONE TO GET WATER FROM THE CREEK!
RIGHT, YOU'RE RIGHT...
I'LL CALL THE FIRE DEPARTMENT!
I ALREADY CALLED THEM, BUT IT'LL JUST BE A FEW VOLUNTEERS FOR A WHILE!
GIVE ME ONE OF THOSE BUCKETS, ALDEN!
THANKS, WILTON!
YOU THINK THIS WAS REALLY A METEORITE?
I DON'T KNOW, I WAS LOOKING UP AT ANOTHER ONE...

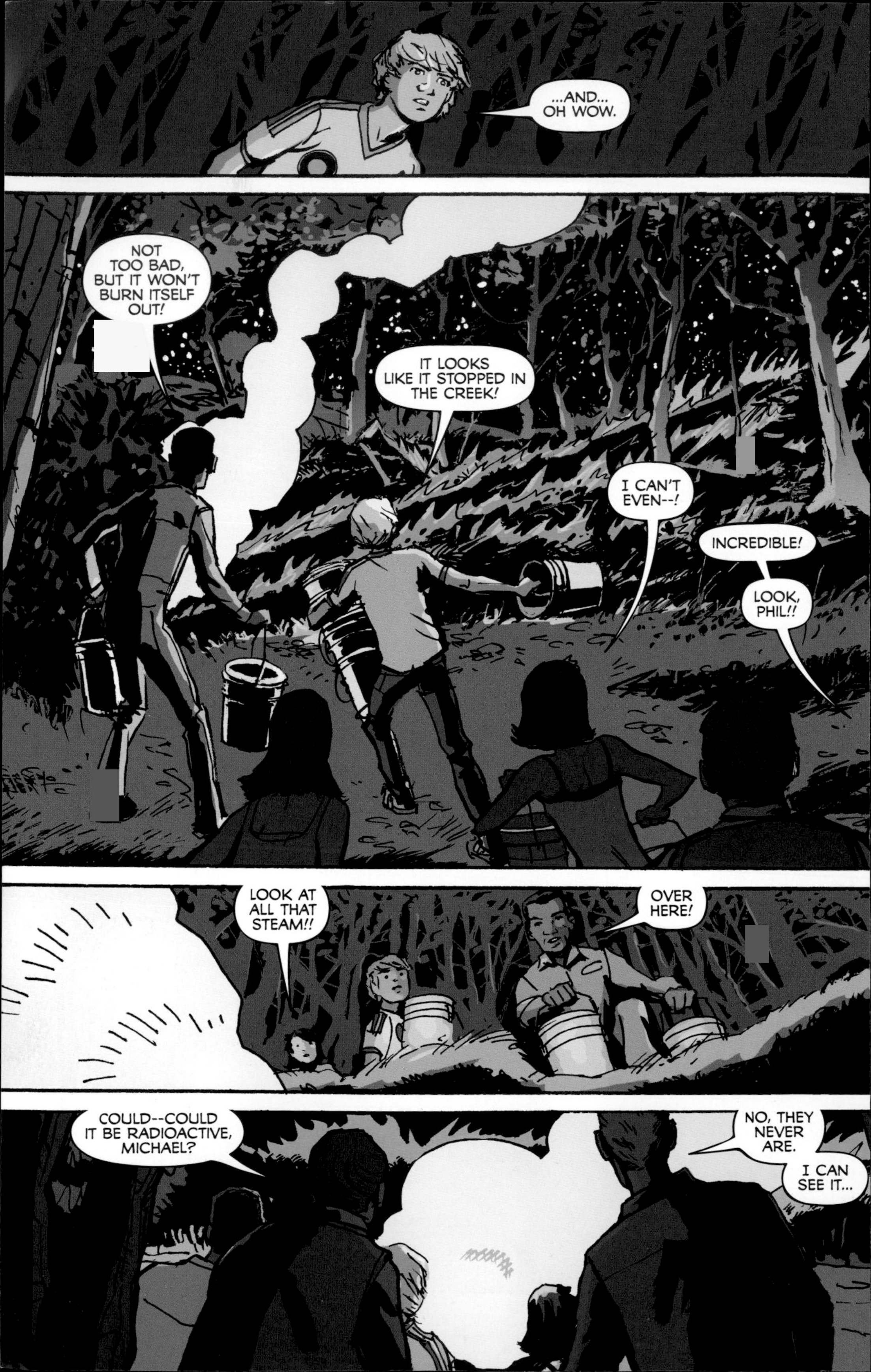
...AND... OH WOW.
NOT TOO BAD, BUT IT WON'T BURN ITSELF OUT!
IT LOOKS LIKE IT STOPPED IN THE CREEK!
I CAN'T EVEN--!
INCREDIBLE!
LOOK, PHIL!!
LOOK AT ALL THAT STEAM!!
OVER HERE!
COULD--COULD IT BE RADIOACTIVE, MICHAEL?
NO, THEY NEVER ARE.
I CAN SEE IT...

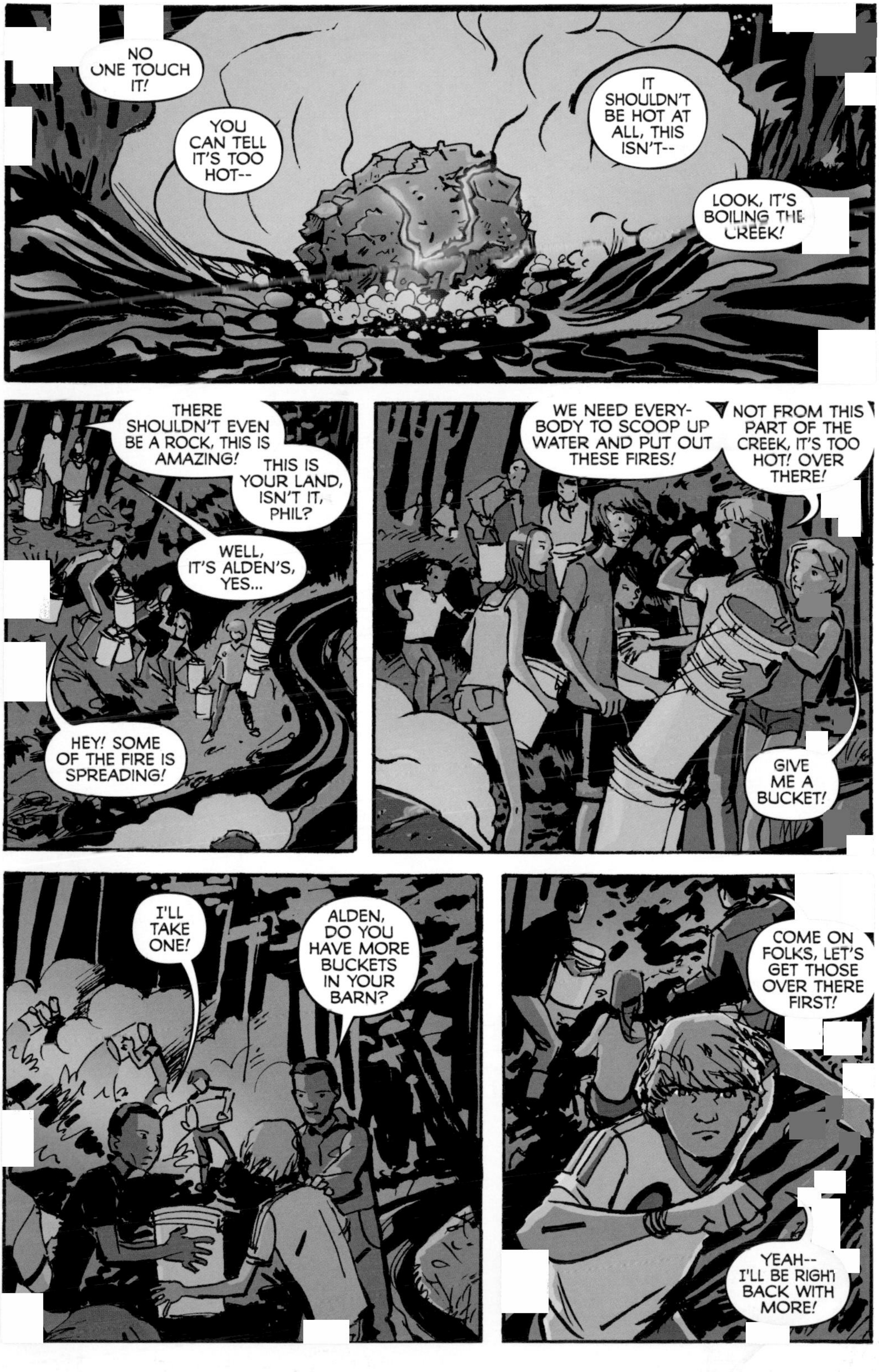
NO ONE TOUCH IT!
YOU CAN TELL IT'S TOO HOT--
IT SHOULDN'T BE HOT AT ALL, THIS ISN'T--
LOOK, IT'S BOILING THE CREEK!
THERE SHOULDN'T EVEN BE A ROCK, THIS IS AMAZING!
THIS IS YOUR LAND, ISN'T IT, PHIL?
WELL, IT'S ALDEN'S, YES...
HEY! SOME OF THE FIRE IS SPREADING!
WE NEED EVERY-BODY TO SCOOP UP WATER AND PUT OUT THESE FIRES!
NOT FROM THIS PART OF THE CREEK, IT'S TOO HOT! OVER THERE!
GIVE ME A BUCKET!
I'LL TAKE ONE!
ALDEN, DO YOU HAVE MORE BUCKETS IN YOUR BARN?
COME ON FOLKS, LET'S GET THOSE OVER THERE FIRST!
YEAH-- I'LL BE RIGHT BACK WITH MORE!

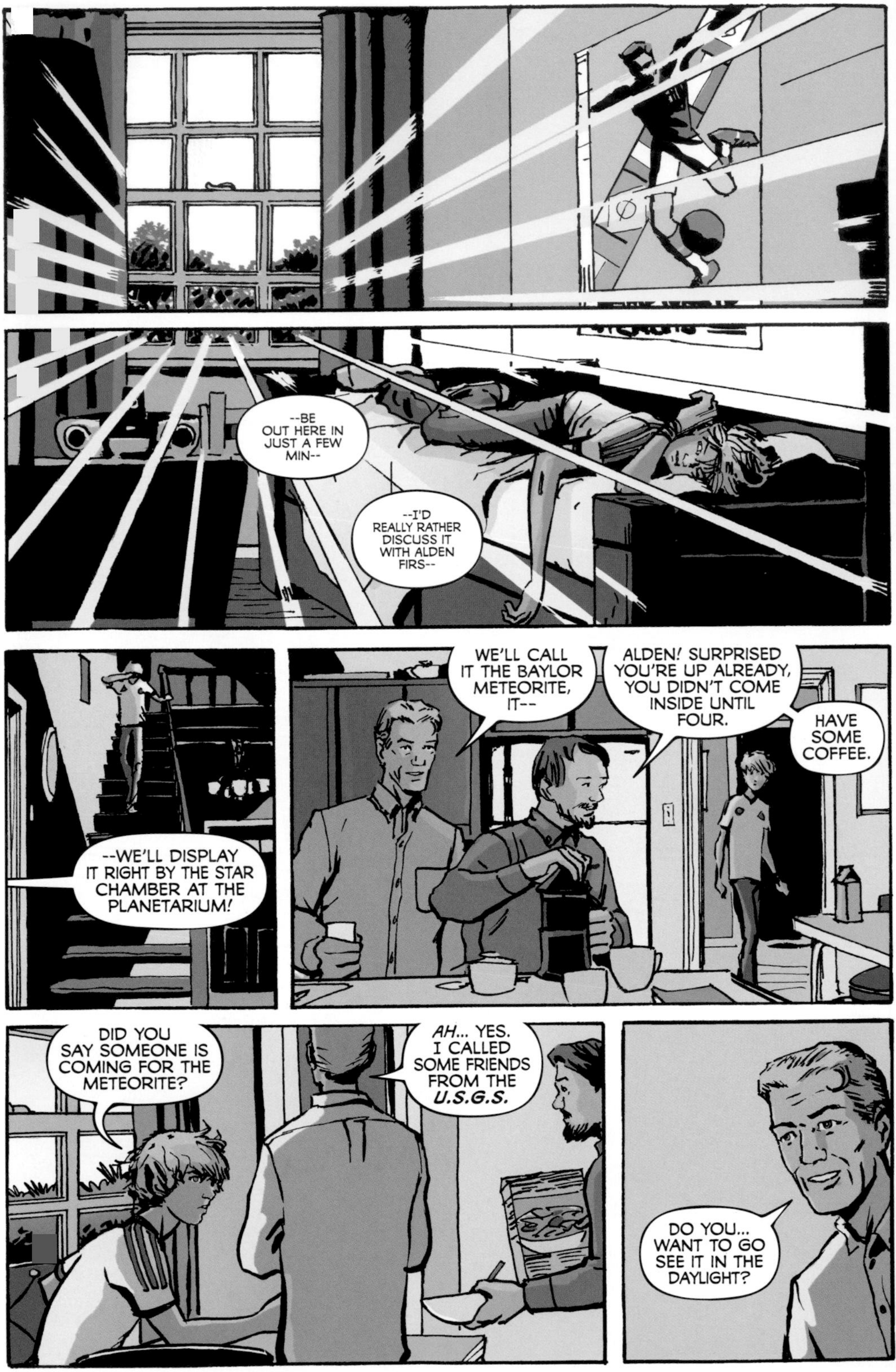
--BE OUT HERE IN JUST A FEW MIN--
--I'D REALLY RATHER DISCUSS IT WITH ALDEN FIRS--
--WE'LL DISPLAY IT RIGHT BY THE STAR CHAMBER AT THE PLANETARIUM!
WE'LL CALL IT THE BAYLOR METEORITE, IT--
ALDEN! SURPRISED YOU'RE UP ALREADY, YOU DIDN'T COME INSIDE UNTIL FOUR.
HAVE SOME COFFEE.
DID YOU SAY SOMEONE IS COMING FOR THE METEORITE?
AH... YES. I CALLED SOME FRIENDS FROM THE ***U.S.G.S.***
DO YOU... WANT TO GO SEE IT IN THE DAYLIGHT?

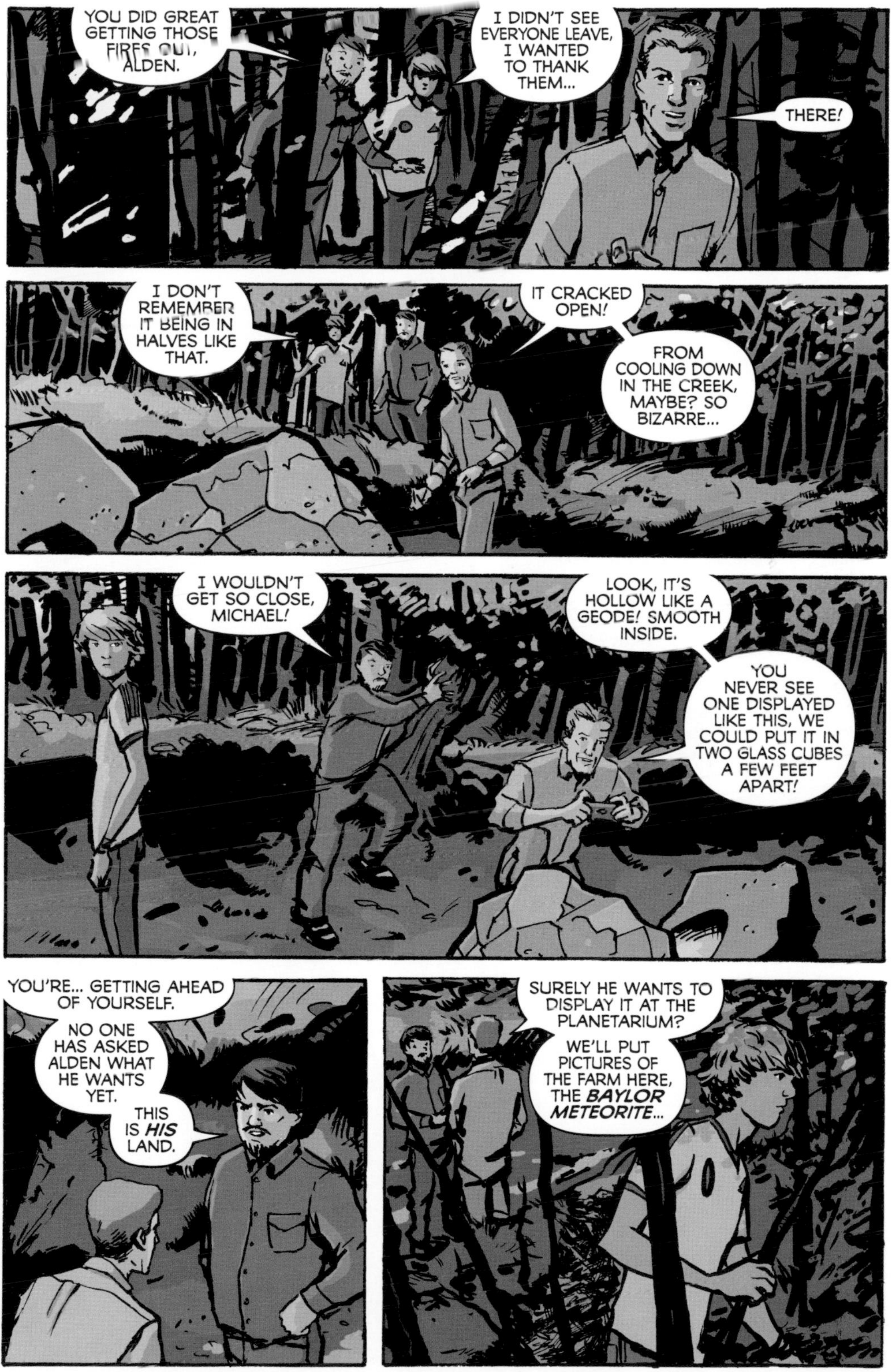
YOU DID GREAT GETTING THOSE FIRES OUT, ALDEN.
I DIDN'T SEE EVERYONE LEAVE, I WANTED TO THANK THEM...
THERE!
I DON'T REMEMBER IT BEING IN HALVES LIKE THAT.
IT CRACKED OPEN!
FROM COOLING DOWN IN THE CREEK, MAYBE? SO BIZARRE...
I WOULDN'T GET SO CLOSE, MICHAEL!
LOOK, IT'S HOLLOW LIKE A GEODE! SMOOTH INSIDE.
YOU NEVER SEE ONE DISPLAYED LIKE THIS, WE COULD PUT IT IN TWO GLASS CUBES A FEW FEET APART!
YOU'RE... GETTING AHEAD OF YOURSELF.
NO ONE HAS ASKED ALDEN WHAT HE WANTS YET.
THIS IS *HIS* LAND.
SURELY HE WANTS TO DISPLAY IT AT THE PLANETARIUM?
WE'LL PUT PICTURES OF THE FARM HERE, THE *BAYLOR METEORITE*...

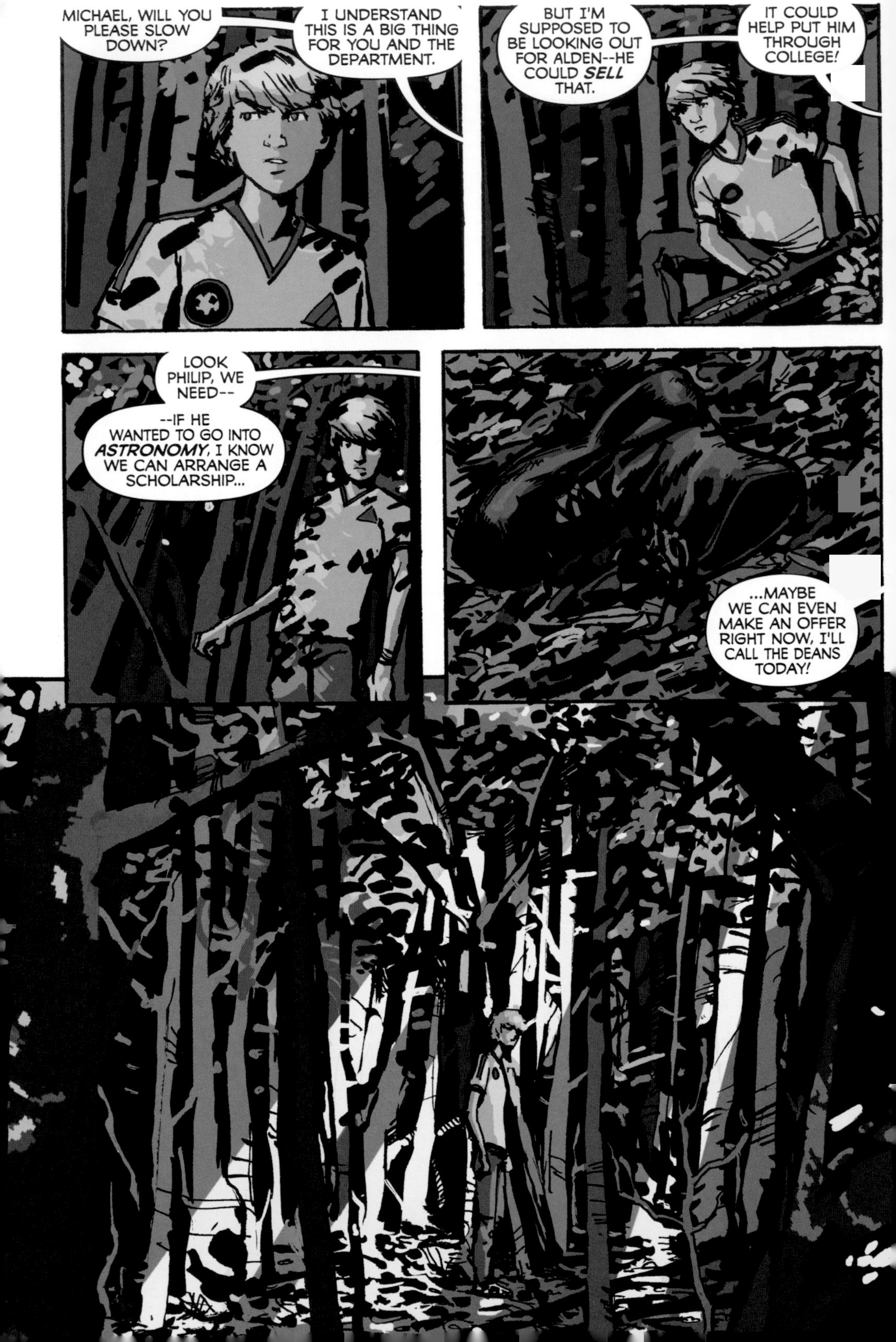
MICHAEL, WILL YOU PLEASE SLOW DOWN?
I UNDERSTAND THIS IS A BIG THING FOR YOU AND THE DEPARTMENT.
BUT I'M SUPPOSED TO BE LOOKING OUT FOR ALDEN--HE COULD SELL THAT.
IT COULD HELP PUT HIM THROUGH COLLEGE!
LOOK PHILIP, WE NEED--
--IF HE WANTED TO GO INTO ASTRONOMY, I KNOW WE CAN ARRANGE A SCHOLARSHIP...
...MAYBE WE CAN EVEN MAKE AN OFFER RIGHT NOW, I'LL CALL THE DEANS TODAY!

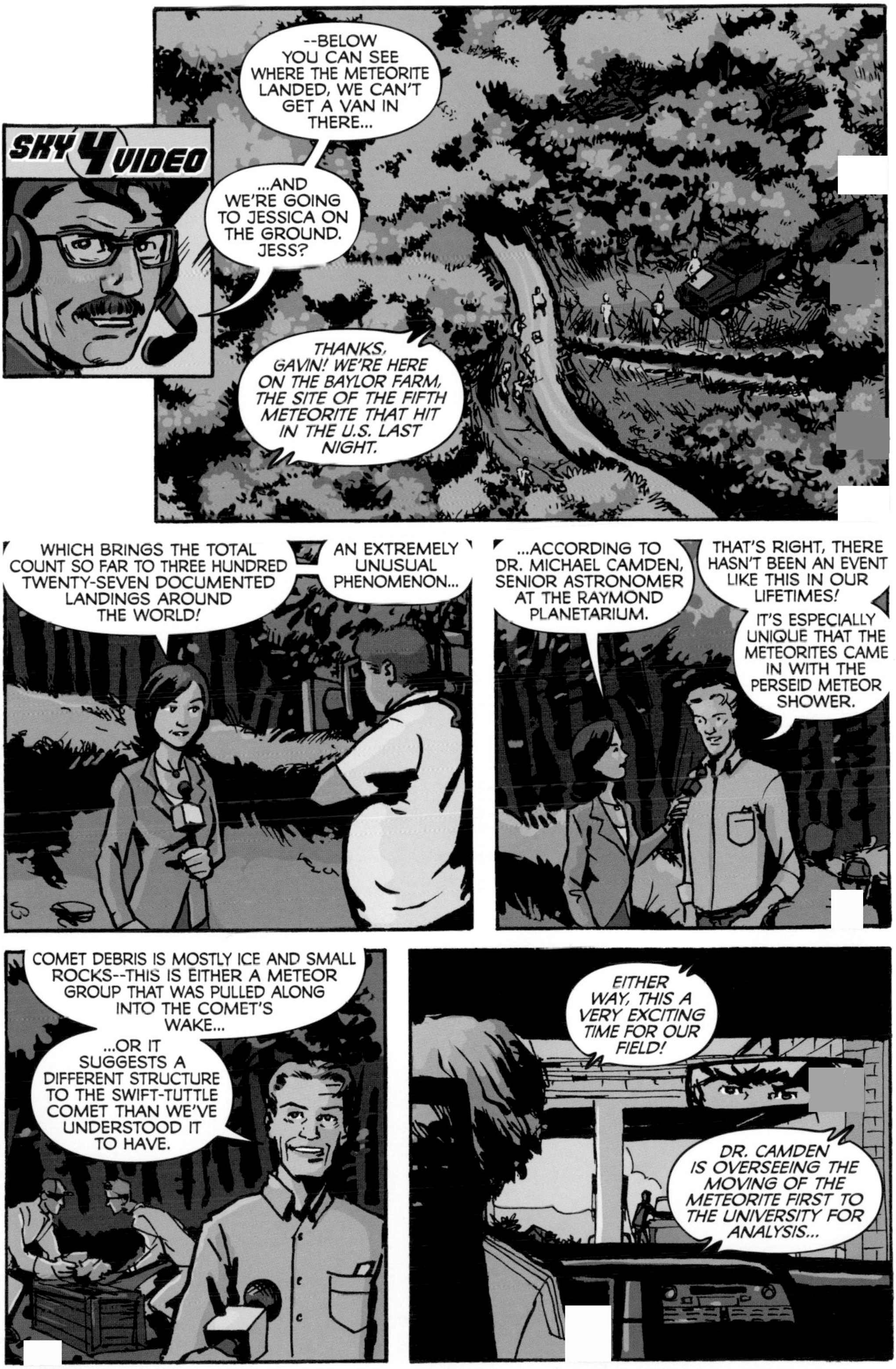
--BELOW YOU CAN SEE WHERE THE METEORITE LANDED, WE CAN'T GET A VAN IN THERE...
SKY 4 VIDEO
...AND WE'RE GOING TO JESSICA ON THE GROUND. JESS?
THANKS, GAVIN! WE'RE HERE ON THE BAYLOR FARM, THE SITE OF THE FIFTH METEORITE THAT HIT IN THE U.S. LAST NIGHT.
WHICH BRINGS THE TOTAL COUNT SO FAR TO THREE HUNDRED TWENTY-SEVEN DOCUMENTED LANDINGS AROUND THE WORLD!
AN EXTREMELY UNUSUAL PHENOMENON...
...ACCORDING TO DR. MICHAEL CAMDEN, SENIOR ASTRONOMER AT THE RAYMOND PLANETARIUM.
THAT'S RIGHT, THERE HASN'T BEEN AN EVENT LIKE THIS IN OUR LIFETIMES!
IT'S ESPECIALLY UNIQUE THAT THE METEORITES CAME IN WITH THE PERSEID METEOR SHOWER.
COMET DEBRIS IS MOSTLY ICE AND SMALL ROCKS--THIS IS EITHER A METEOR GROUP THAT WAS PULLED ALONG INTO THE COMET'S WAKE...
...OR IT SUGGESTS A DIFFERENT STRUCTURE TO THE SWIFT-TUTTLE COMET THAN WE'VE UNDERSTOOD IT TO HAVE.
EITHER WAY, THIS A VERY EXCITING TIME FOR OUR FIELD!
DR. CAMDEN IS OVERSEEING THE MOVING OF THE METEORITE FIRST TO THE UNIVERSITY FOR ANALYSIS...

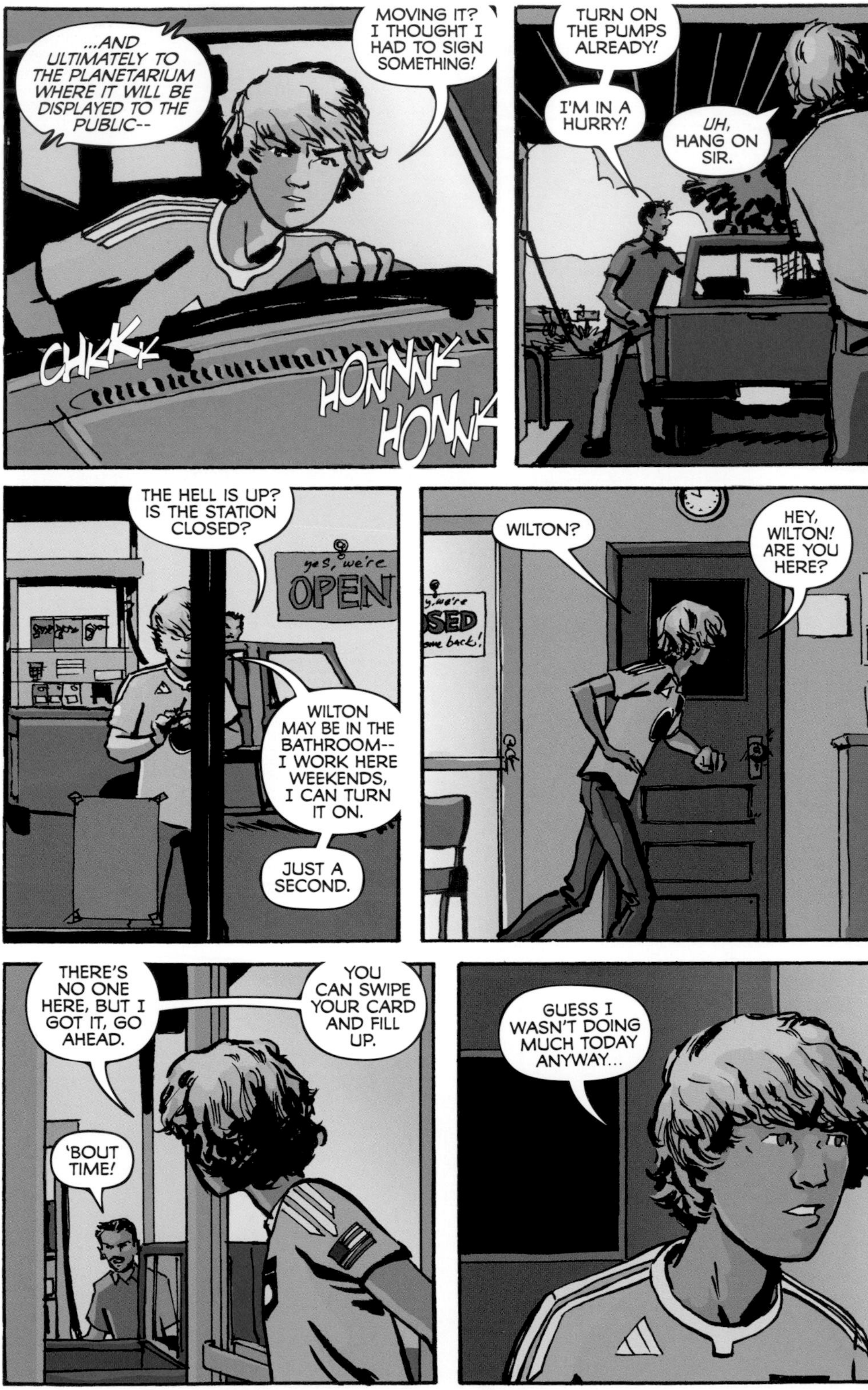

...AND ULTIMATELY TO THE PLANETARIUM WHERE IT WILL BE DISPLAYED TO THE PUBLIC--
MOVING IT? I THOUGHT I HAD TO SIGN SOMETHING!
CHKKK
HONNNK
HONNK
TURN ON THE PUMPS ALREADY!
I'M IN A HURRY!
UH, HANG ON SIR.
THE HELL IS UP? IS THE STATION CLOSED?
yes, we're OPEN
WILTON MAY BE IN THE BATHROOM-- I WORK HERE WEEKENDS, I CAN TURN IT ON.
JUST A SECOND.
WILTON?
HEY, WILTON! ARE YOU HERE?
THERE'S NO ONE HERE, BUT I GOT IT, GO AHEAD.
YOU CAN SWIPE YOUR CARD AND FILL UP.
'BOUT TIME!
GUESS I WASN'T DOING MUCH TODAY ANYWAY...

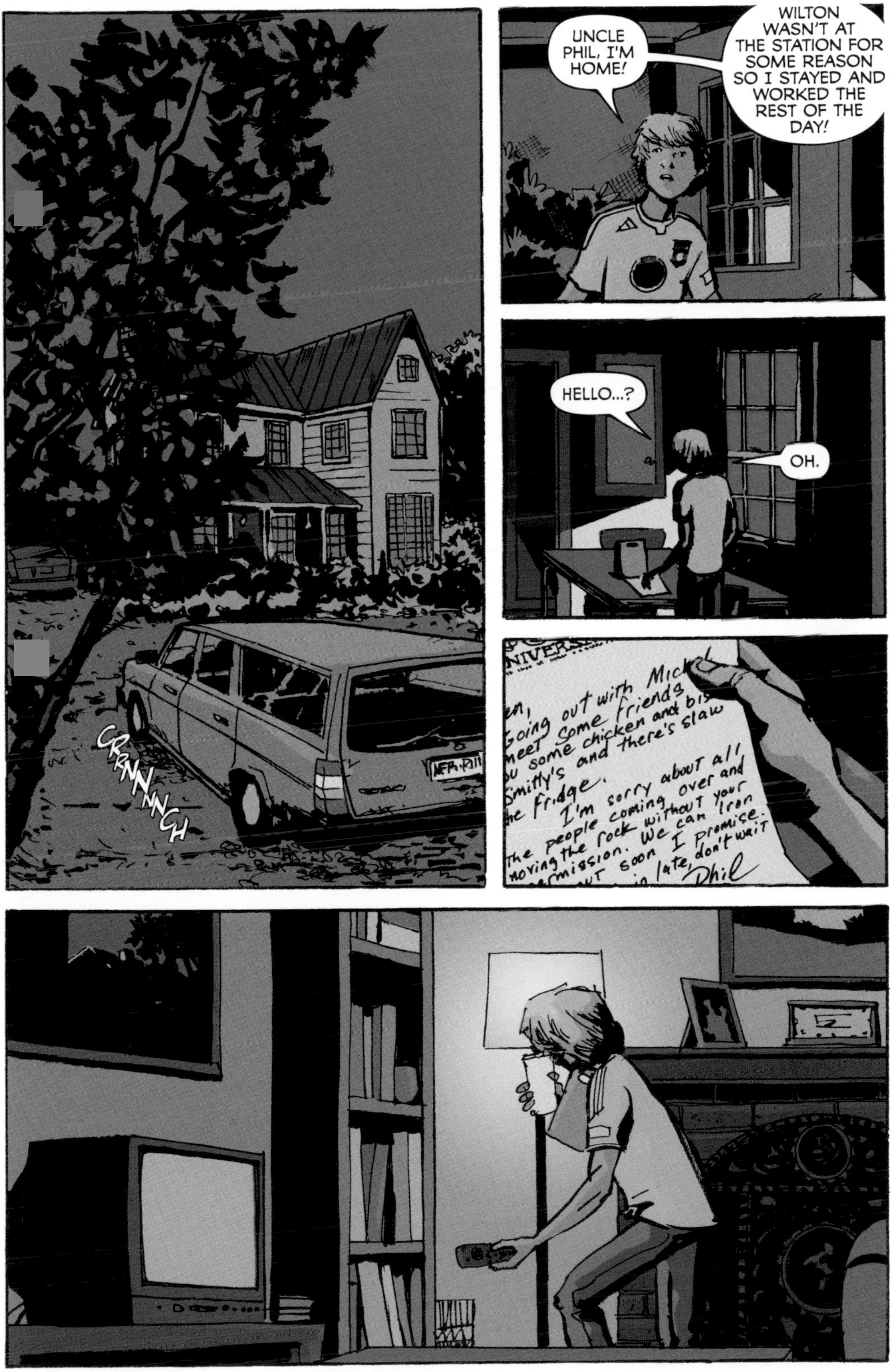
CRRNNNNCH
UNCLE PHIL, I'M HOME!
WILTON WASN'T AT THE STATION FOR SOME REASON SO I STAYED AND WORKED THE REST OF THE DAY!
HELLO...?
OH.
I'm sorry about all
Phil

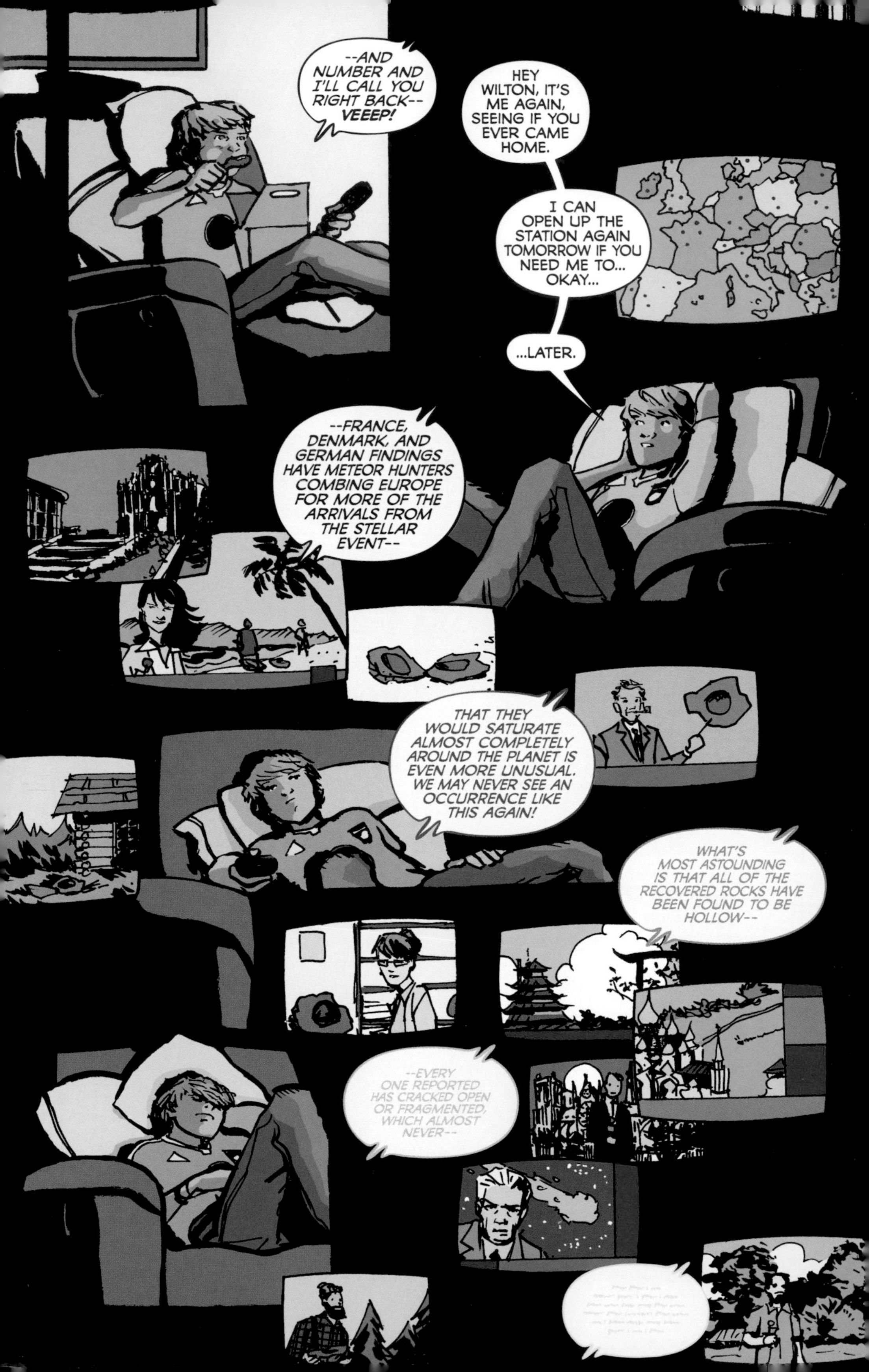
--AND NUMBER AND I'LL CALL YOU RIGHT BACK-- VEEEP!
HEY WILTON, IT'S ME AGAIN, SEEING IF YOU EVER CAME HOME.
I CAN OPEN UP THE STATION AGAIN TOMORROW IF YOU NEED ME TO... OKAY...
...LATER.
--FRANCE, DENMARK, AND GERMAN FINDINGS HAVE METEOR HUNTERS COMBING EUROPE FOR MORE OF THE ARRIVALS FROM THE STELLAR EVENT--
THAT THEY WOULD SATURATE ALMOST COMPLETELY AROUND THE PLANET IS EVEN MORE UNUSUAL. WE MAY NEVER SEE AN OCCURRENCE LIKE THIS AGAIN!
WHAT'S MOST ASTOUNDING IS THAT ALL OF THE RECOVERED ROCKS HAVE BEEN FOUND TO BE HOLLOW--
--EVERY ONE REPORTED HAS CRACKED OPEN OR FRAGMENTED, WHICH ALMOST NEVER--

ALDEN.

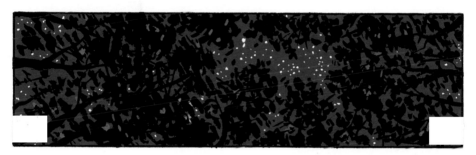

ALDEN.

ALDEN,
I'M STILL
HERE.

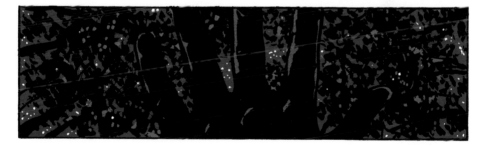

ALDEN.

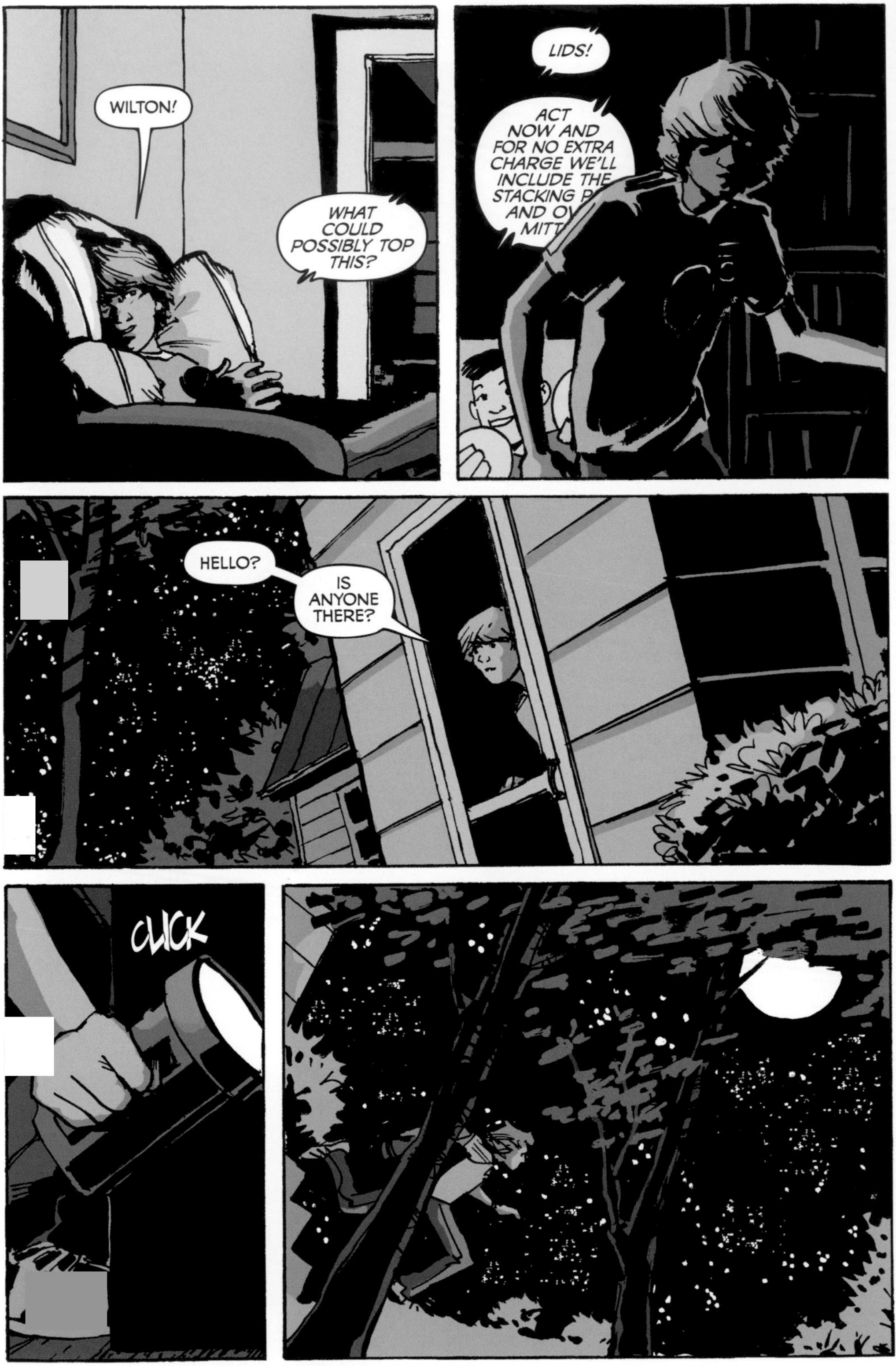
WILTON!
WHAT COULD POSSIBLY TOP THIS?
LIDS!
ACT NOW AND FOR NO EXTRA CHARGE WE'LL INCLUDE THE STACKING P
AND OV
MITT
HELLO?
IS ANYONE THERE?
CLICK

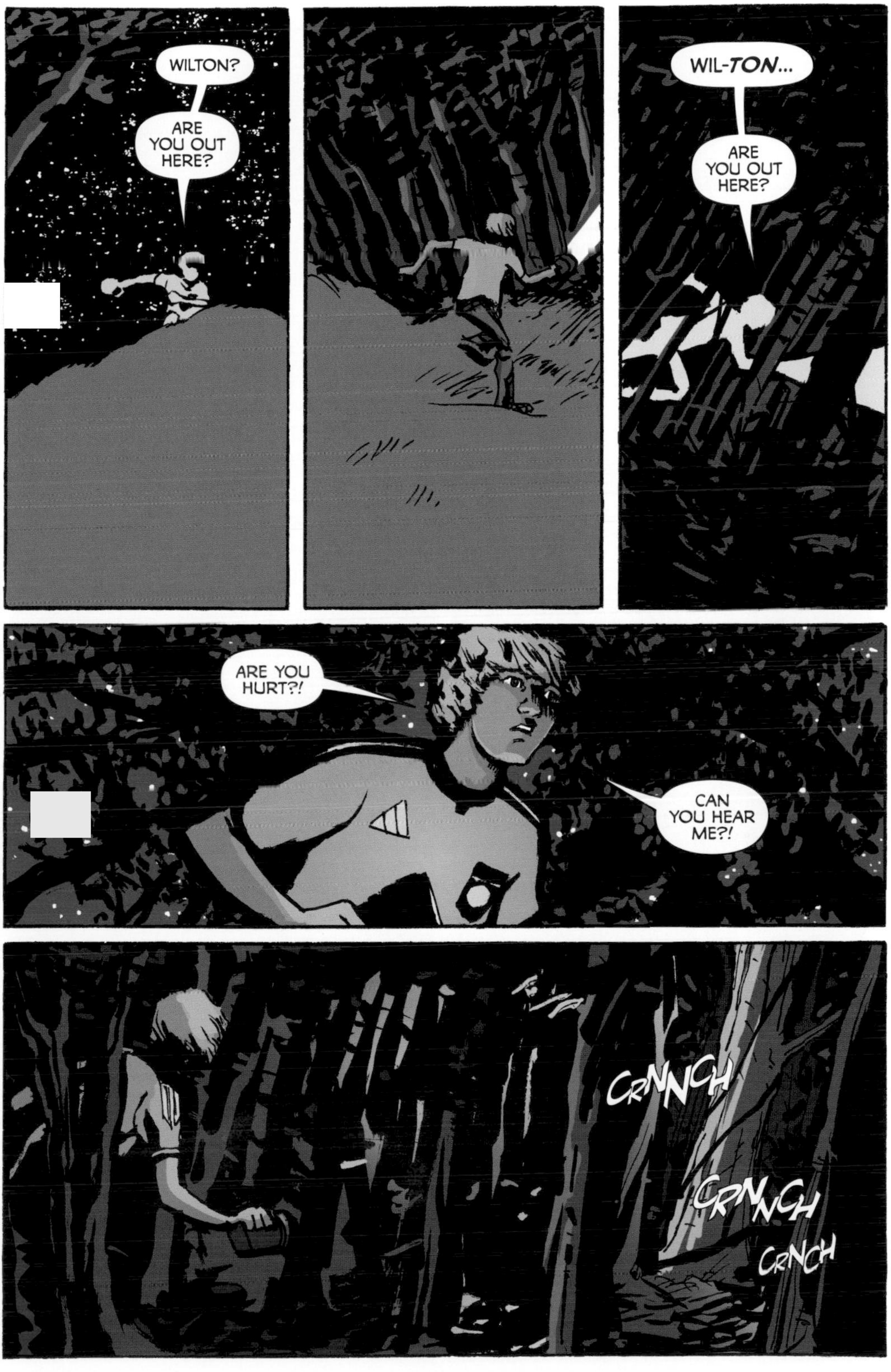
WILTON?
ARE YOU OUT HERE?
WIL-TON...
ARE YOU OUT HERE?
ARE YOU HURT?!
CAN YOU HEAR ME?!
CRNNCH
CRNNCH
CRNCH

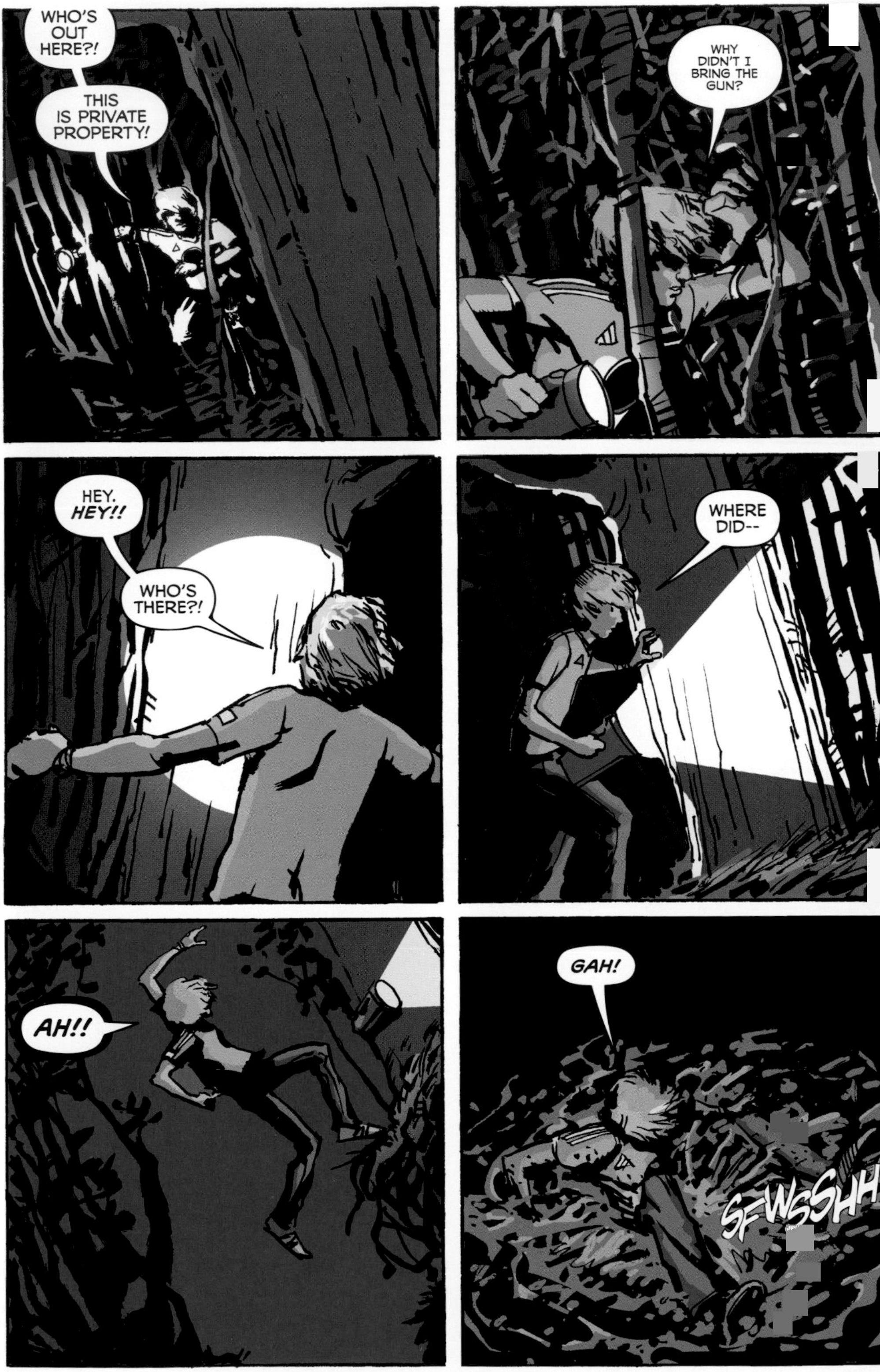
WHO'S OUT HERE?!
THIS IS PRIVATE PROPERTY!
WHY DIDN'T I BRING THE GUN?
HEY. *HEY!!*
WHO'S THERE?!
WHERE DID--
AH!!
GAH!
SFWSSHH

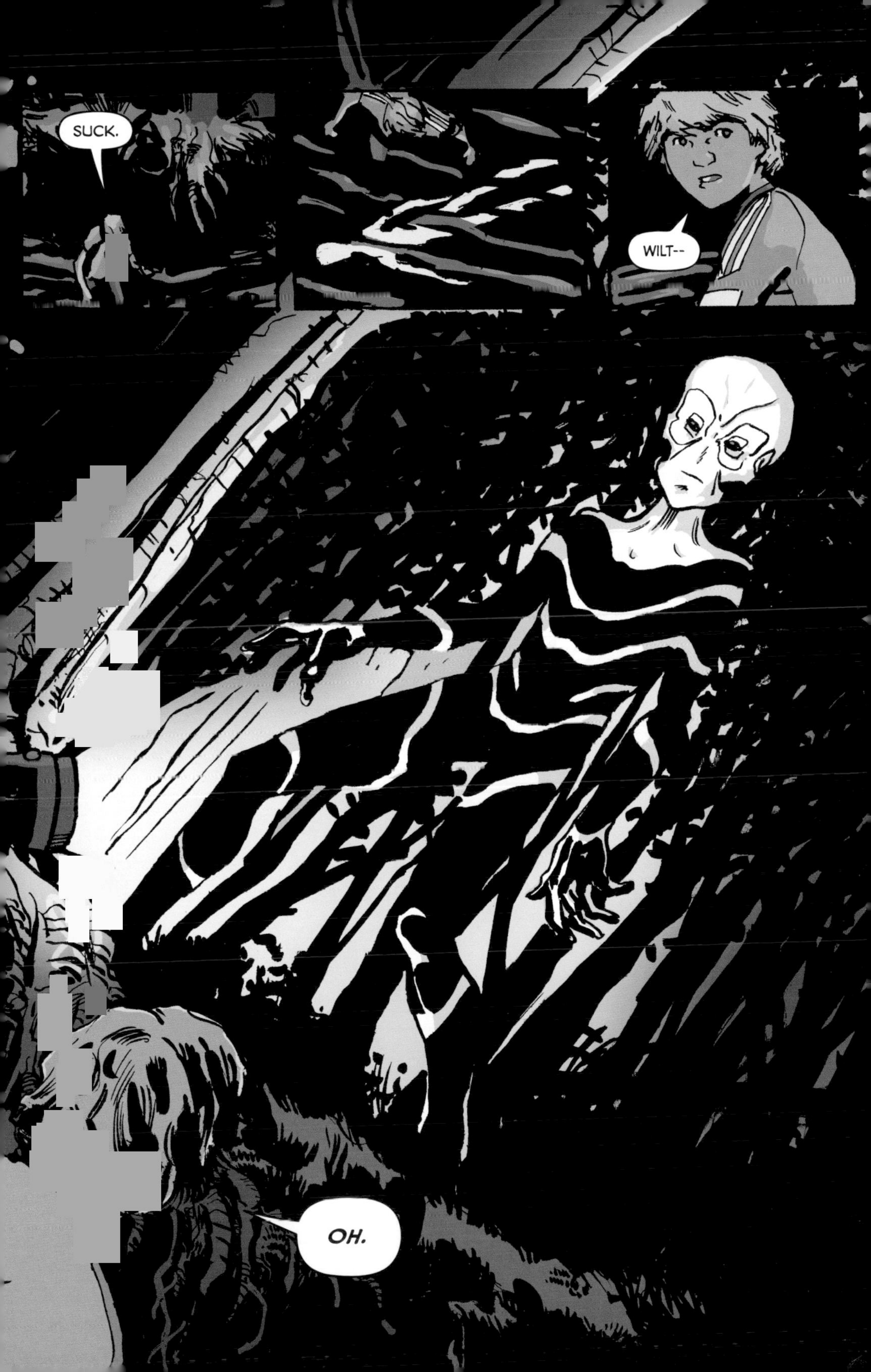
SUCK.
WILT--
OH.

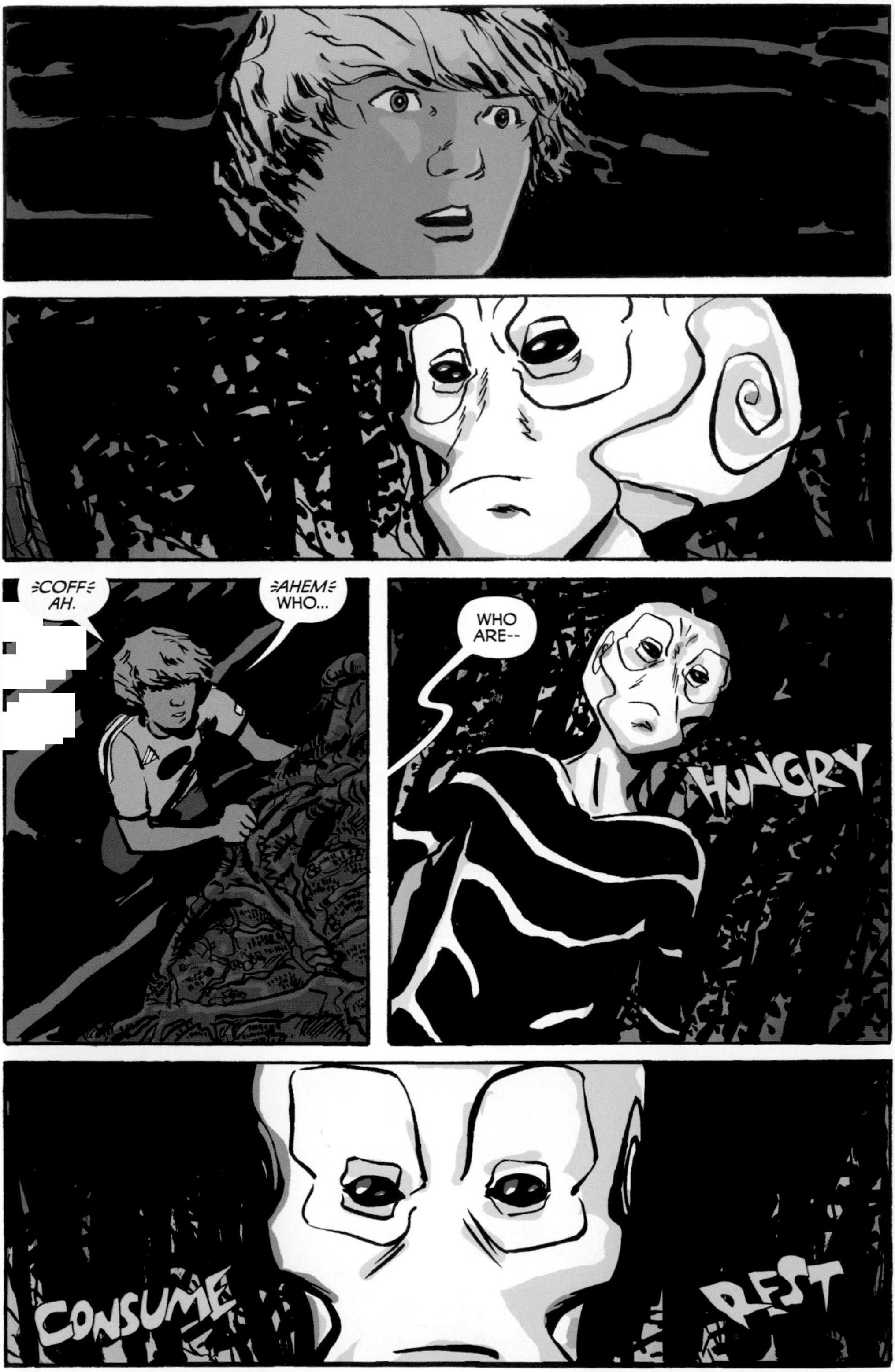

≶COFF≷ AH.
≶AHEM≷ WHO...
WHO ARE--
HUNGRY
CONSUME
REST

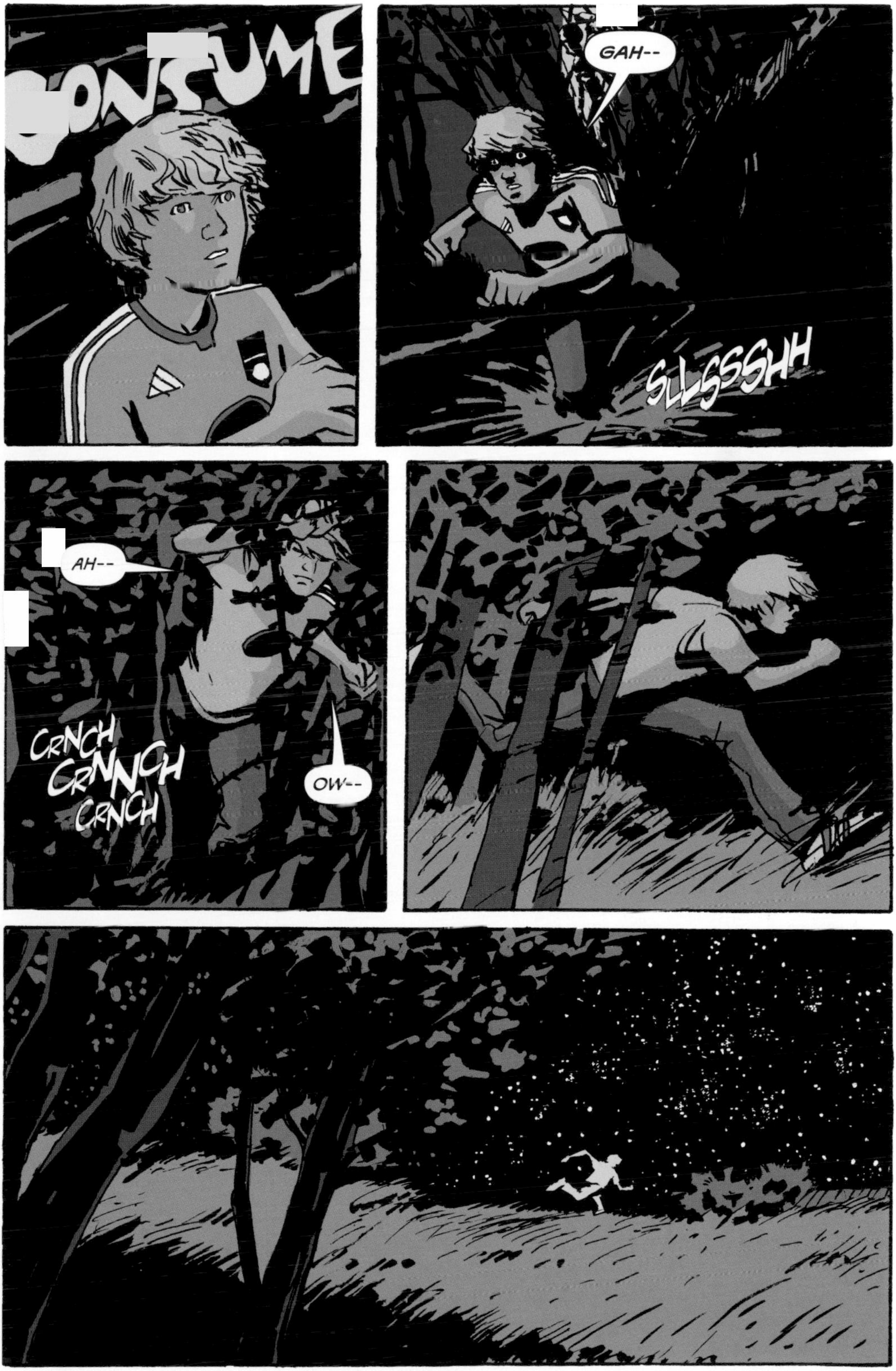
CONSUME
GAH--
SLLSSSHH
AH--
CRNCH
CRNNCH
CRNCH
OW--

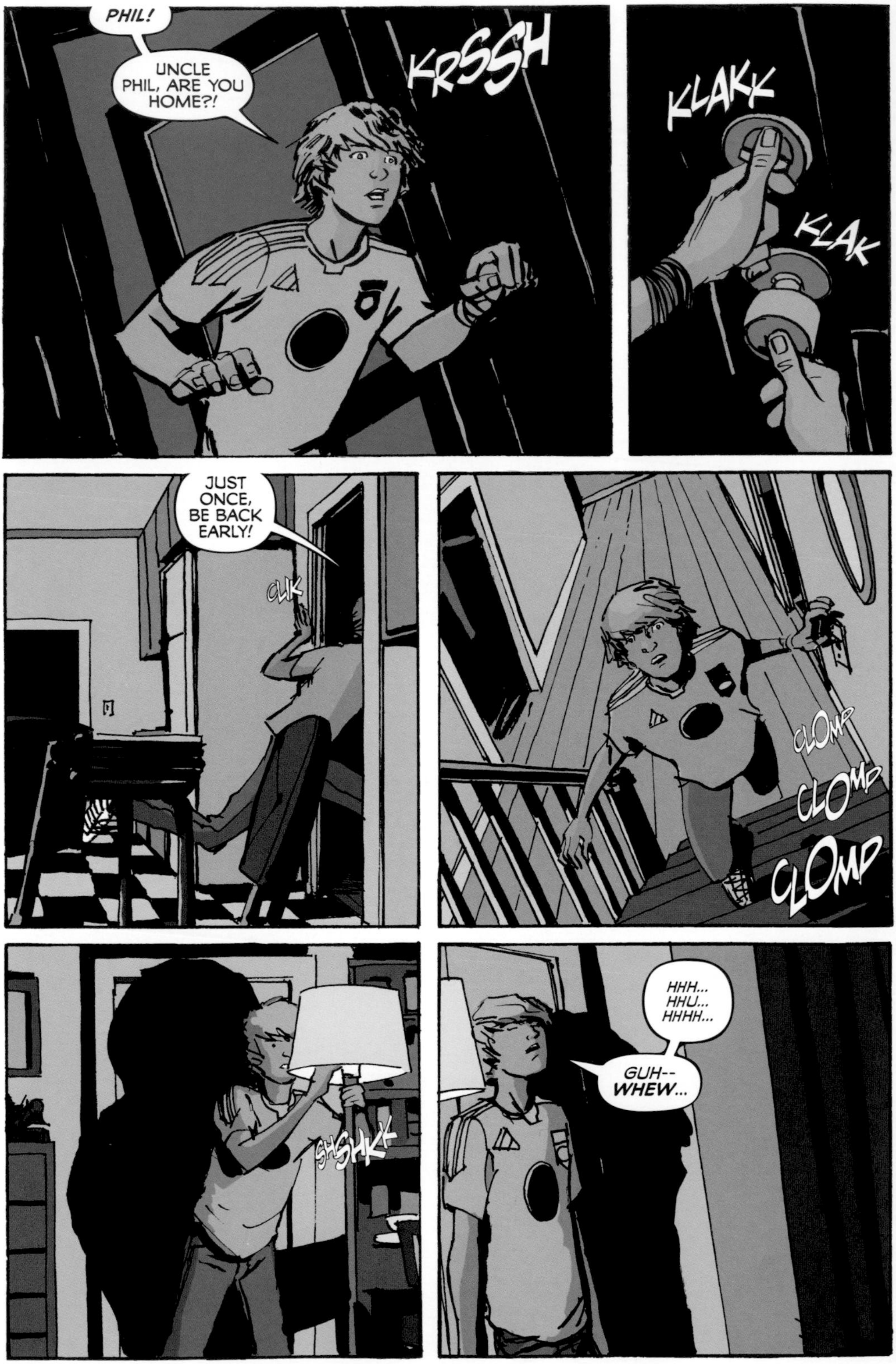
PHIL!
UNCLE PHIL, ARE YOU HOME?!
KRSSH
KLAKK
KLAK
JUST ONCE, BE BACK EARLY!
CLIK
CLOMP
CLOMP
CLOMP
SHSHKK
HHH... HHU... HHHH...
GUH-- WHEW...

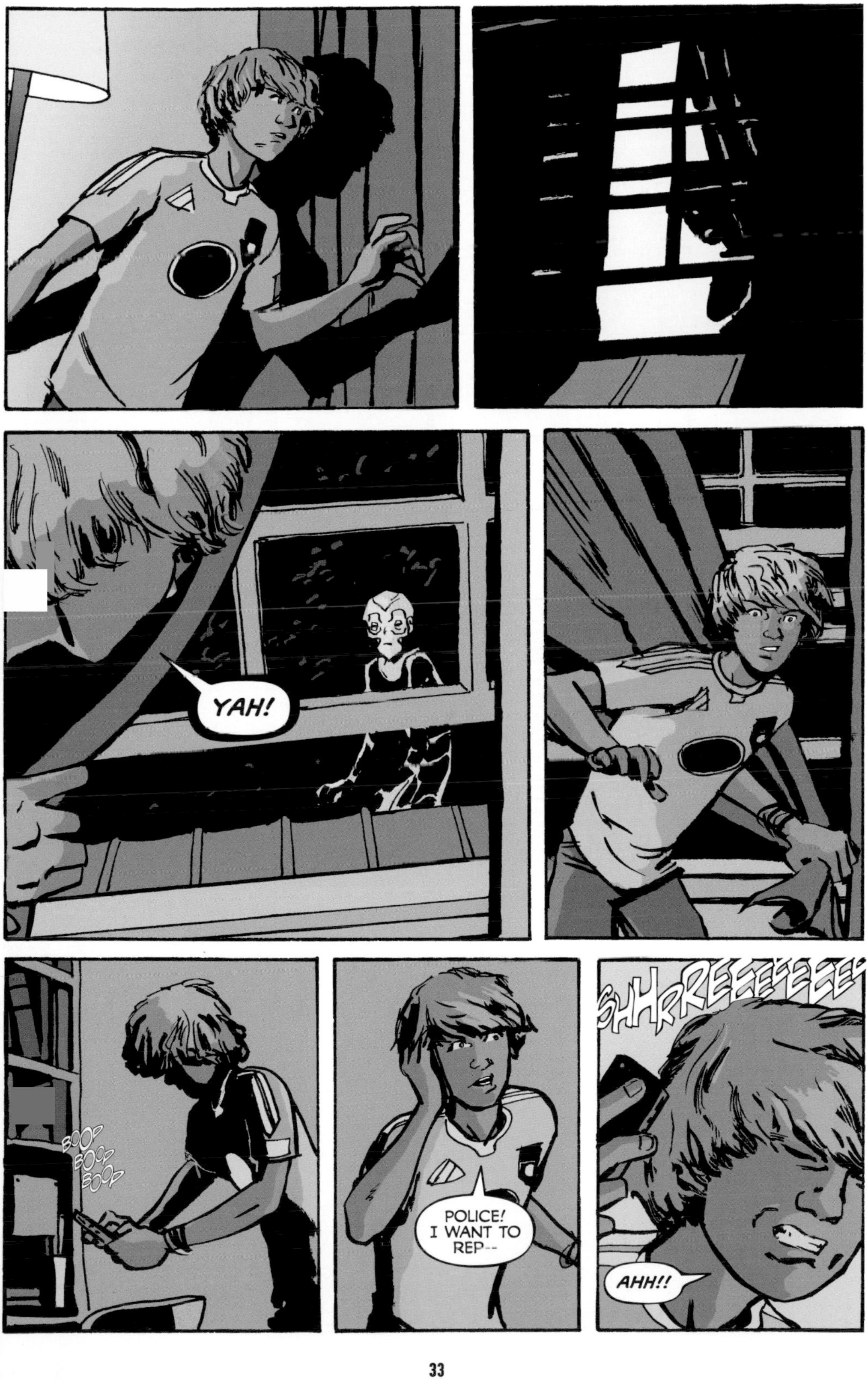
YAH!
BOOP
BOOP
BOOP
POLICE! I WANT TO REP--
SHHRREEEEEEEEE
AHH!!

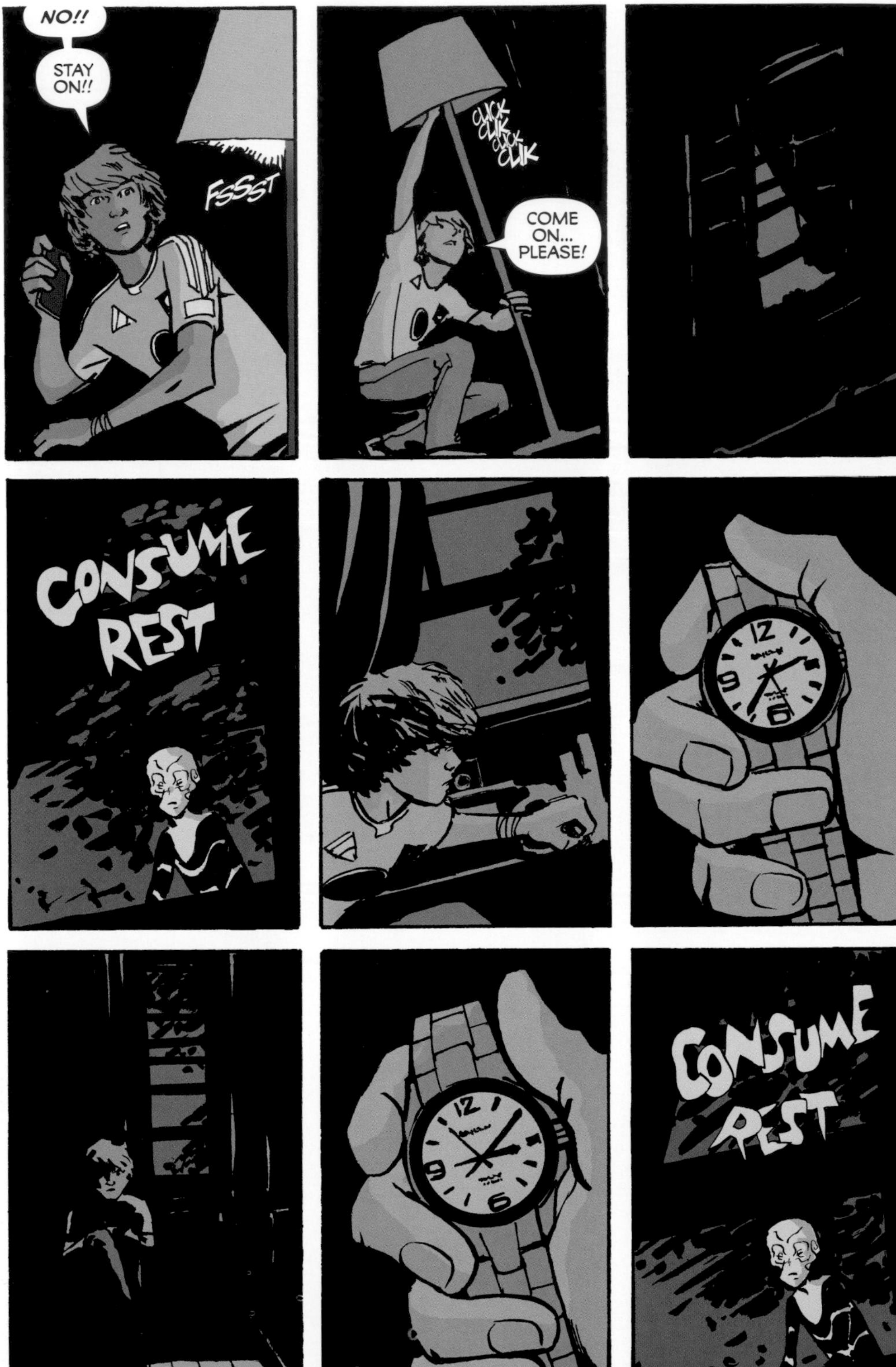
NO!!
STAY ON!!
FSSST
CLICK CLIK CLICK CLIK
COME ON... PLEASE!
CONSUME REST
CONSUME REST

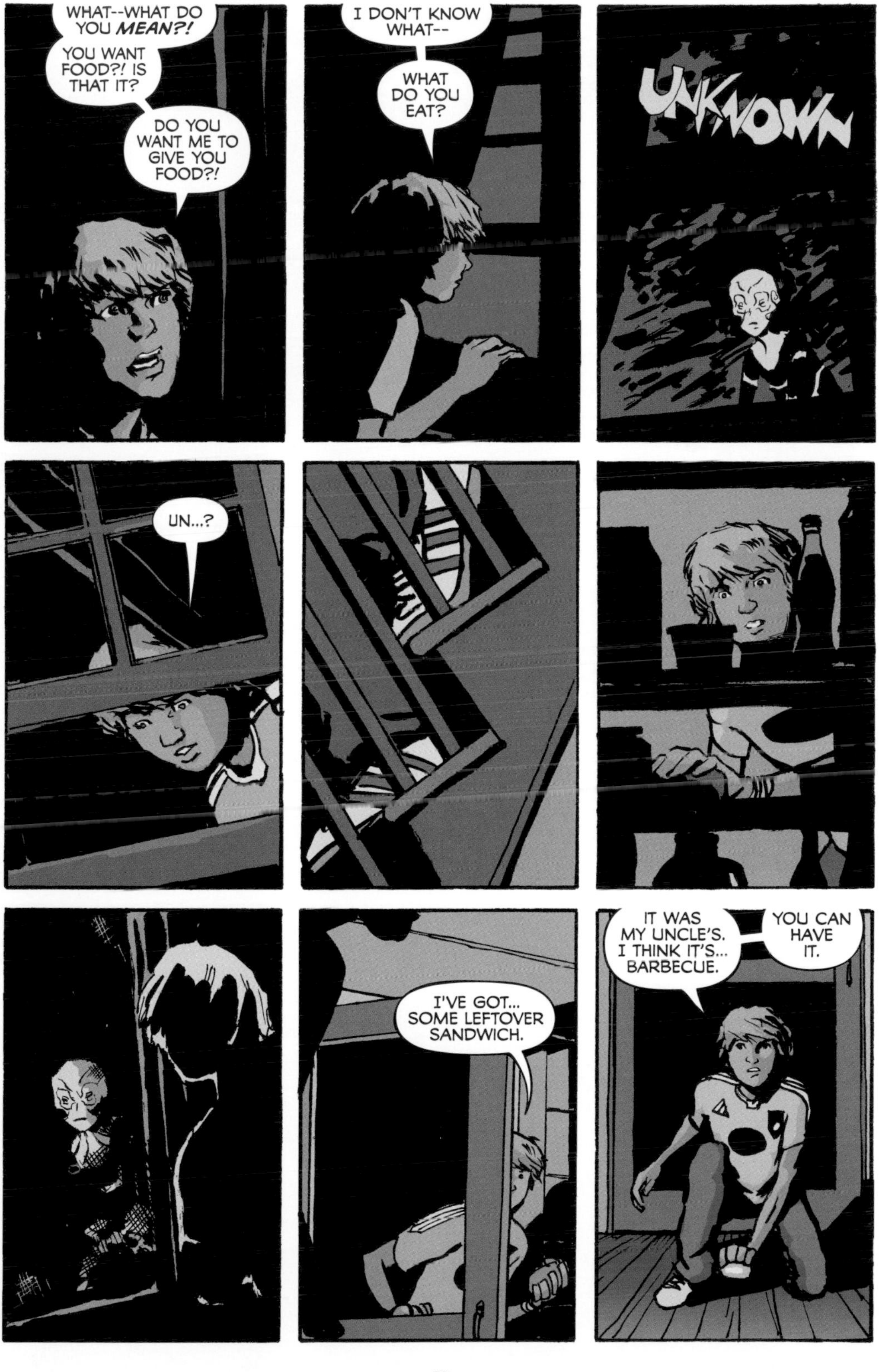
WHAT--WHAT DO YOU *MEAN?!*
YOU WANT FOOD?! IS THAT IT?
DO YOU WANT ME TO GIVE YOU FOOD?!
I DON'T KNOW WHAT--
WHAT DO YOU EAT?
UNKNOWN
UN...?
I'VE GOT... SOME LEFTOVER SANDWICH.
IT WAS MY UNCLE'S. I THINK IT'S... BARBECUE.
YOU CAN HAVE IT.

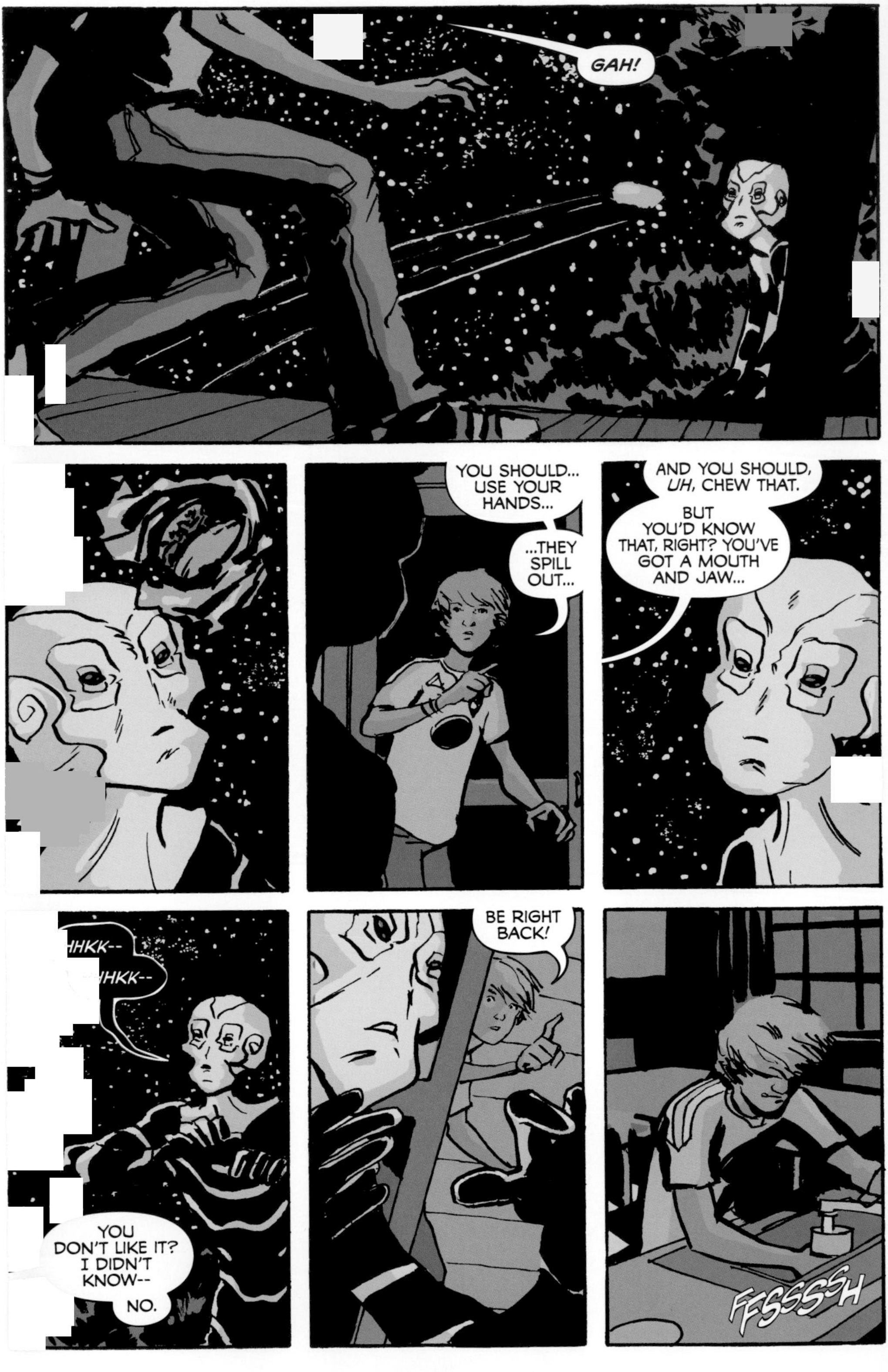
GAH!
YOU SHOULD... USE YOUR HANDS...
...THEY SPILL OUT...
AND YOU SHOULD, *UH*, CHEW THAT.
BUT YOU'D KNOW THAT, RIGHT? YOU'VE GOT A MOUTH AND JAW...
HHKK--
HHKK--
YOU DON'T LIKE IT? I DIDN'T KNOW--
NO.
BE RIGHT BACK!
FFSSSSH

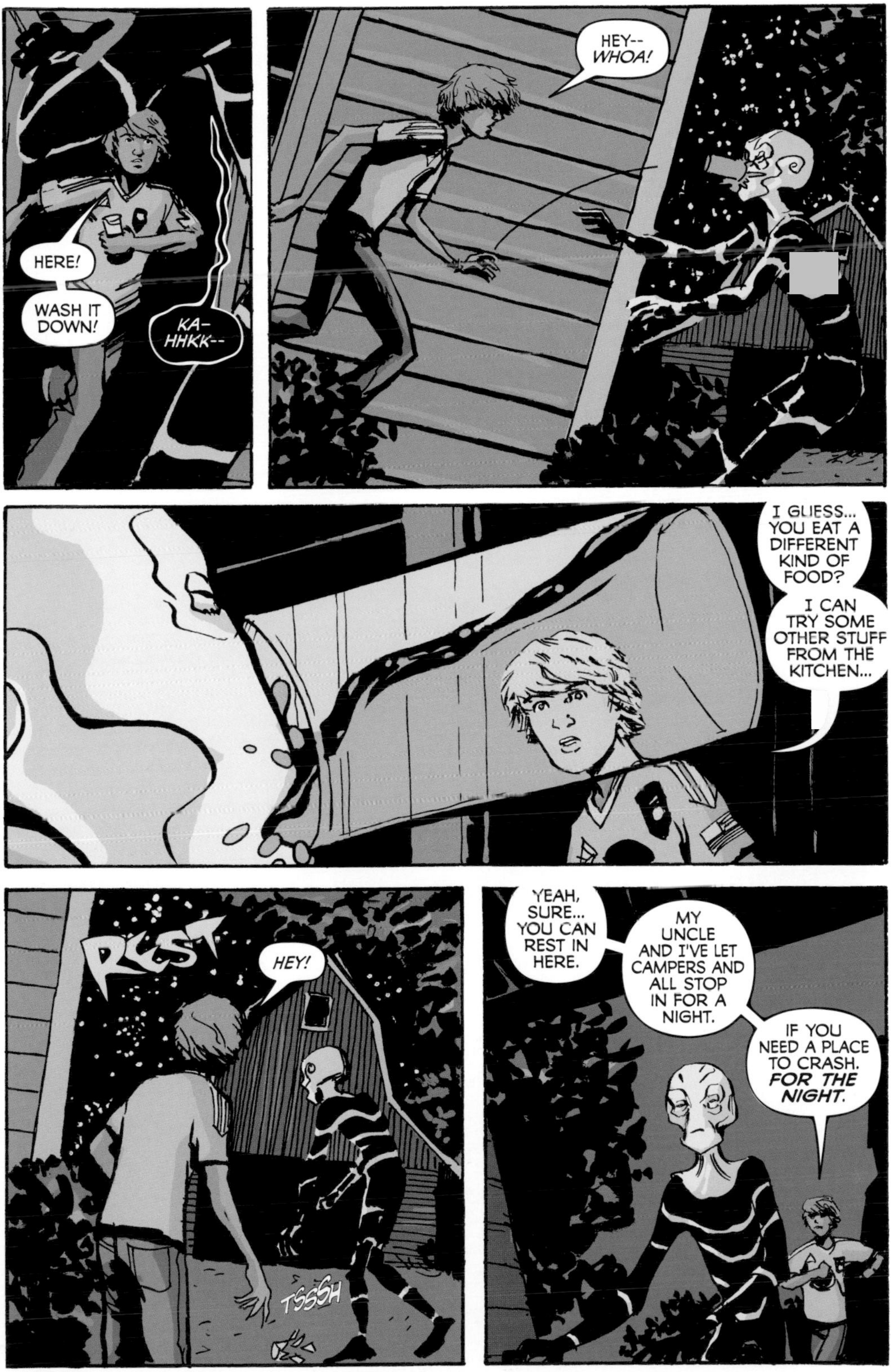
HERE!
WASH IT DOWN!
KA-HHKK--
HEY-- WHOA!
I GUESS... YOU EAT A DIFFERENT KIND OF FOOD?
I CAN TRY SOME OTHER STUFF FROM THE KITCHEN...
RUST
HEY!
TSSSH
YEAH, SURE... YOU CAN REST IN HERE.
MY UNCLE AND I'VE LET CAMPERS AND ALL STOP IN FOR A NIGHT.
IF YOU NEED A PLACE TO CRASH. FOR THE NIGHT.

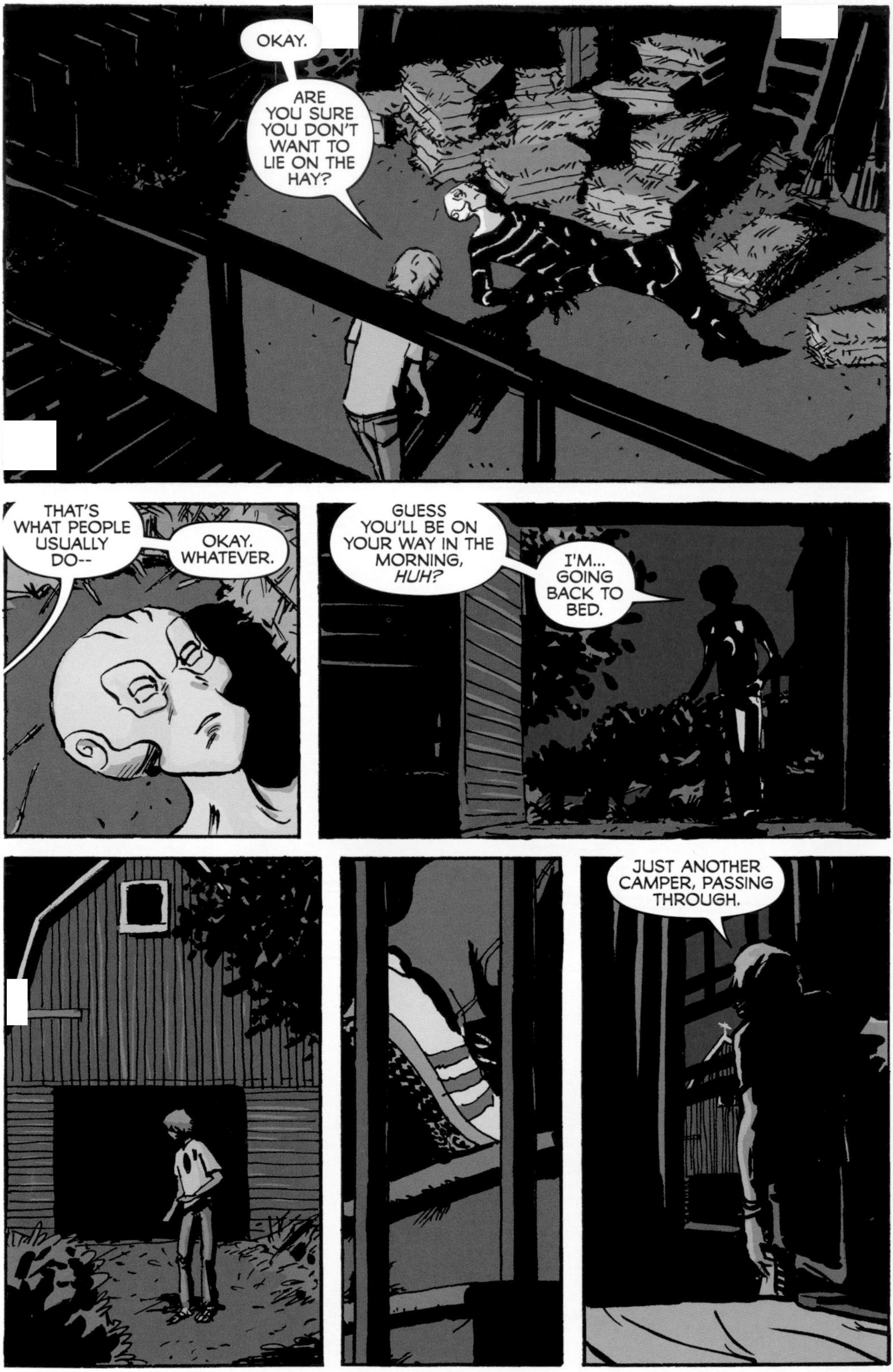

OKAY.
ARE YOU SURE YOU DON'T WANT TO LIE ON THE HAY?
THAT'S WHAT PEOPLE USUALLY DO--
OKAY. WHATEVER.
GUESS YOU'LL BE ON YOUR WAY IN THE MORNING, *HUH?*
I'M... GOING BACK TO BED.
JUST ANOTHER CAMPER, PASSING THROUGH.

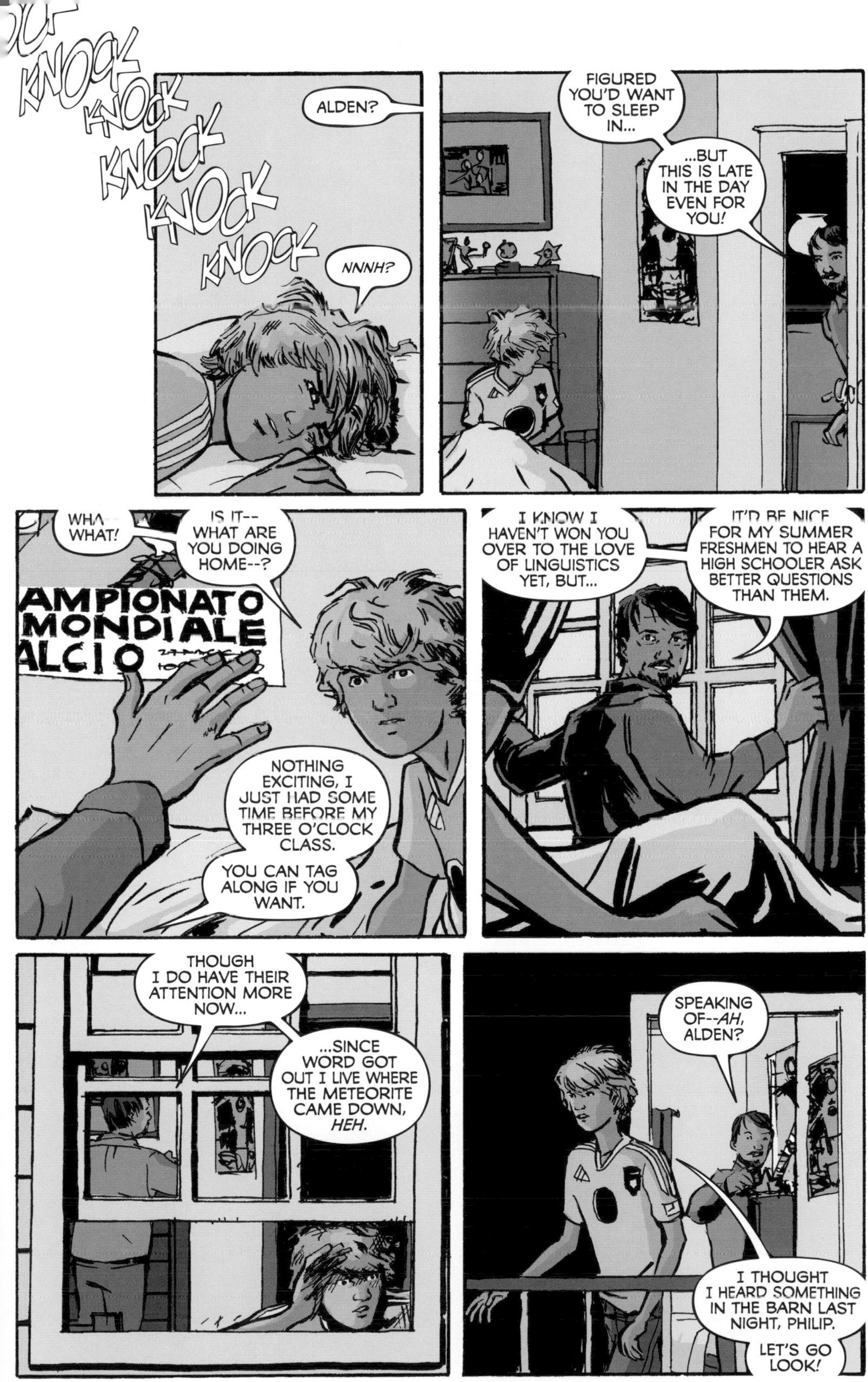
KNOCK
KNOCK
KNOCK
KNOCK
KNOCK
ALDEN?
NNNH?
FIGURED YOU'D WANT TO SLEEP IN...
...BUT THIS IS LATE IN THE DAY EVEN FOR YOU!
WHA-WHAT!
IS IT-- WHAT ARE YOU DOING HOME--?
AMPIONATO MONDIALE ALCIO
NOTHING EXCITING, I JUST HAD SOME TIME BEFORE MY THREE O'CLOCK CLASS.
YOU CAN TAG ALONG IF YOU WANT.
I KNOW I HAVEN'T WON YOU OVER TO THE LOVE OF LINGUISTICS YET, BUT...
IT'D BE NICE FOR MY SUMMER FRESHMEN TO HEAR A HIGH SCHOOLER ASK BETTER QUESTIONS THAN THEM.
THOUGH I DO HAVE THEIR ATTENTION MORE NOW...
...SINCE WORD GOT OUT I LIVE WHERE THE METEORITE CAME DOWN, *HEH*.
SPEAKING OF--*AH*, ALDEN?
I THOUGHT I HEARD SOMETHING IN THE BARN LAST NIGHT, PHILIP.
LET'S GO LOOK!

SURE, BUT I JUST WANT TO REASSURE YOU...

...MICHAEL *ISN'T* TRYING TO LAY CLAIM TO THE METEOR.

HE KNOWS IT LANDED ON THIS PROPERTY, AND IT'S *YOURS*.

HE JUST WANTED TO PROTECT--WELL, THERE'S ALREADY BEEN LOTS OF STORIES OF PEOPLE MAKING OFF WITH THE OTHER SPACE ROCKS THAT LANDED.

I ASSUME THEY'LL BUST THEM UP AND SELL PIECES.

I DON'T THINK THAT'S THE RIGHT THING TO DO WITH SOMETHING LIKE THIS, ALDEN.

BUT I'VE MADE IT CLEAR, THIS IS YOUR PROPERTY!

YOU KNOW, YOU MAY BE ABLE TO GET A FREE RIDE AT THE UNIVERSITY--

IF WE HANDLE THIS--*WHEW*--WAIT...

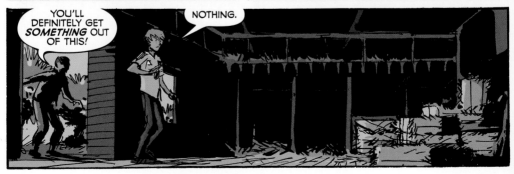

YOU'LL DEFINITELY GET *SOMETHING* OUT OF THIS!

NOTHING.

40

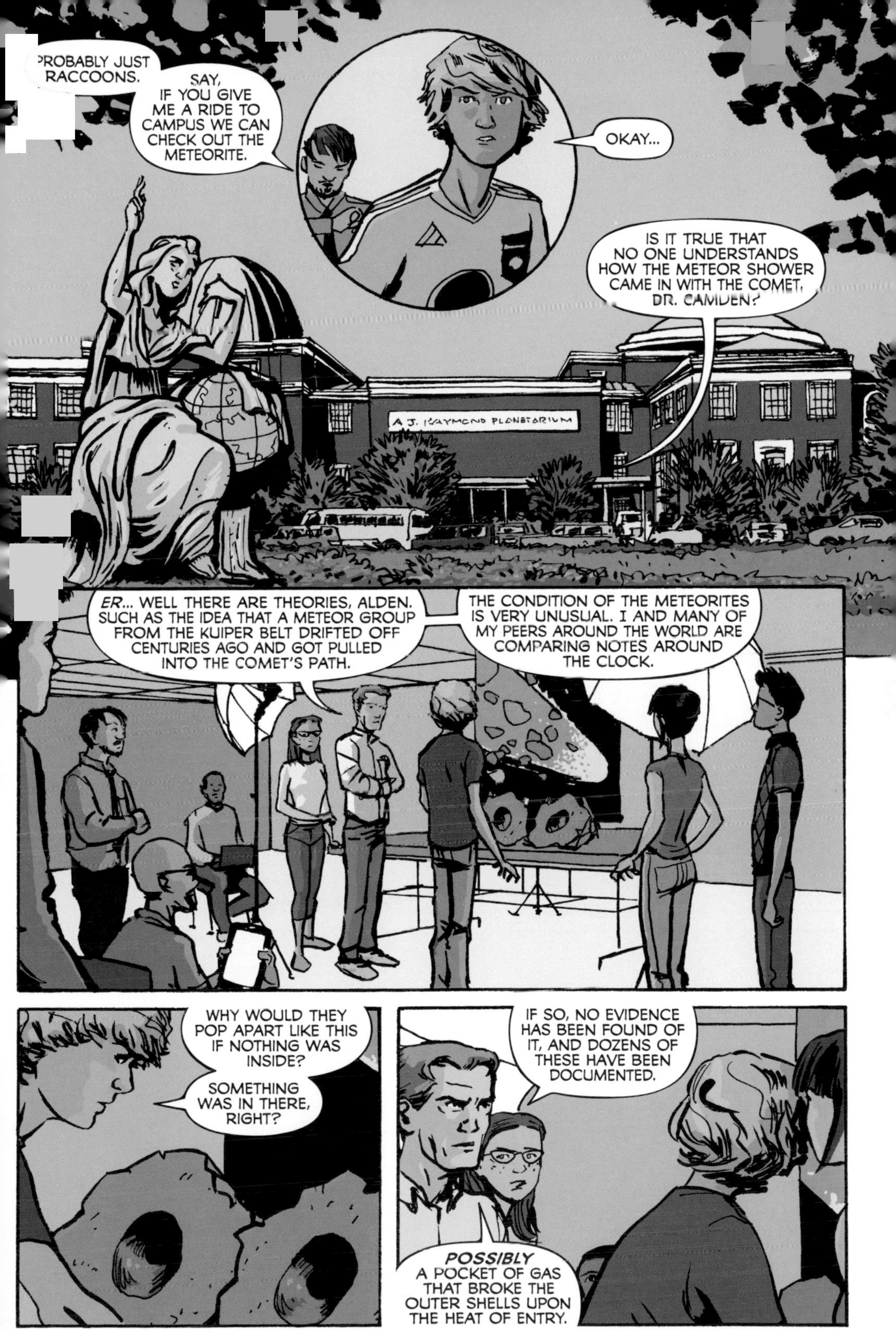
PROBABLY JUST RACCOONS.
SAY, IF YOU GIVE ME A RIDE TO CAMPUS WE CAN CHECK OUT THE METEORITE.
OKAY...
IS IT TRUE THAT NO ONE UNDERSTANDS HOW THE METEOR SHOWER CAME IN WITH THE COMET, DR. CAMDEN?
A. J. RAYMOND PLANETARIUM
ER... WELL THERE ARE THEORIES, ALDEN. SUCH AS THE IDEA THAT A METEOR GROUP FROM THE KUIPER BELT DRIFTED OFF CENTURIES AGO AND GOT PULLED INTO THE COMET'S PATH.
THE CONDITION OF THE METEORITES IS VERY UNUSUAL. I AND MANY OF MY PEERS AROUND THE WORLD ARE COMPARING NOTES AROUND THE CLOCK.
WHY WOULD THEY POP APART LIKE THIS IF NOTHING WAS INSIDE?
SOMETHING WAS IN THERE, RIGHT?
IF SO, NO EVIDENCE HAS BEEN FOUND OF IT, AND DOZENS OF THESE HAVE BEEN DOCUMENTED.
POSSIBLY A POCKET OF GAS THAT BROKE THE OUTER SHELLS UPON THE HEAT OF ENTRY.

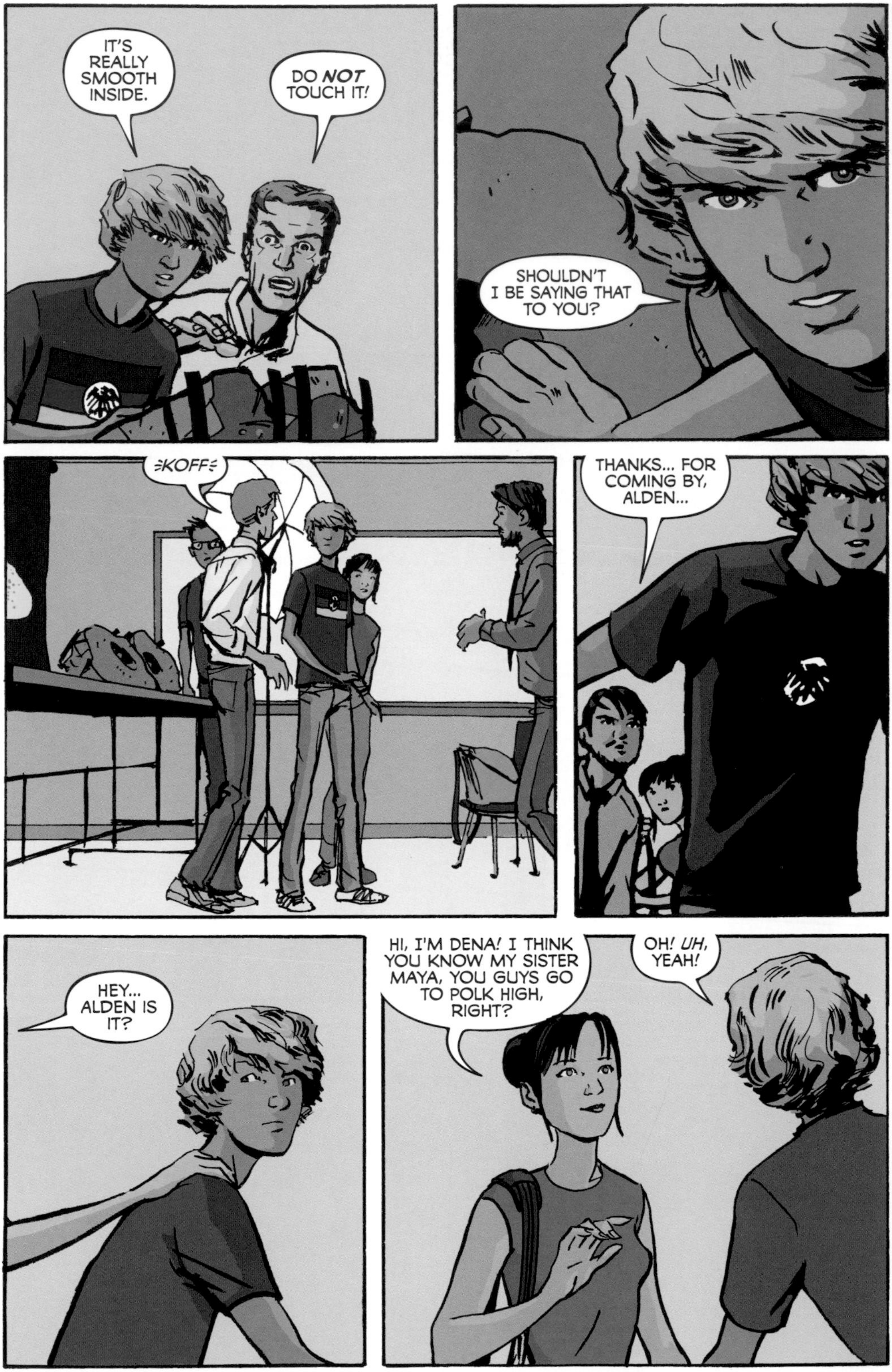
IT'S REALLY SMOOTH INSIDE.
DO NOT TOUCH IT!
SHOULDN'T I BE SAYING THAT TO YOU?
KOFF
THANKS... FOR COMING BY, ALDEN...
HEY... ALDEN IS IT?
HI, I'M DENA! I THINK YOU KNOW MY SISTER MAYA, YOU GUYS GO TO POLK HIGH, RIGHT?
OH! UH, YEAH!

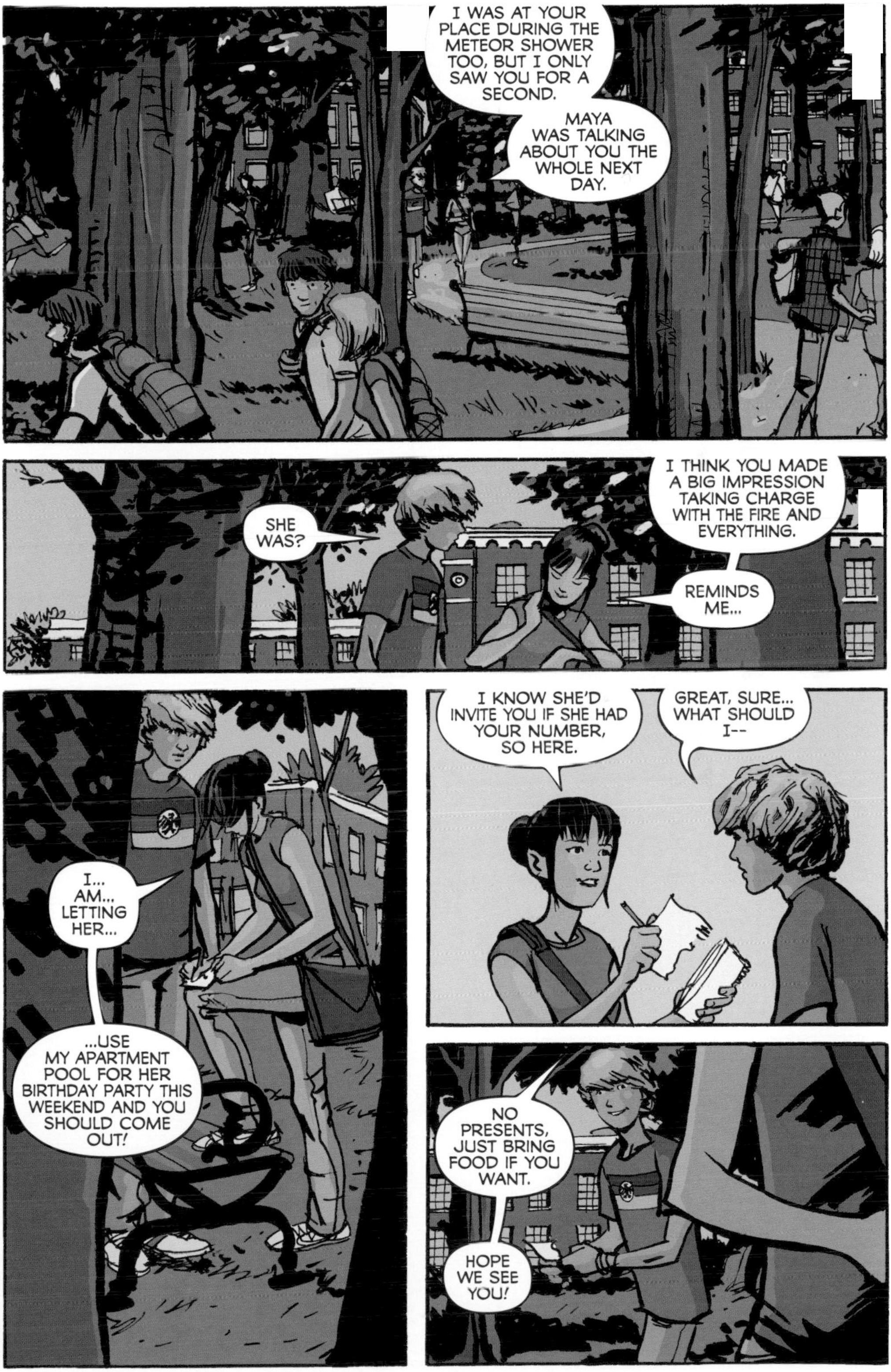
I WAS AT YOUR PLACE DURING THE METEOR SHOWER TOO, BUT I ONLY SAW YOU FOR A SECOND.
MAYA WAS TALKING ABOUT YOU THE WHOLE NEXT DAY.
SHE WAS?
I THINK YOU MADE A BIG IMPRESSION TAKING CHARGE WITH THE FIRE AND EVERYTHING.
REMINDS ME...
I... AM... LETTING HER...
...USE MY APARTMENT POOL FOR HER BIRTHDAY PARTY THIS WEEKEND AND YOU SHOULD COME OUT!
I KNOW SHE'D INVITE YOU IF SHE HAD YOUR NUMBER, SO HERE.
GREAT, SURE... WHAT SHOULD I--
NO PRESENTS, JUST BRING FOOD IF YOU WANT.
HOPE WE SEE YOU!

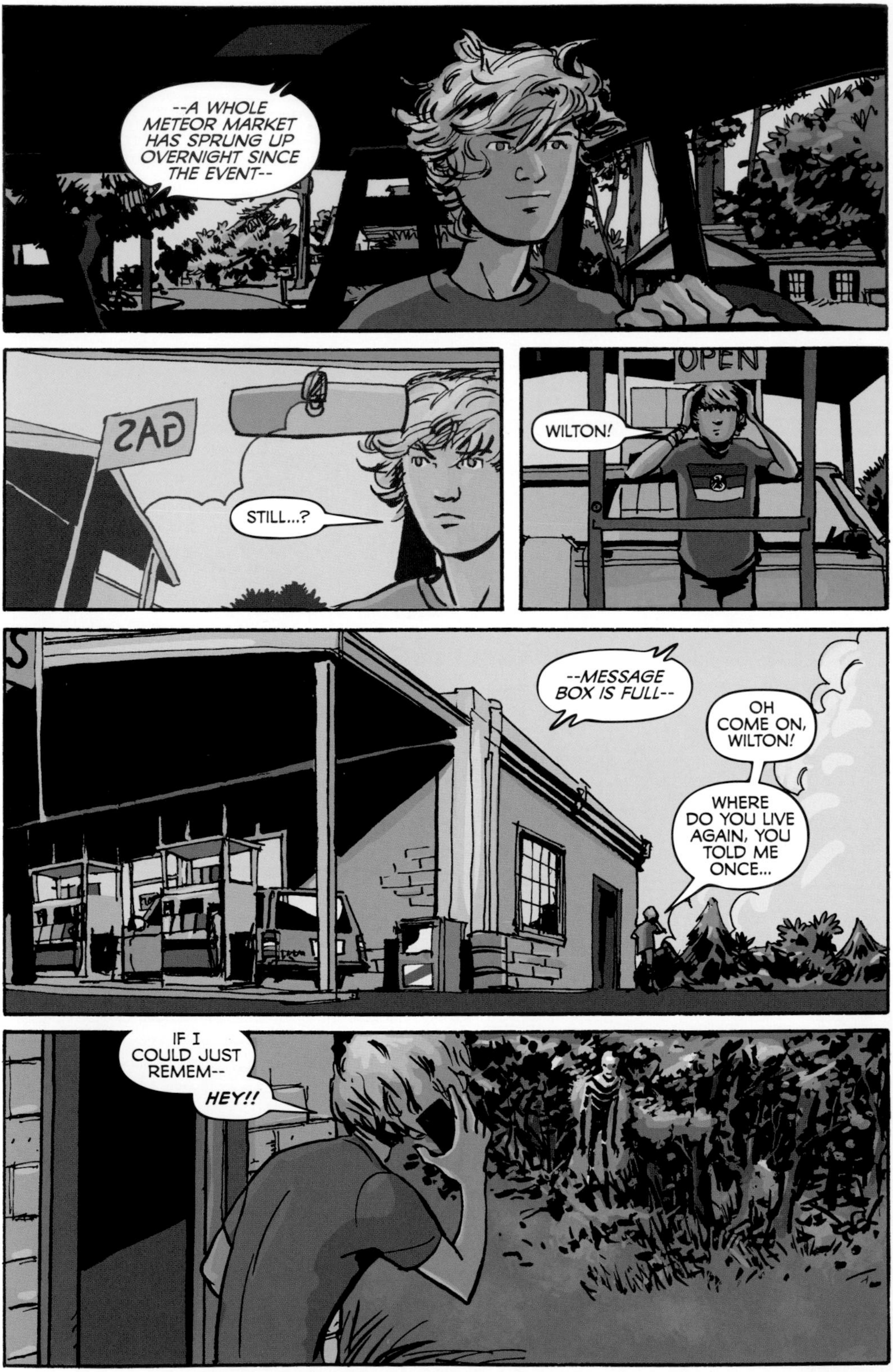
--A WHOLE METEOR MARKET HAS SPRUNG UP OVERNIGHT SINCE THE EVENT--
GAS
STILL...?
OPEN
WILTON!
--MESSAGE BOX IS FULL--
OH COME ON, WILTON!
WHERE DO YOU LIVE AGAIN, YOU TOLD ME ONCE...
IF I COULD JUST REMEM--
HEY!!

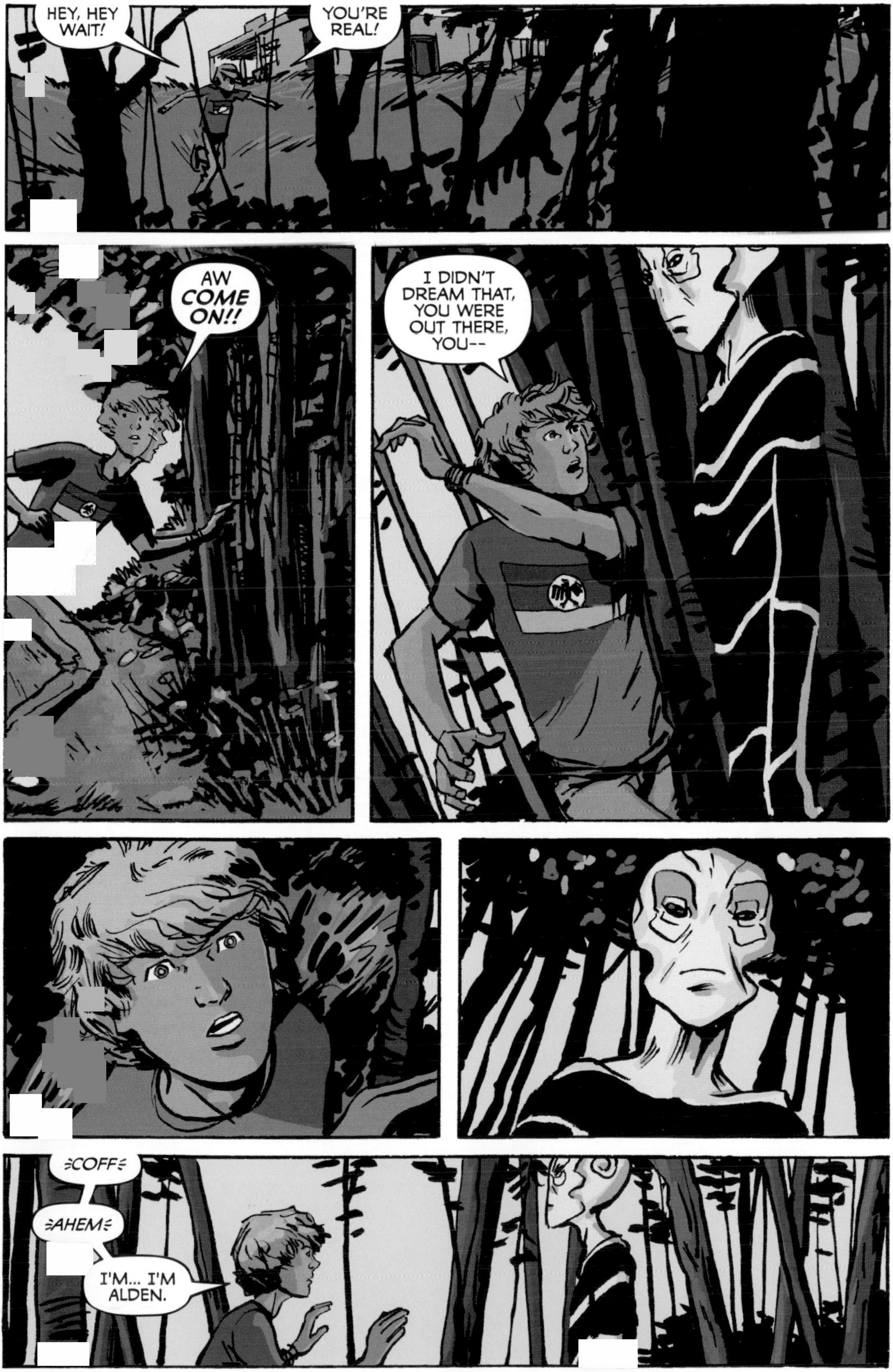
HEY, HEY WAIT!
YOU'RE REAL!
AW COME ON!!
I DIDN'T DREAM THAT, YOU WERE OUT THERE, YOU--
COFF
AHEM
I'M... I'M ALDEN.

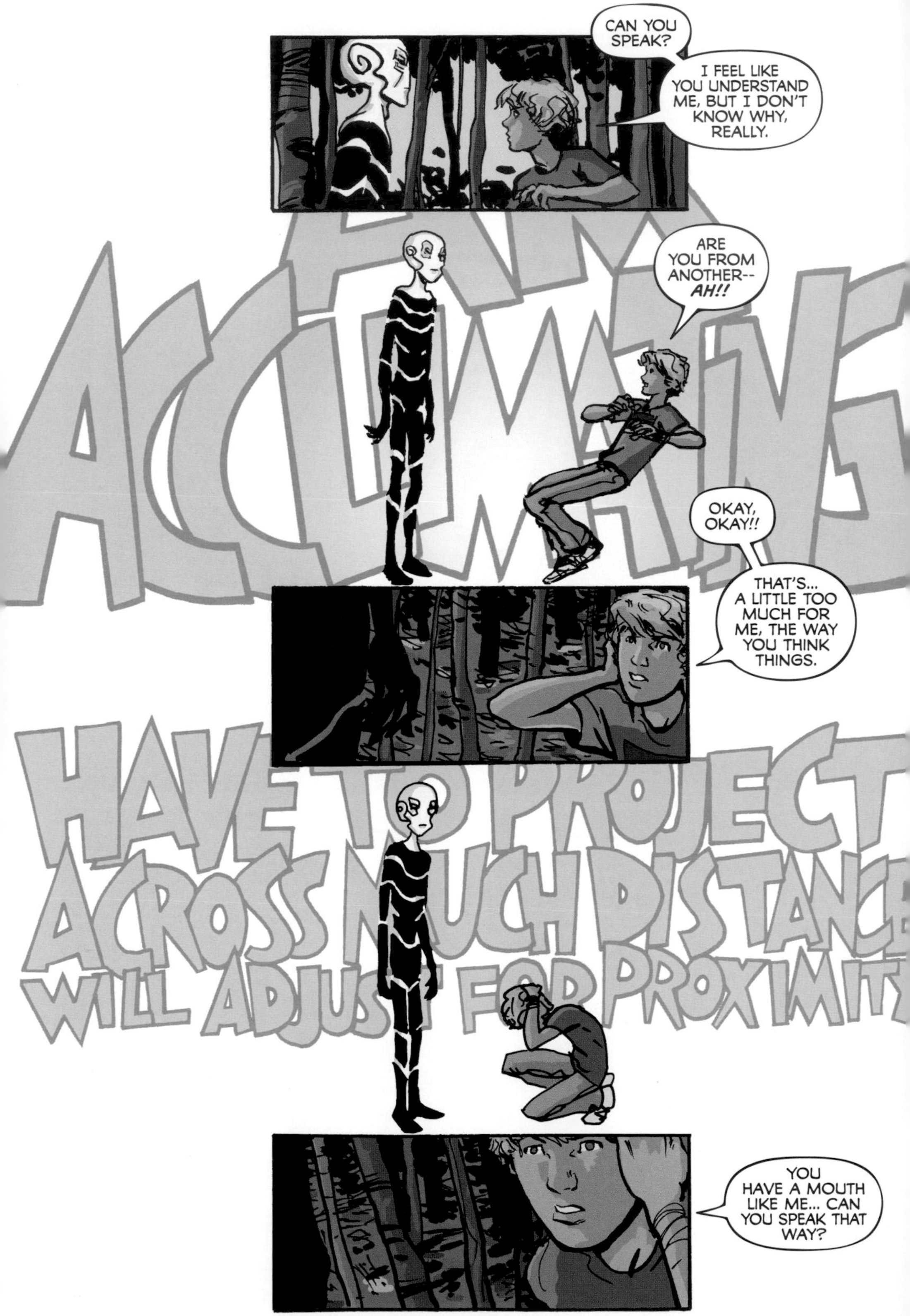
CAN YOU SPEAK?
I FEEL LIKE YOU UNDERSTAND ME, BUT I DON'T KNOW WHY, REALLY.
ARE YOU FROM ANOTHER-- *AH!!*
OKAY, OKAY!!
THAT'S... A LITTLE TOO MUCH FOR ME, THE WAY YOU THINK THINGS.
HAVE TO PROJECT
YOU HAVE A MOUTH LIKE ME... CAN YOU SPEAK THAT WAY?

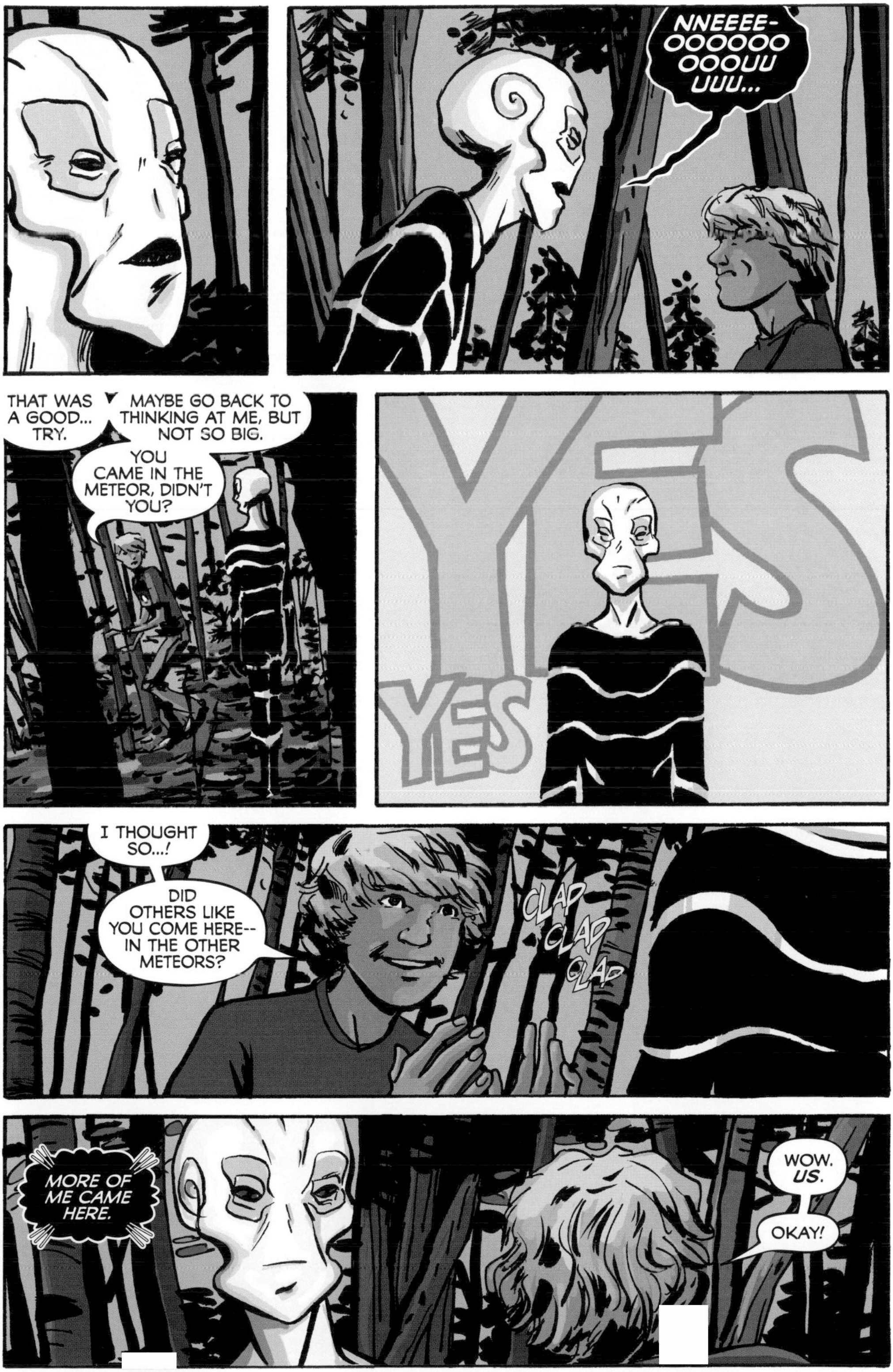
NNEEEE-OOOOOO OOOUU UUU...
THAT WAS A GOOD... TRY.
MAYBE GO BACK TO THINKING AT ME, BUT NOT SO BIG.
YOU CAME IN THE METEOR, DIDN'T YOU?
YES
YES
I THOUGHT SO...!
DID OTHERS LIKE YOU COME HERE-- IN THE OTHER METEORS?
CLAP CLAP CLAP
MORE OF ME CAME HERE.
WOW. US.
OKAY!

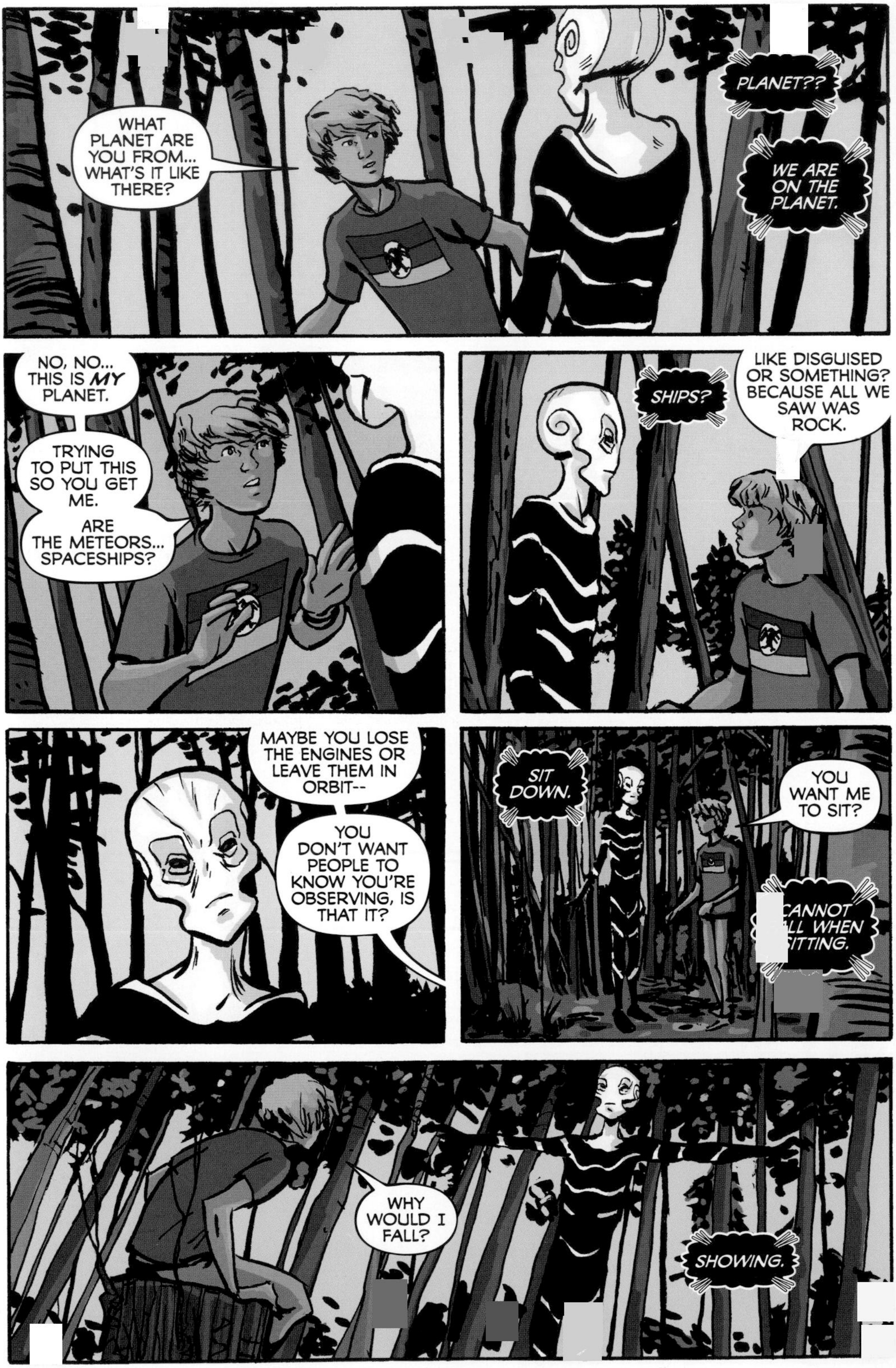
WHAT PLANET ARE YOU FROM... WHAT'S IT LIKE THERE?
PLANET??
WE ARE ON THE PLANET.
NO, NO... THIS IS *MY* PLANET.
TRYING TO PUT THIS SO YOU GET ME.
ARE THE METEORS... SPACESHIPS?
SHIPS?
LIKE DISGUISED OR SOMETHING? BECAUSE ALL WE SAW WAS ROCK.
MAYBE YOU LOSE THE ENGINES OR LEAVE THEM IN ORBIT--
YOU DON'T WANT PEOPLE TO KNOW YOU'RE OBSERVING, IS THAT IT?
SIT DOWN.
YOU WANT ME TO SIT?
CANNOT
LL WHEN
ITTING.
WHY WOULD I FALL?
SHOWING.

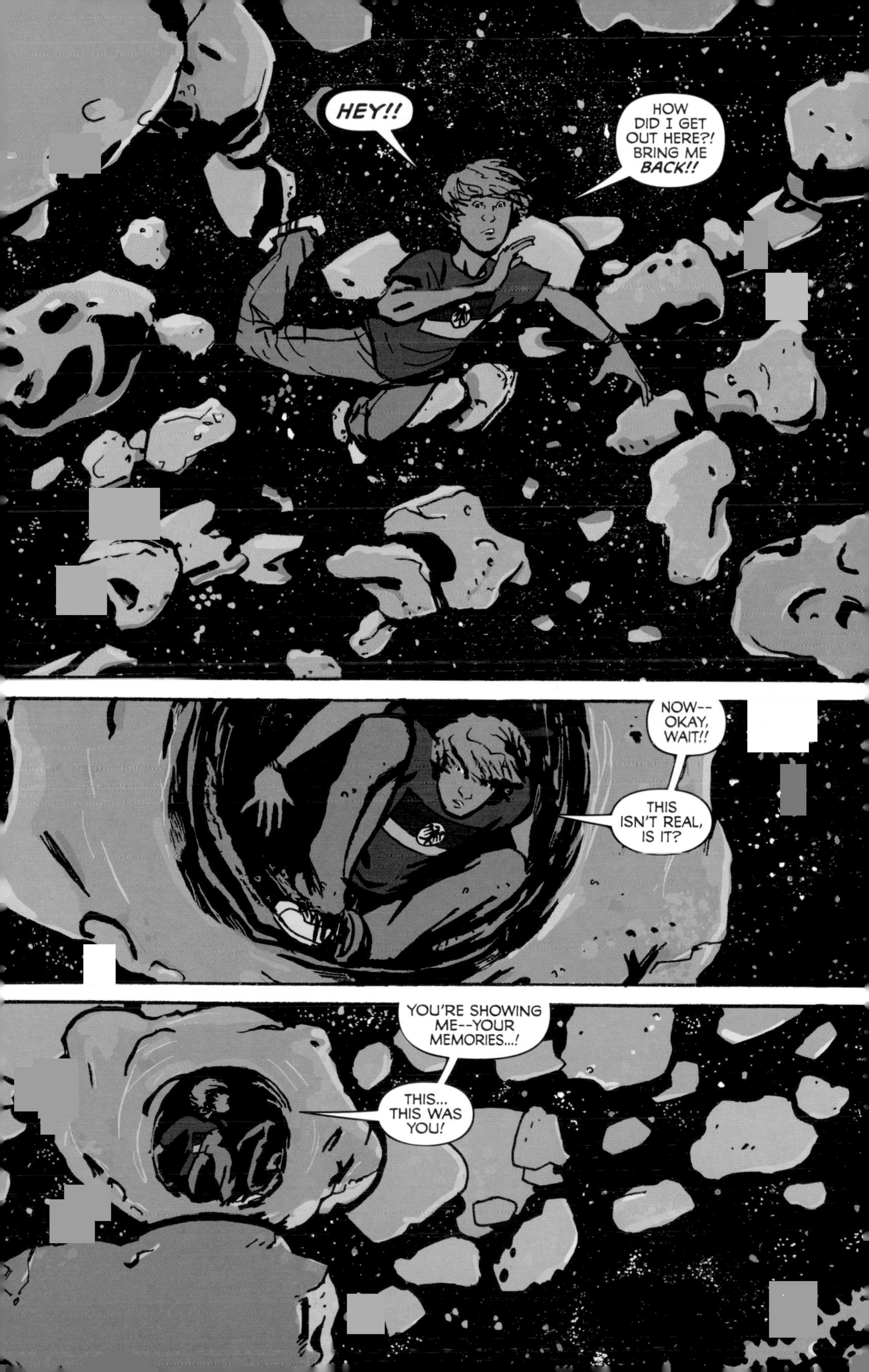
HEY!!
HOW DID I GET OUT HERE?! BRING ME BACK!!
NOW-- OKAY, WAIT!!
THIS ISN'T REAL, IS IT?
YOU'RE SHOWING ME--YOUR MEMORIES...!
THIS... THIS WAS YOU!

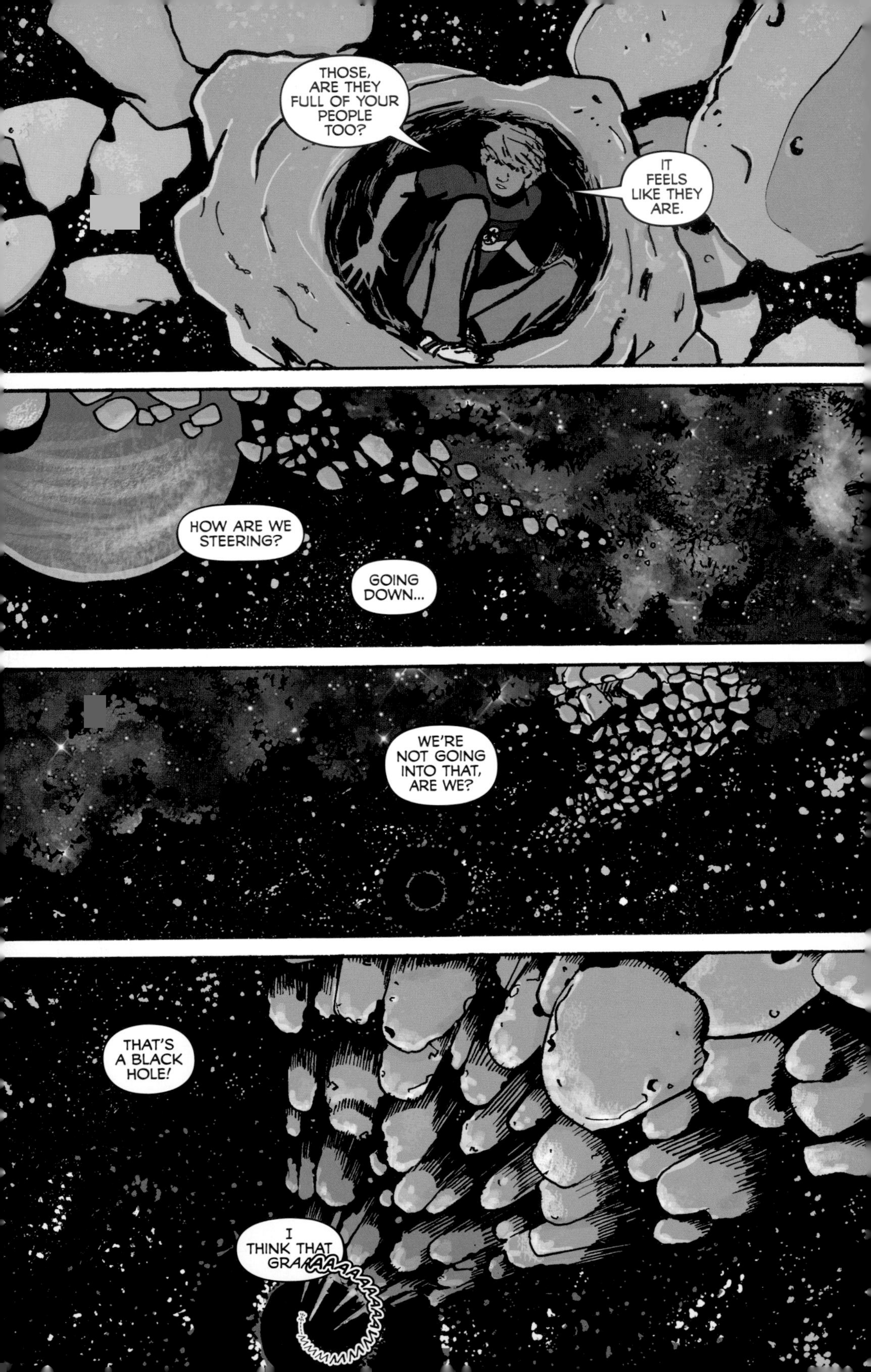
THOSE, ARE THEY FULL OF YOUR PEOPLE TOO?
IT FEELS LIKE THEY ARE.
HOW ARE WE STEERING?
GOING DOWN...
WE'RE NOT GOING INTO THAT, ARE WE?
THAT'S A BLACK HOLE!
I THINK THAT GRA
AAAAAAAAAAAAAAAAAAAA

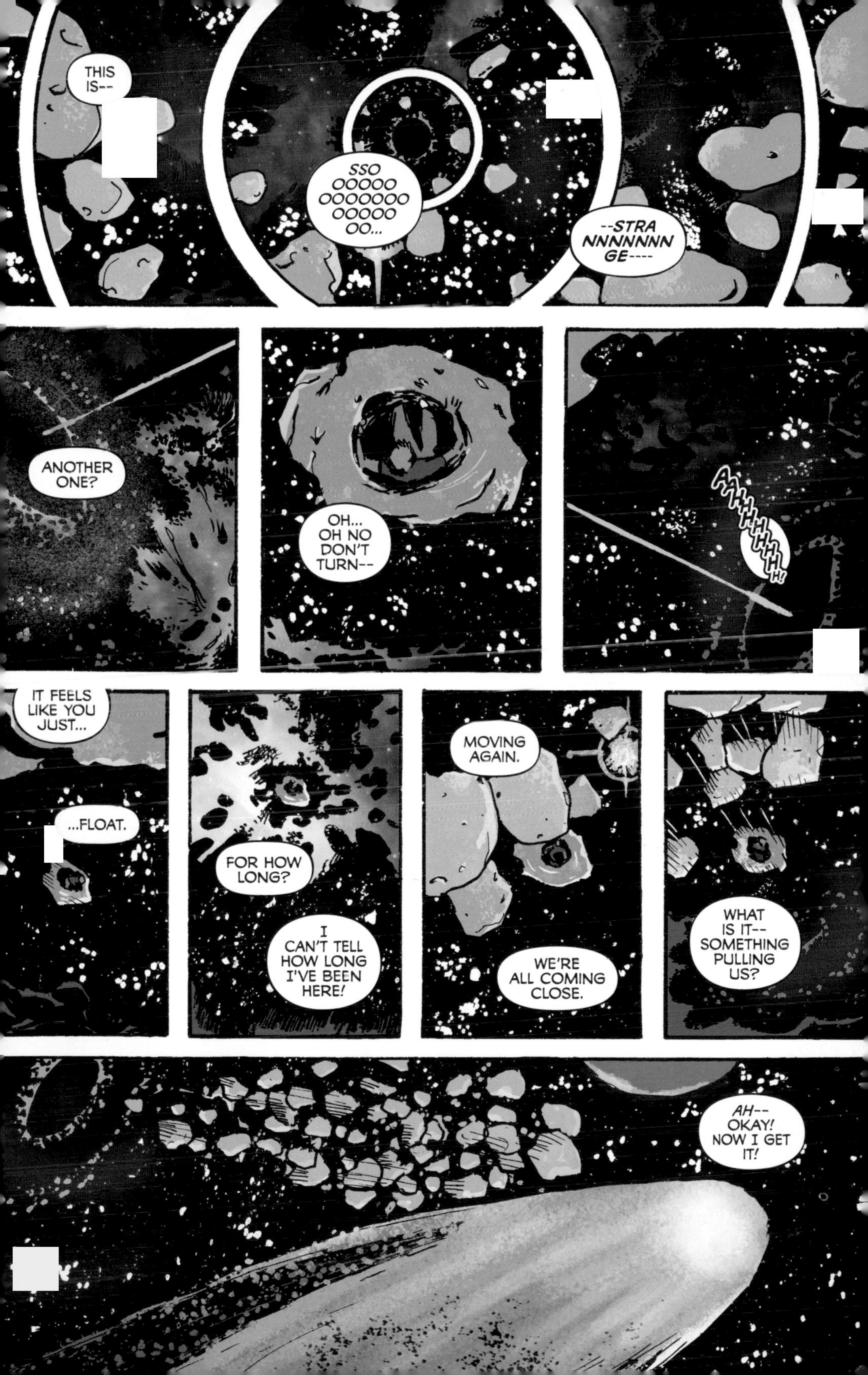
THIS IS--
SSO OOOOO OOOOOOO OOOOO OO...
--STRA NNNNNNN GE----
ANOTHER ONE?
OH... OH NO DON'T TURN--
AAHHHHHHHH!
IT FEELS LIKE YOU JUST...
...FLOAT.
FOR HOW LONG?
I CAN'T TELL HOW LONG I'VE BEEN HERE!
MOVING AGAIN.
WE'RE ALL COMING CLOSE.
WHAT IS IT-- SOMETHING PULLING US?
AH-- OKAY! NOW I GET IT!

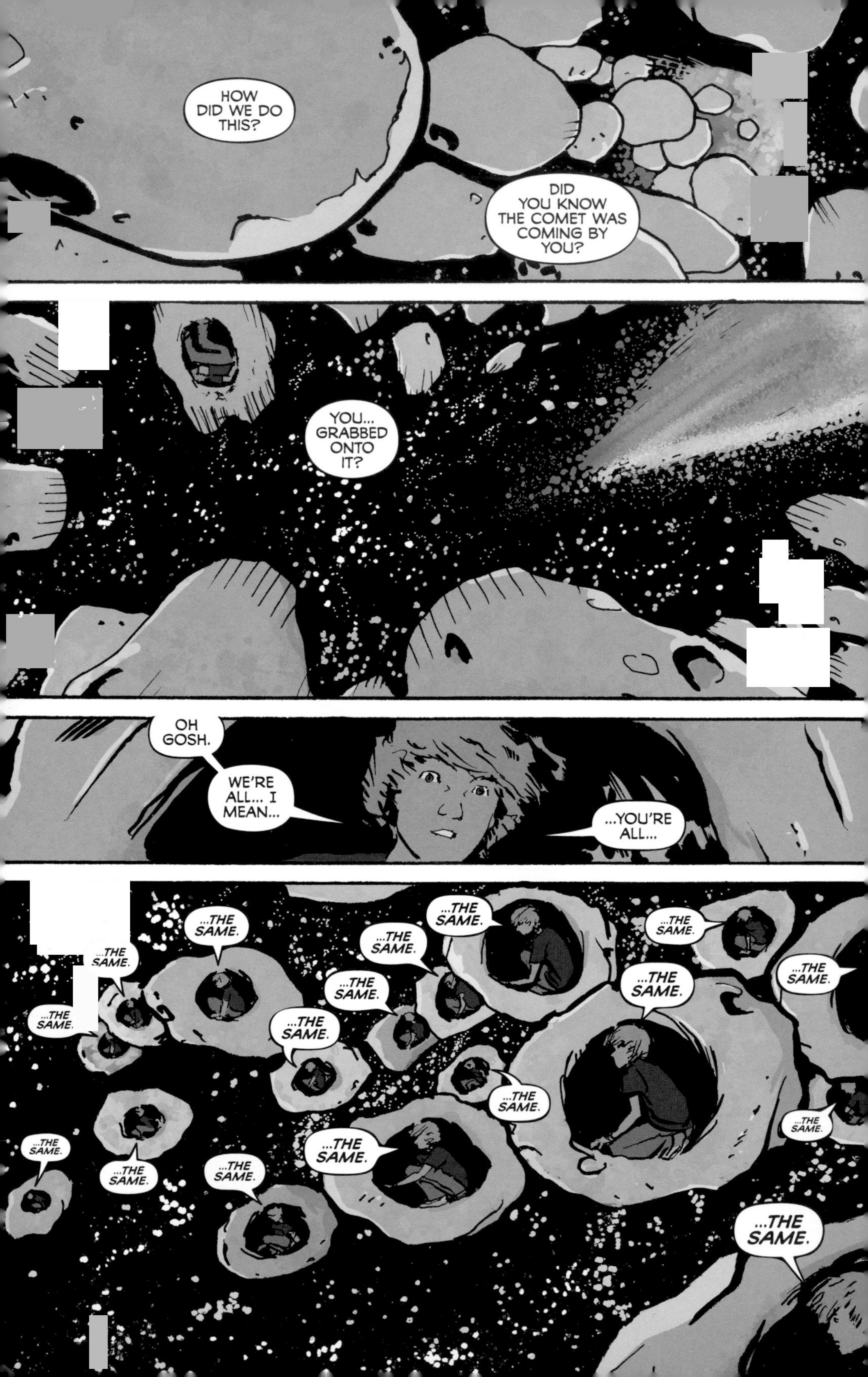
HOW DID WE DO THIS?
DID YOU KNOW THE COMET WAS COMING BY YOU?
YOU... GRABBED ONTO IT?
OH GOSH.
WE'RE ALL... I MEAN...
...YOU'RE ALL...
...THE SAME.
...THE SAME.
...THE SAME.
...THE SAME.
...THE SAME.
...THE SAME.
...THE SAME.
...THE SAME.
...THE SAME.
...THE SAME.
...THE SAME.
...THE SAME.
...THE SAME.
...THE SAME.
...THE SAME.
...THE SAME.
...THE SAME.

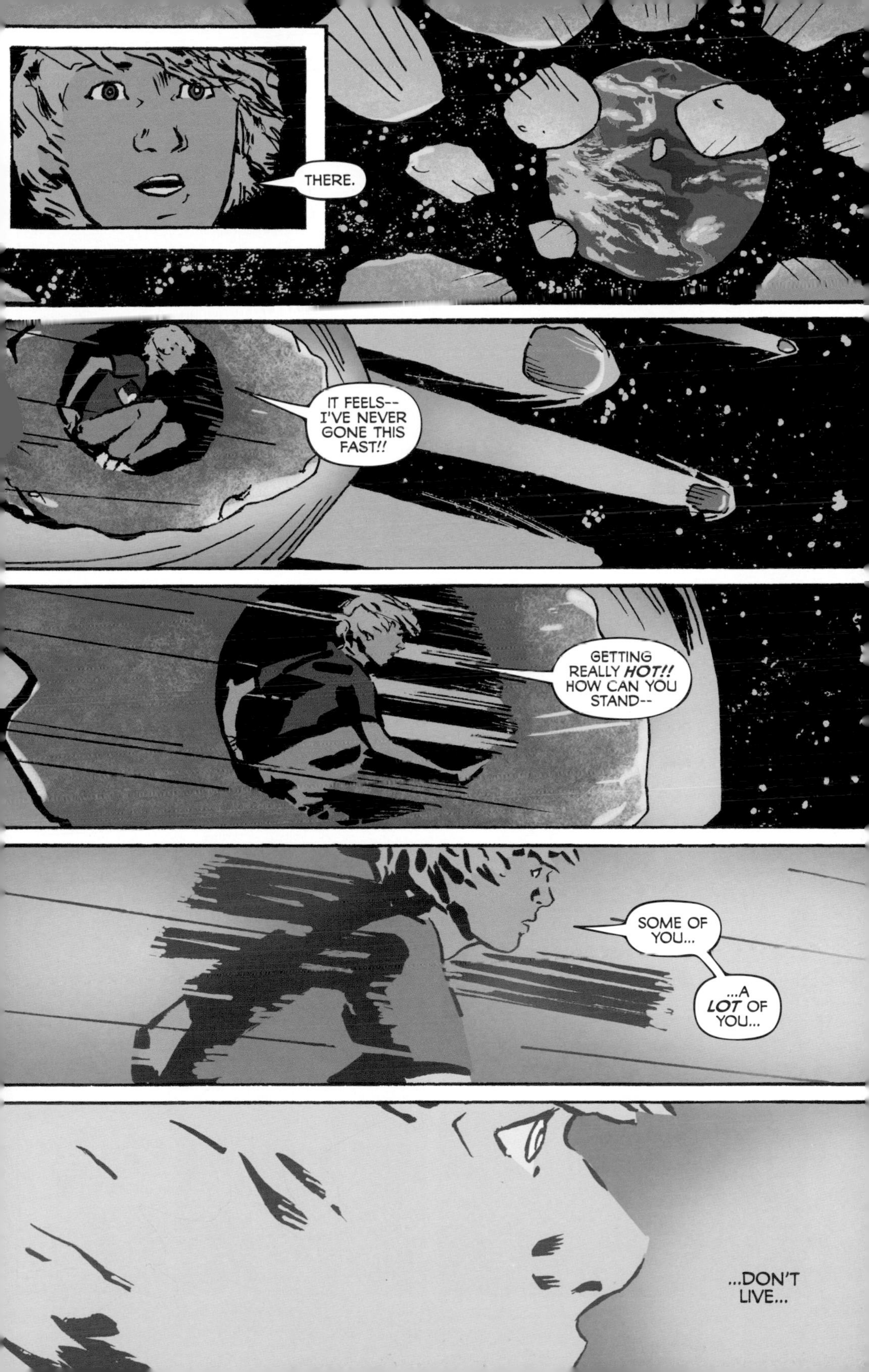
THERE.
IT FEELS-- I'VE NEVER GONE THIS FAST!!
GETTING REALLY HOT!! HOW CAN YOU STAND--
SOME OF YOU...
...A LOT OF YOU...
...DON'T LIVE...

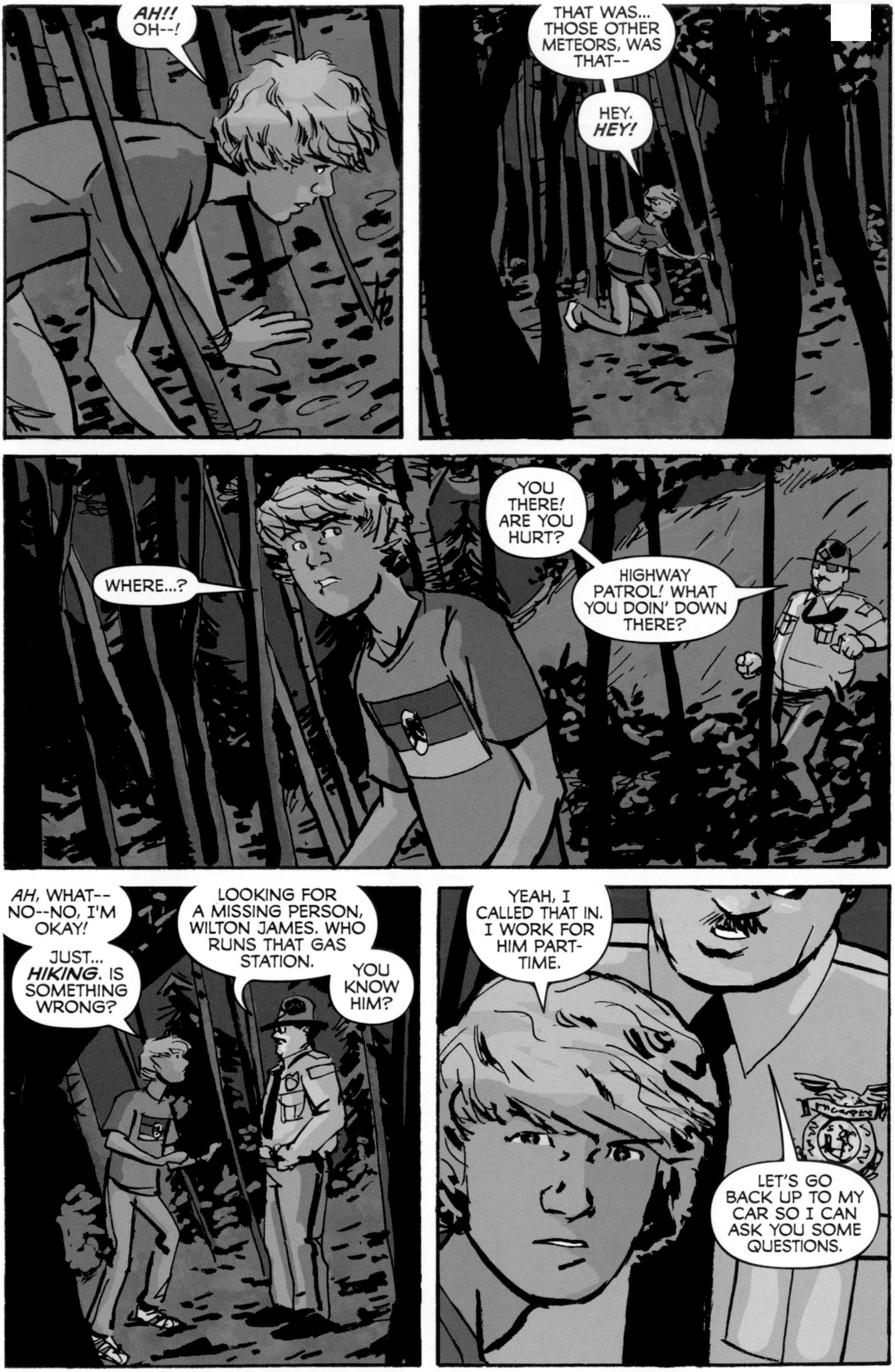
AH!! OH--!
THAT WAS... THOSE OTHER METEORS, WAS THAT--
HEY. HEY!
YOU THERE! ARE YOU HURT?
WHERE...?
HIGHWAY PATROL! WHAT YOU DOIN' DOWN THERE?
AH, WHAT-- NO--NO, I'M OKAY!
JUST... HIKING. IS SOMETHING WRONG?
LOOKING FOR A MISSING PERSON, WILTON JAMES. WHO RUNS THAT GAS STATION.
YOU KNOW HIM?
YEAH, I CALLED THAT IN. I WORK FOR HIM PART-TIME.
LET'S GO BACK UP TO MY CAR SO I CAN ASK YOU SOME QUESTIONS.

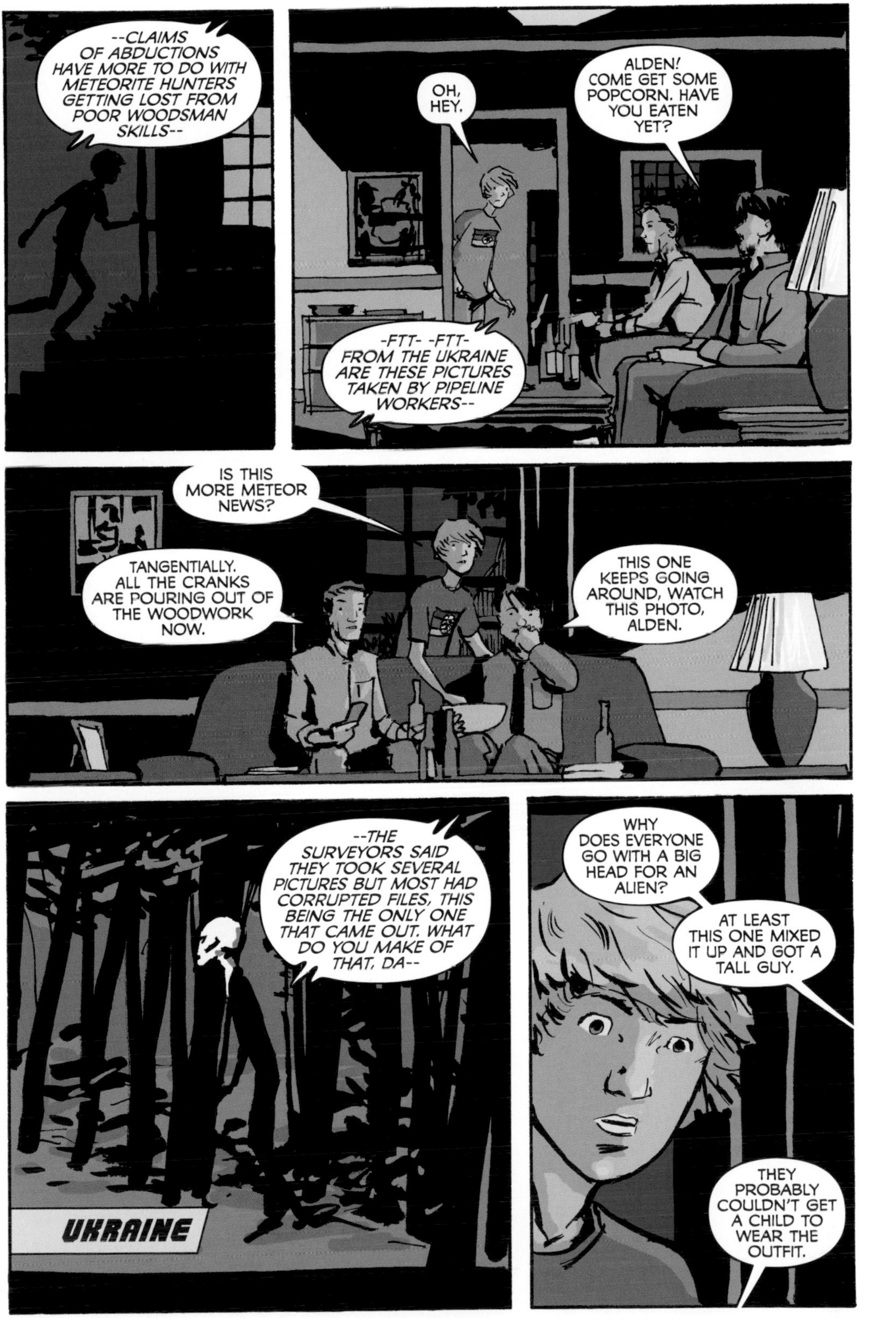
--CLAIMS OF ABDUCTIONS HAVE MORE TO DO WITH METEORITE HUNTERS GETTING LOST FROM POOR WOODSMAN SKILLS--
OH, HEY.
ALDEN! COME GET SOME POPCORN. HAVE YOU EATEN YET?
-FTT- -FTT- FROM THE UKRAINE ARE THESE PICTURES TAKEN BY PIPELINE WORKERS--
IS THIS MORE METEOR NEWS?
TANGENTIALLY. ALL THE CRANKS ARE POURING OUT OF THE WOODWORK NOW.
THIS ONE KEEPS GOING AROUND, WATCH THIS PHOTO, ALDEN.
--THE SURVEYORS SAID THEY TOOK SEVERAL PICTURES BUT MOST HAD CORRUPTED FILES, THIS BEING THE ONLY ONE THAT CAME OUT. WHAT DO YOU MAKE OF THAT, DA--
UKRAINE
WHY DOES EVERYONE GO WITH A BIG HEAD FOR AN ALIEN?
AT LEAST THIS ONE MIXED IT UP AND GOT A TALL GUY.
THEY PROBABLY COULDN'T GET A CHILD TO WEAR THE OUTFIT.

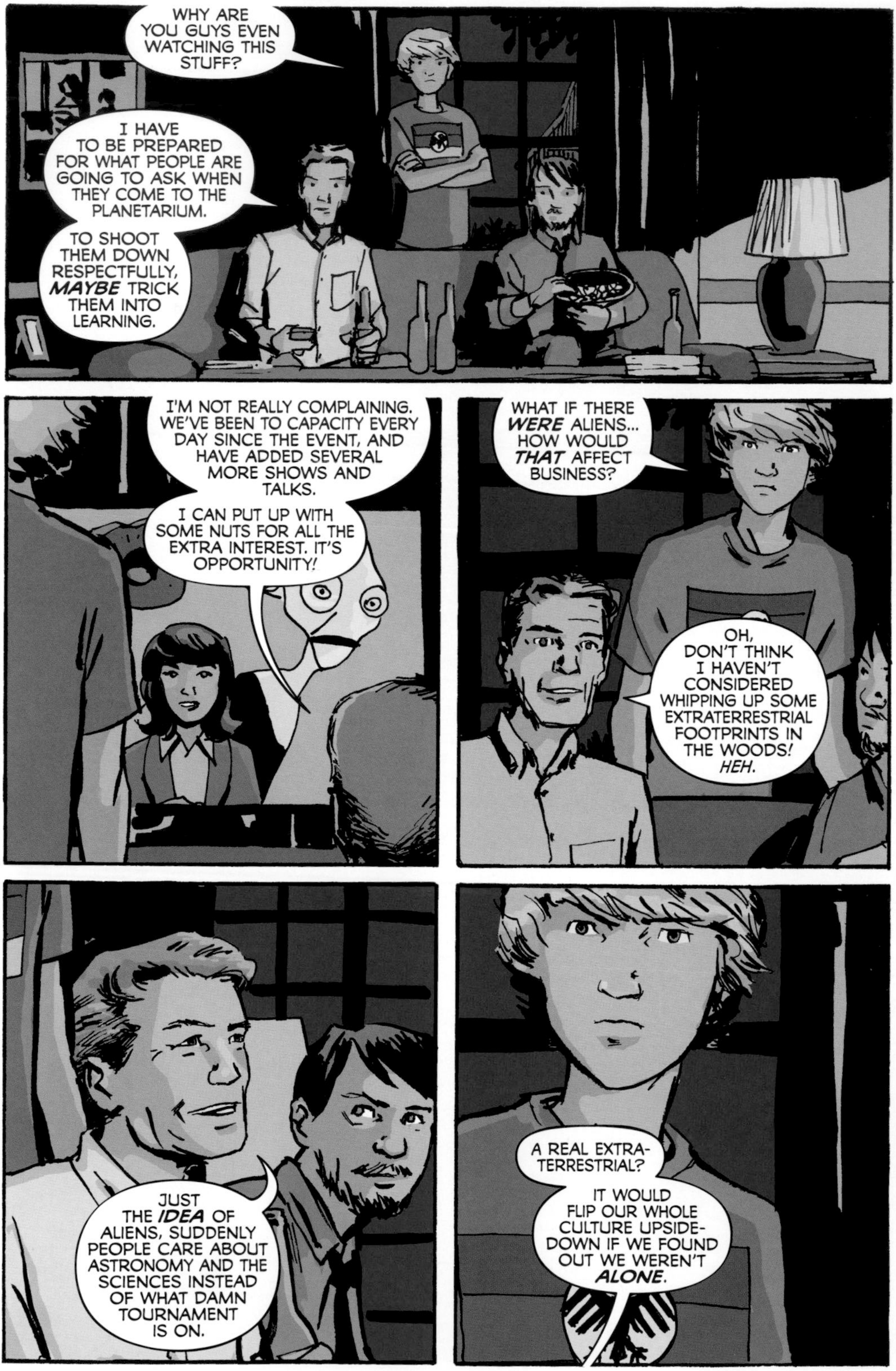
WHY ARE YOU GUYS EVEN WATCHING THIS STUFF?
I HAVE TO BE PREPARED FOR WHAT PEOPLE ARE GOING TO ASK WHEN THEY COME TO THE PLANETARIUM.
TO SHOOT THEM DOWN RESPECTFULLY, *MAYBE* TRICK THEM INTO LEARNING.
I'M NOT REALLY COMPLAINING. WE'VE BEEN TO CAPACITY EVERY DAY SINCE THE EVENT, AND HAVE ADDED SEVERAL MORE SHOWS AND TALKS.
I CAN PUT UP WITH SOME NUTS FOR ALL THE EXTRA INTEREST. IT'S OPPORTUNITY!
WHAT IF THERE *WERE* ALIENS... HOW WOULD *THAT* AFFECT BUSINESS?
OH, DON'T THINK I HAVEN'T CONSIDERED WHIPPING UP SOME EXTRATERRESTRIAL FOOTPRINTS IN THE WOODS! *HEH*.
JUST THE *IDEA* OF ALIENS, SUDDENLY PEOPLE CARE ABOUT ASTRONOMY AND THE SCIENCES INSTEAD OF WHAT DAMN TOURNAMENT IS ON.
A REAL EXTRA-TERRESTRIAL?
IT WOULD FLIP OUR WHOLE CULTURE UPSIDE-DOWN IF WE FOUND OUT WE WEREN'T *ALONE*.

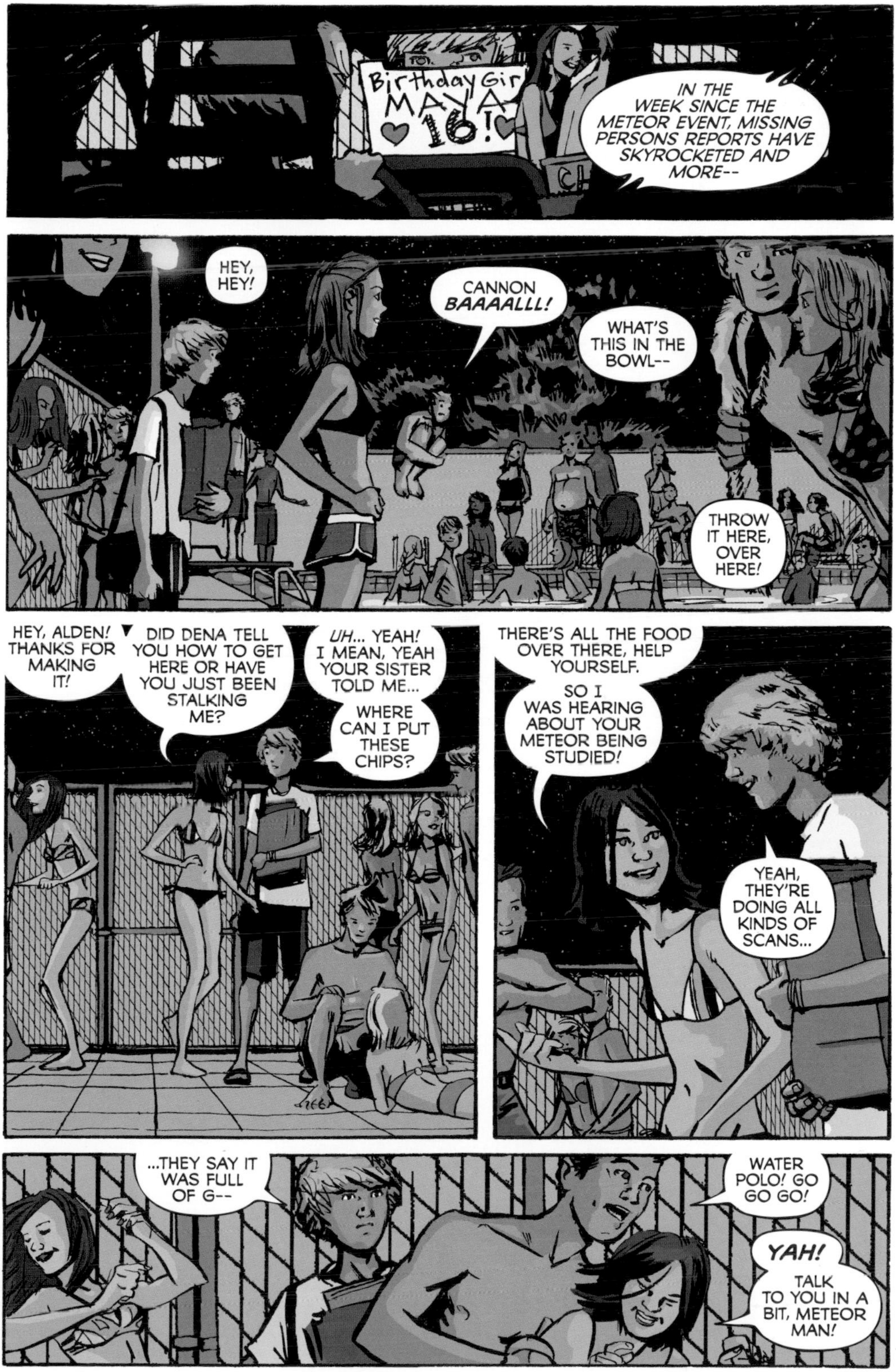
Birthday Girl MAYA 16!
TO:
CH
IN THE WEEK SINCE THE METEOR EVENT, MISSING PERSONS REPORTS HAVE SKYROCKETED AND MORE--
HEY, HEY!
CANNON *BAAAALLL!*
WHAT'S THIS IN THE BOWL--
THROW IT HERE, OVER HERE!
HEY, ALDEN! THANKS FOR MAKING IT!
DID DENA TELL YOU HOW TO GET HERE OR HAVE YOU JUST BEEN STALKING ME?
UH... YEAH! I MEAN, YEAH YOUR SISTER TOLD ME...
WHERE CAN I PUT THESE CHIPS?
THERE'S ALL THE FOOD OVER THERE, HELP YOURSELF.
SO I WAS HEARING ABOUT YOUR METEOR BEING STUDIED!
YEAH, THEY'RE DOING ALL KINDS OF SCANS...
...THEY SAY IT WAS FULL OF G--
WATER POLO! GO GO GO!
YAH!
TALK TO YOU IN A BIT, METEOR MAN!

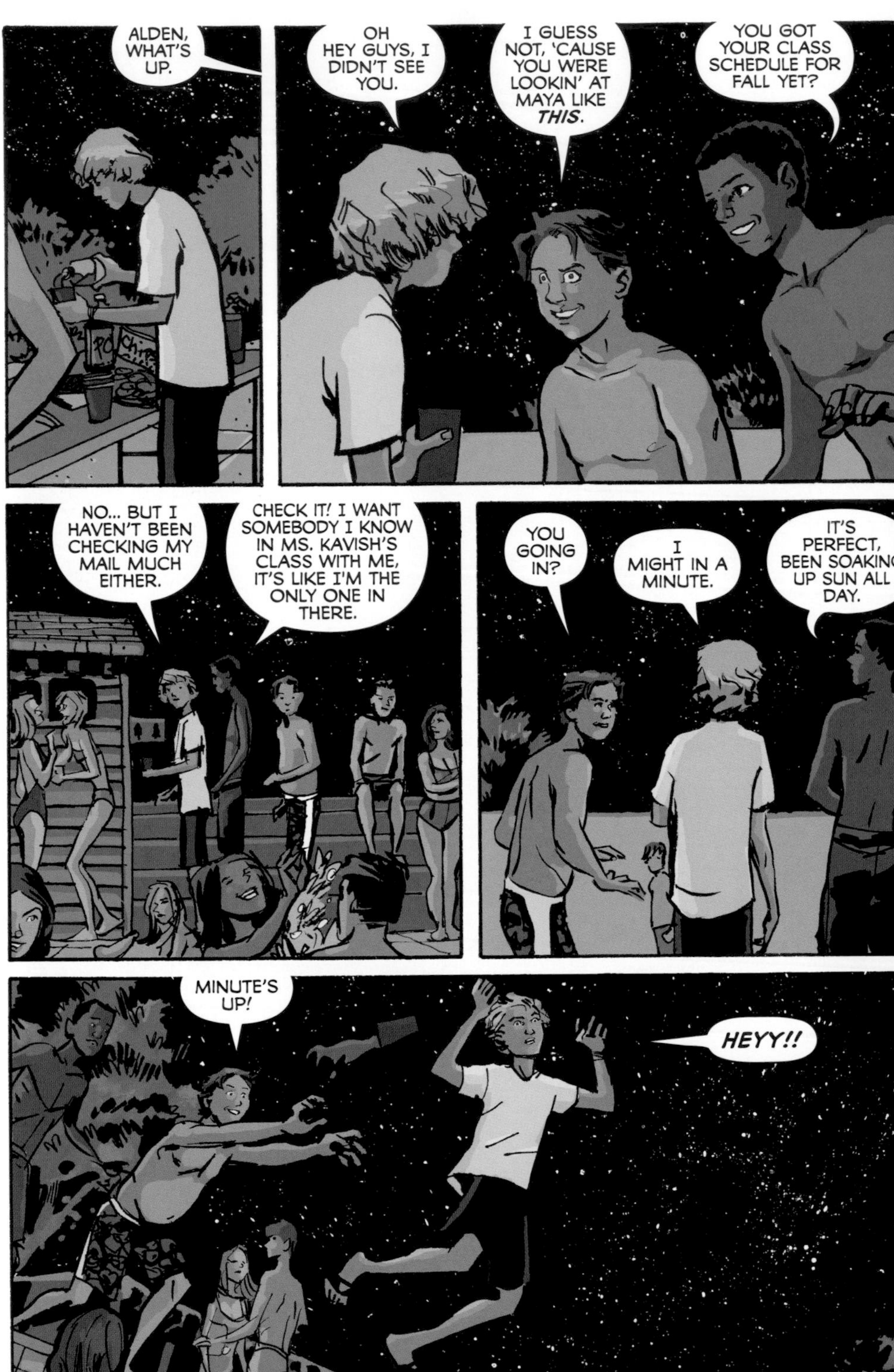
ALDEN, WHAT'S UP.
OH HEY GUYS, I DIDN'T SEE YOU.
I GUESS NOT, 'CAUSE YOU WERE LOOKIN' AT MAYA LIKE *THIS*.
YOU GOT YOUR CLASS SCHEDULE FOR FALL YET?
NO... BUT I HAVEN'T BEEN CHECKING MY MAIL MUCH EITHER.
CHECK IT! I WANT SOMEBODY I KNOW IN MS. KAVISH'S CLASS WITH ME, IT'S LIKE I'M THE ONLY ONE IN THERE.
YOU GOING IN?
I MIGHT IN A MINUTE.
IT'S PERFECT, BEEN SOAKING UP SUN ALL DAY.
MINUTE'S UP!
HEYY!!

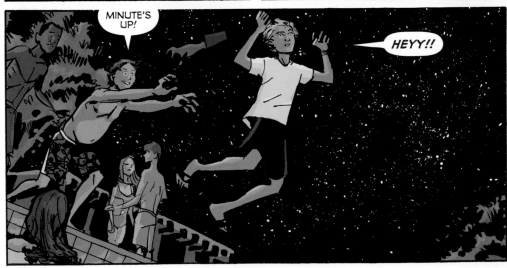

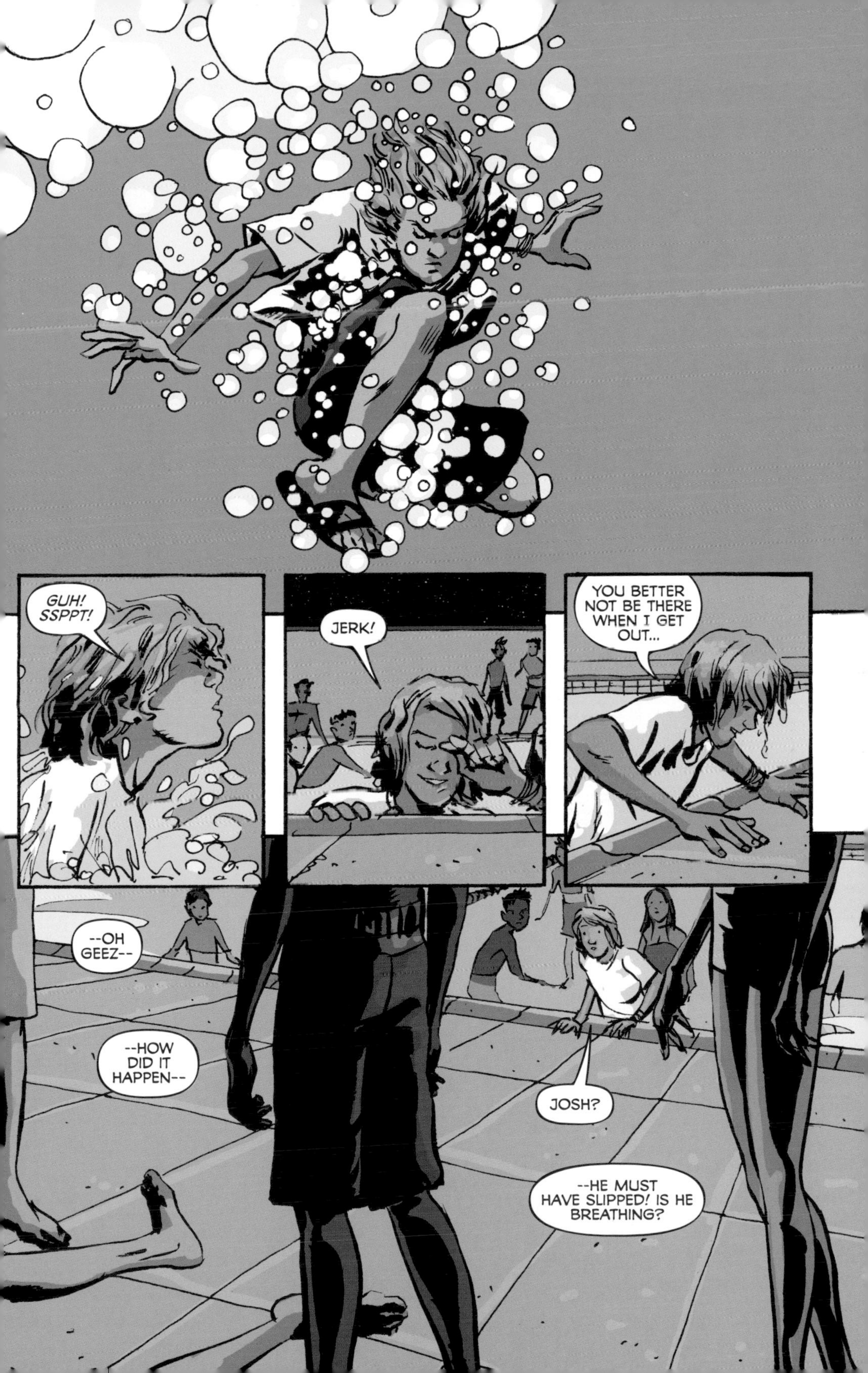
GUH! SSPPT!
JERK!
YOU BETTER NOT BE THERE WHEN I GET OUT...
--OH GEEZ--
--HOW DID IT HAPPEN--
JOSH?
--HE MUST HAVE SLIPPED! IS HE BREATHING?

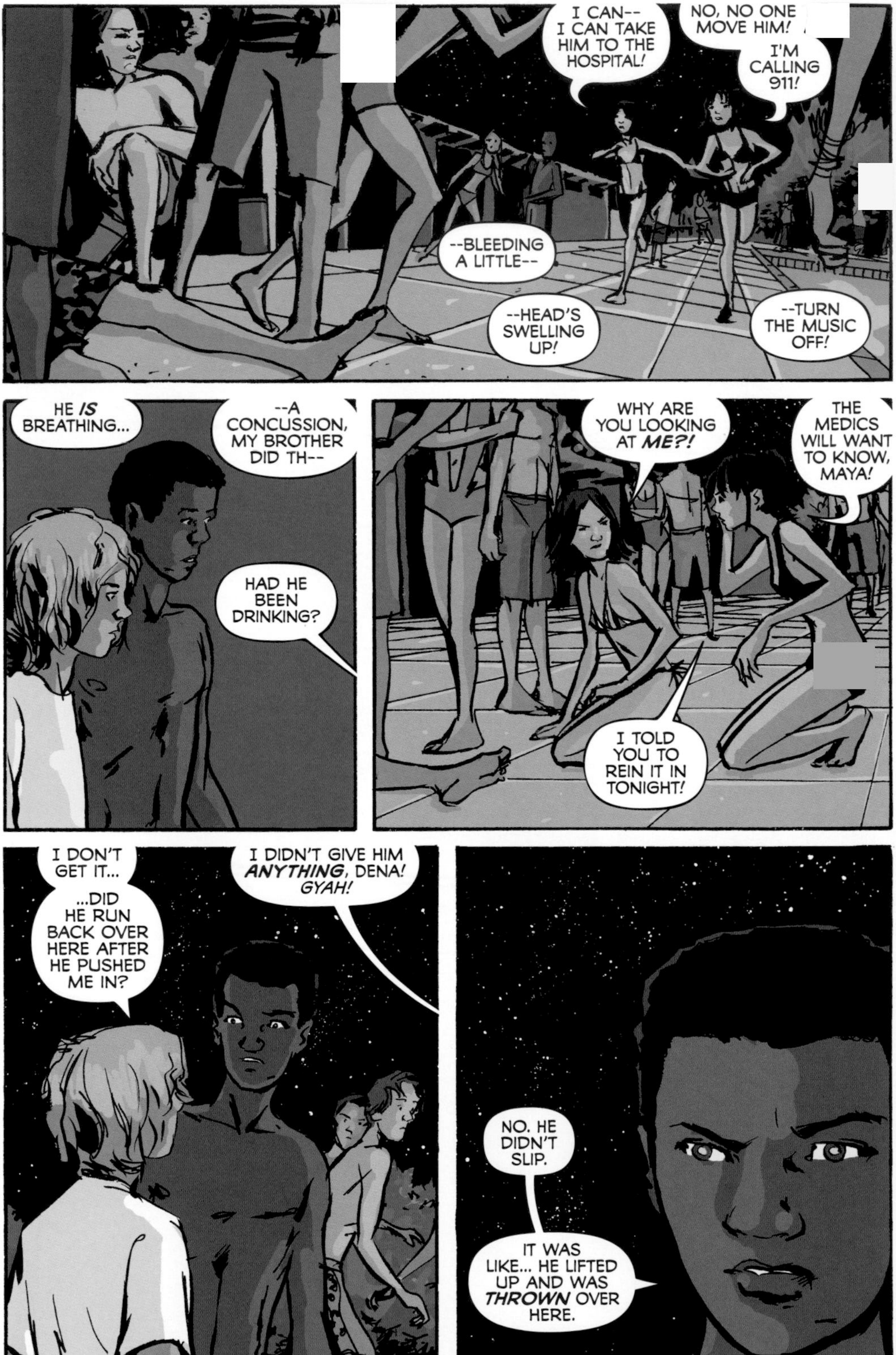
I CAN-- I CAN TAKE HIM TO THE HOSPITAL!
NO, NO ONE MOVE HIM!
I'M CALLING 911!
--BLEEDING A LITTLE--
--HEAD'S SWELLING UP!
--TURN THE MUSIC OFF!
HE *IS* BREATHING...
--A CONCUSSION, MY BROTHER DID TH--
HAD HE BEEN DRINKING?
WHY ARE YOU LOOKING AT *ME?!*
THE MEDICS WILL WANT TO KNOW, MAYA!
I TOLD YOU TO REIN IT IN TONIGHT!
I DON'T GET IT...
...DID HE RUN BACK OVER HERE AFTER HE PUSHED ME IN?
I DIDN'T GIVE HIM *ANYTHING*, DENA! *GYAH!*
NO. HE DIDN'T SLIP.
IT WAS LIKE... HE LIFTED UP AND WAS *THROWN* OVER HERE.

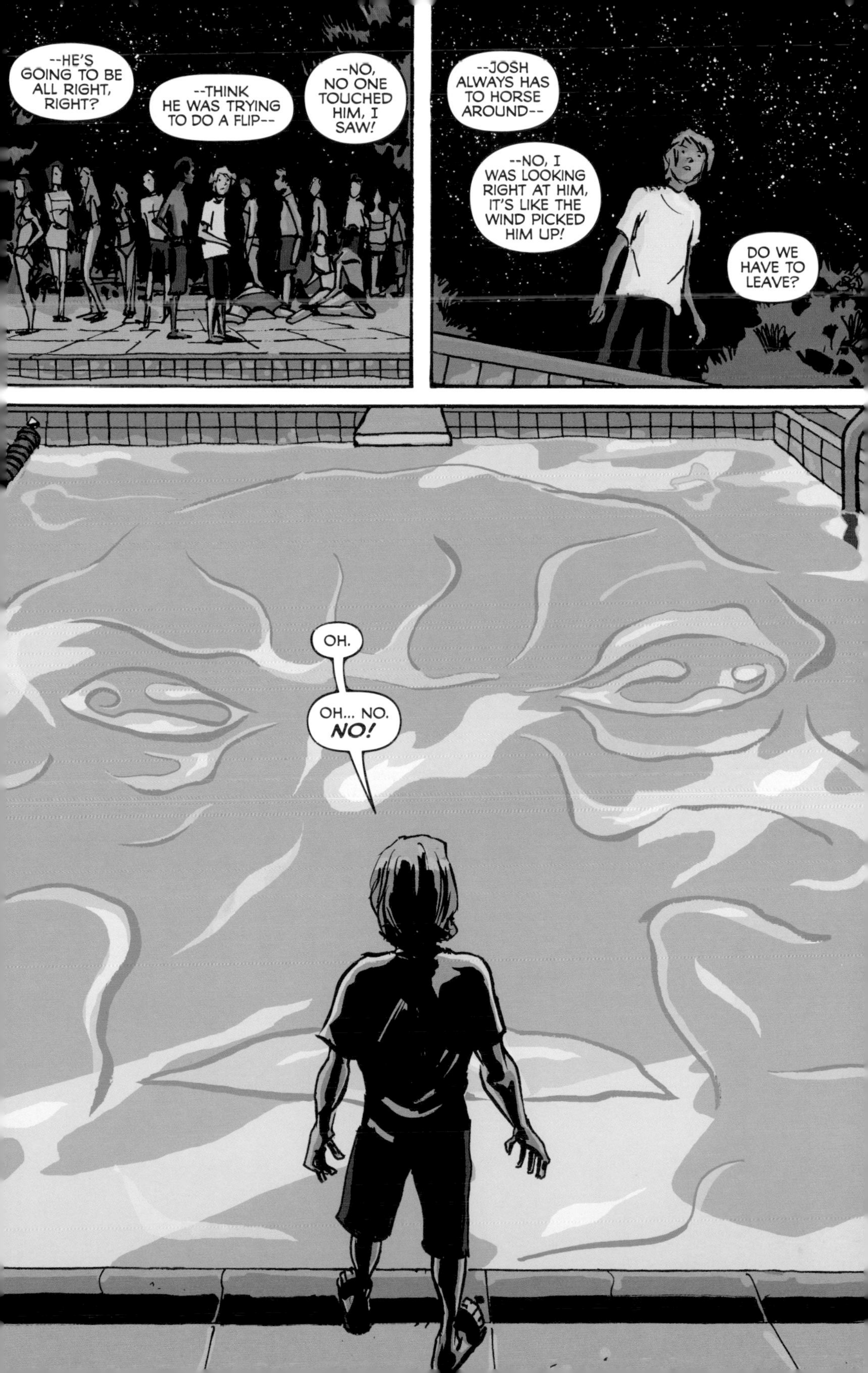
--HE'S GOING TO BE ALL RIGHT, RIGHT?
--THINK HE WAS TRYING TO DO A FLIP--
--NO, NO ONE TOUCHED HIM, I SAW!
--JOSH ALWAYS HAS TO HORSE AROUND--
--NO, I WAS LOOKING RIGHT AT HIM, IT'S LIKE THE WIND PICKED HIM UP!
DO WE HAVE TO LEAVE?
OH.
OH... NO. *NO!*

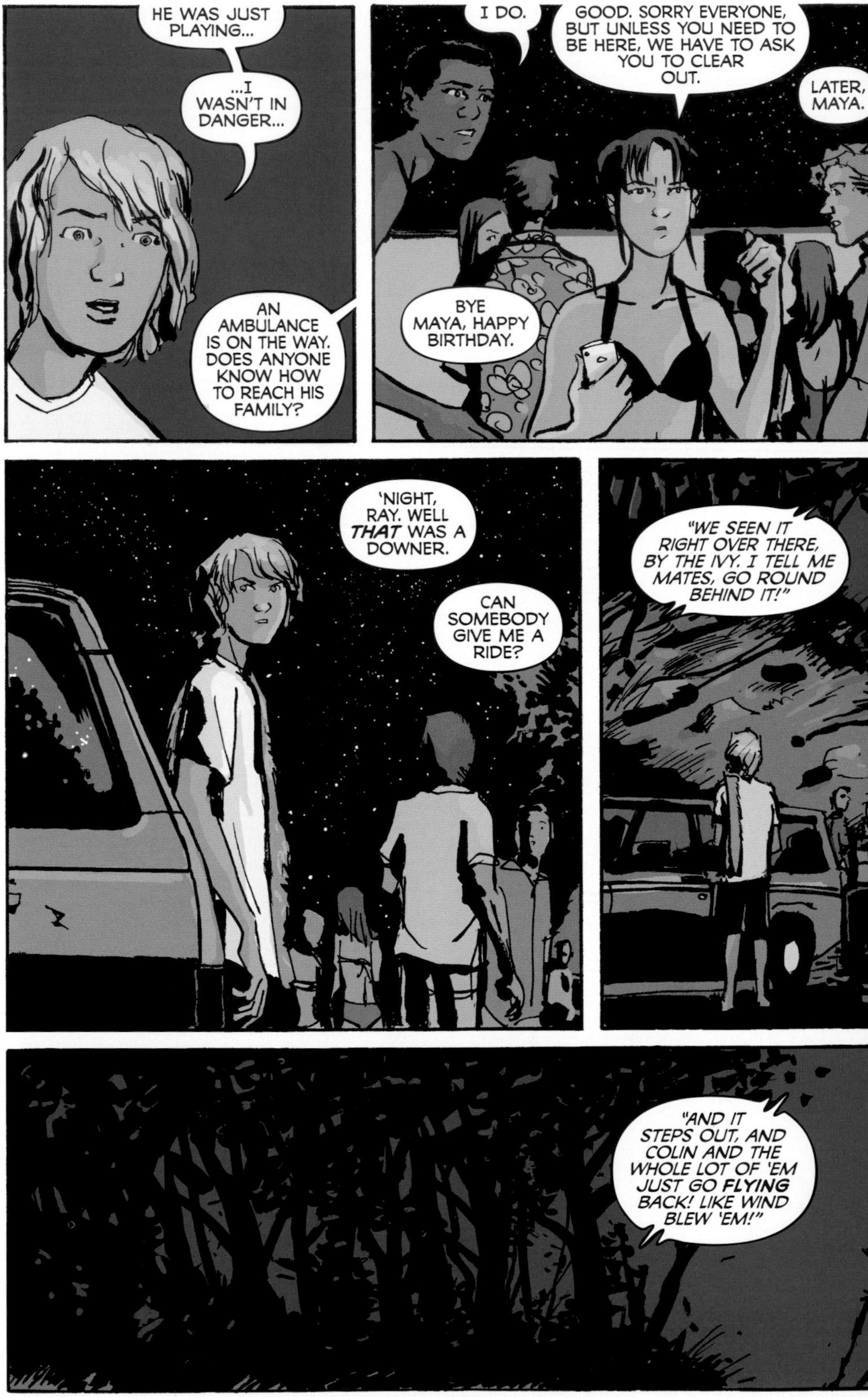
HE WAS JUST PLAYING...
...I WASN'T IN DANGER...
AN AMBULANCE IS ON THE WAY. DOES ANYONE KNOW HOW TO REACH HIS FAMILY?
I DO.
GOOD. SORRY EVERYONE, BUT UNLESS YOU NEED TO BE HERE, WE HAVE TO ASK YOU TO CLEAR OUT.
LATER, MAYA.
BYE MAYA, HAPPY BIRTHDAY.
'NIGHT, RAY. WELL *THAT* WAS A DOWNER.
CAN SOMEBODY GIVE ME A RIDE?
"WE SEEN IT RIGHT OVER THERE, BY THE IVY. I TELL ME MATES, GO ROUND BEHIND IT!"
"AND IT STEPS OUT, AND COLIN AND THE WHOLE LOT OF 'EM JUST GO ***FLYING*** *BACK! LIKE WIND BLEW 'EM!"*

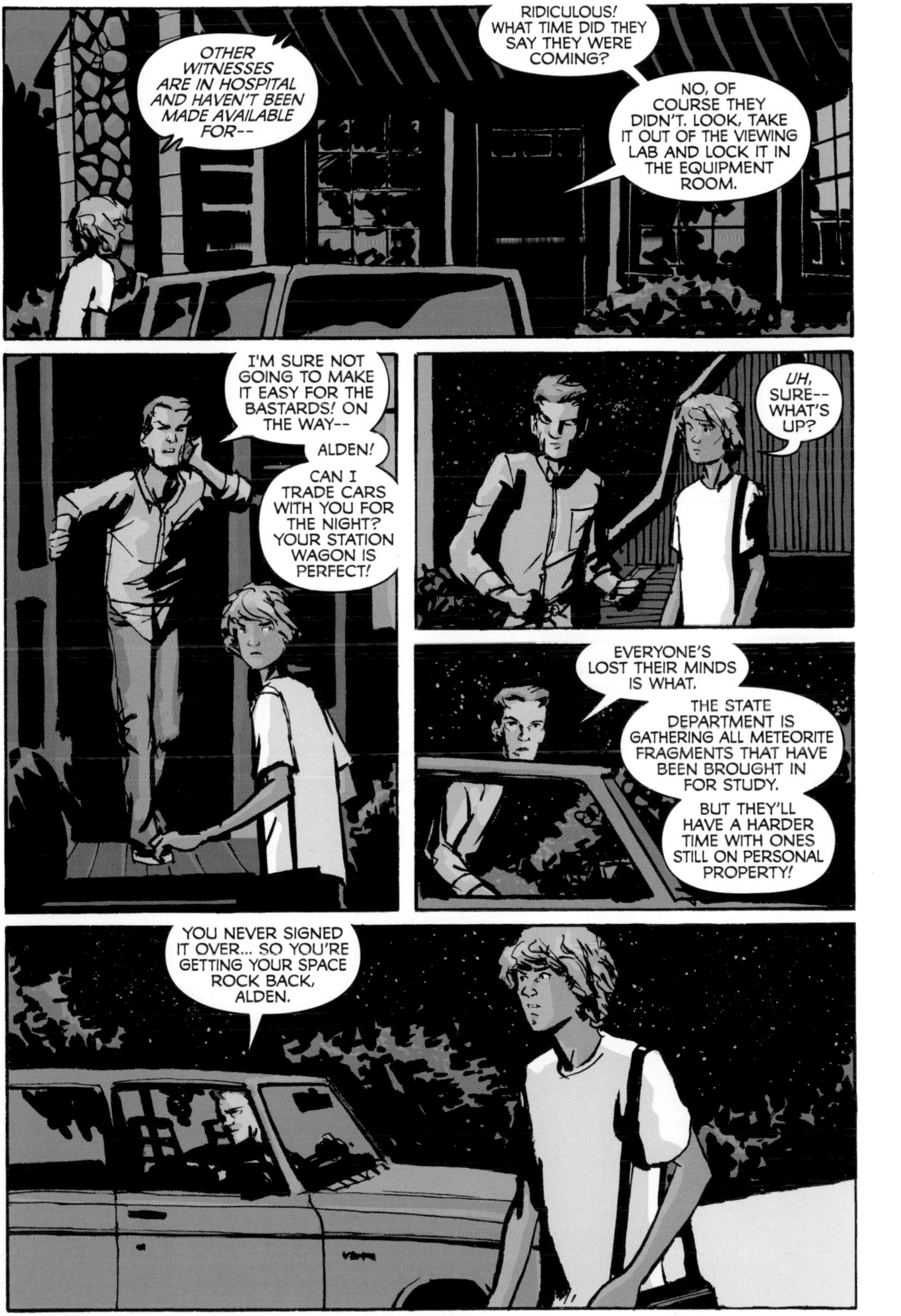
OTHER WITNESSES ARE IN HOSPITAL AND HAVEN'T BEEN MADE AVAILABLE FOR--
RIDICULOUS! WHAT TIME DID THEY SAY THEY WERE COMING?
NO, OF COURSE THEY DIDN'T. LOOK, TAKE IT OUT OF THE VIEWING LAB AND LOCK IT IN THE EQUIPMENT ROOM.
I'M SURE NOT GOING TO MAKE IT EASY FOR THE BASTARDS! ON THE WAY--
ALDEN!
CAN I TRADE CARS WITH YOU FOR THE NIGHT? YOUR STATION WAGON IS PERFECT!
UH, SURE-- WHAT'S UP?
EVERYONE'S LOST THEIR MINDS IS WHAT.
THE STATE DEPARTMENT IS GATHERING ALL METEORITE FRAGMENTS THAT HAVE BEEN BROUGHT IN FOR STUDY.
BUT THEY'LL HAVE A HARDER TIME WITH ONES STILL ON PERSONAL PROPERTY!
YOU NEVER SIGNED IT OVER... SO YOU'RE GETTING YOUR SPACE ROCK BACK, ALDEN.

SOUNDS LIKE DR. CAMDEN IS PRETTY UPSET.

ALDEN? YOU'RE BACK EARLY.

--THIS ONE FROM SRI LANKA HAS ANOTHER ACCOUNT OF THE SKY WALKING..

THIS SAME SCENE WAS CAUGHT BY TWO DIFFERENT CAMERAS AS YOU'LL SEE--

A KID GOT HURT AT THE PARTY, HE FELL DOWN...

...IS THIS REAL?

WHILE MANY HOAXES HAVE EMERGED IN THE PAST WEEK, THESE PHOTOS WERE FROM TWO SEPARATE TOURISTS FROM DIFFERENT COUNTRIES WITH NO CONNECTION.

THIS STUFF HAS STARTED COMING IN TODAY--MICHAEL THINKS THE GOVERNMENT IS STARTING TO TAKE IT SERIOUSLY.

I THINK THEY'RE JUST USING IT ALL AS AN EXCUSE TO COLLECT THE METEORS BECAUSE THEY DIDN'T GET THEIR HANDS ON MANY WHEN THE EVENT HAPPENED.

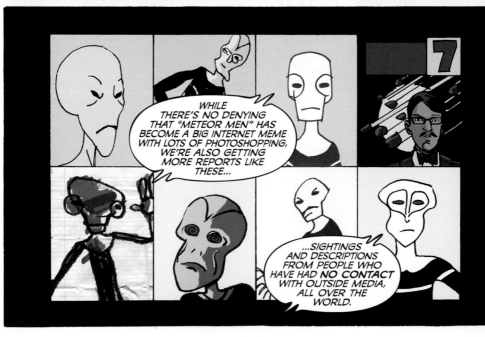

WHILE THERE'S NO DENYING THAT "METEOR MEN" HAS BECOME A BIG INTERNET MEME WITH LOTS OF PHOTOSHOPPING, WE'RE ALSO GETTING MORE REPORTS LIKE THESE...

...SIGHTINGS AND DESCRIPTIONS FROM PEOPLE WHO HAVE HAD **NO CONTACT** WITH OUTSIDE MEDIA, ALL OVER THE WORLD.

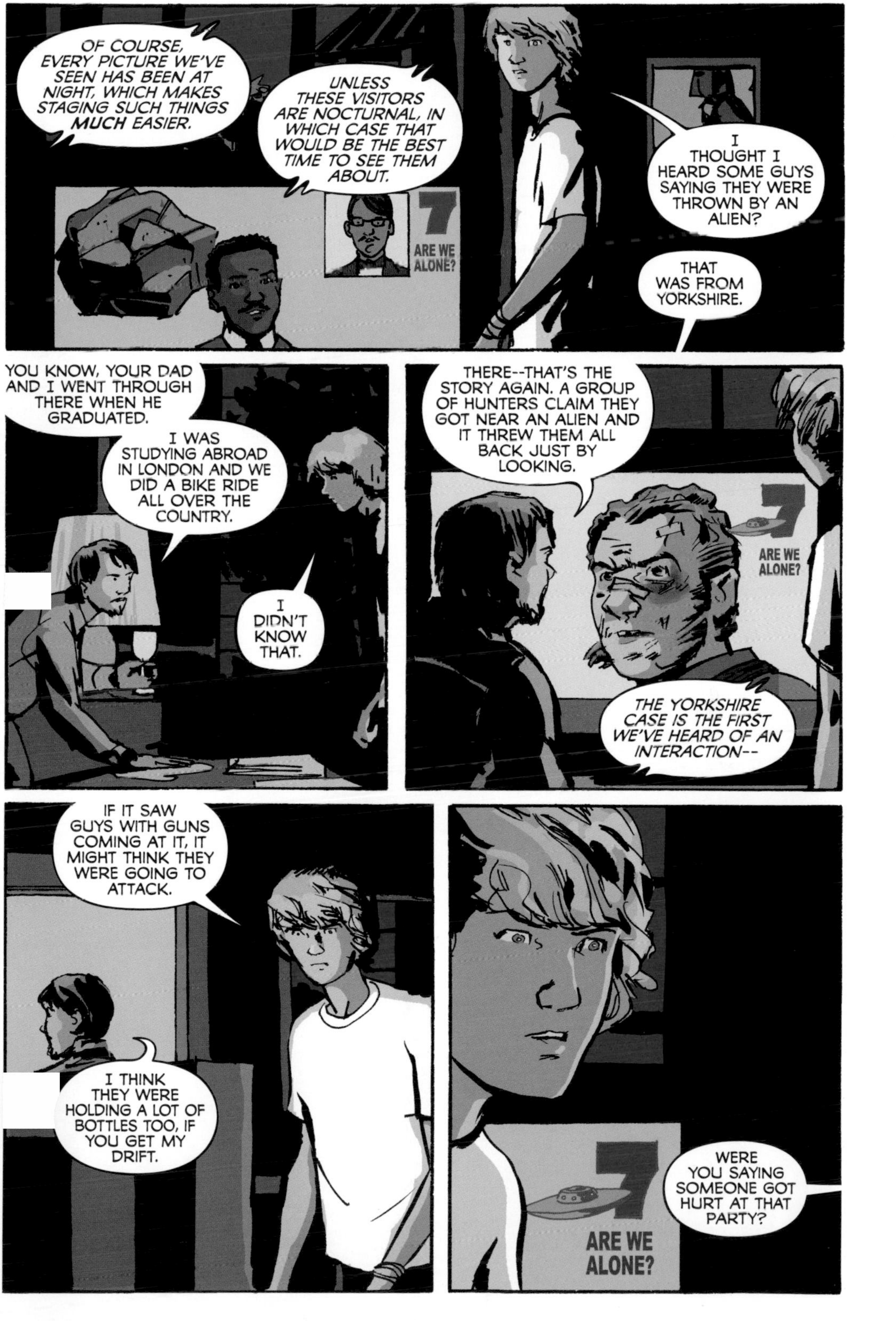
OF COURSE, EVERY PICTURE WE'VE SEEN HAS BEEN AT NIGHT, WHICH MAKES STAGING SUCH THINGS MUCH EASIER.
UNLESS THESE VISITORS ARE NOCTURNAL, IN WHICH CASE THAT WOULD BE THE BEST TIME TO SEE THEM ABOUT.
7 ARE WE ALONE?
I THOUGHT I HEARD SOME GUYS SAYING THEY WERE THROWN BY AN ALIEN?
THAT WAS FROM YORKSHIRE.
YOU KNOW, YOUR DAD AND I WENT THROUGH THERE WHEN HE GRADUATED.
I WAS STUDYING ABROAD IN LONDON AND WE DID A BIKE RIDE ALL OVER THE COUNTRY.
I DIDN'T KNOW THAT.
THERE--THAT'S THE STORY AGAIN. A GROUP OF HUNTERS CLAIM THEY GOT NEAR AN ALIEN AND IT THREW THEM ALL BACK JUST BY LOOKING.
7 ARE WE ALONE?
THE YORKSHIRE CASE IS THE FIRST WE'VE HEARD OF AN INTERACTION--
IF IT SAW GUYS WITH GUNS COMING AT IT, IT MIGHT THINK THEY WERE GOING TO ATTACK.
I THINK THEY WERE HOLDING A LOT OF BOTTLES TOO, IF YOU GET MY DRIFT.
7 ARE WE ALONE?
WERE YOU SAYING SOMEONE GOT HURT AT THAT PARTY?

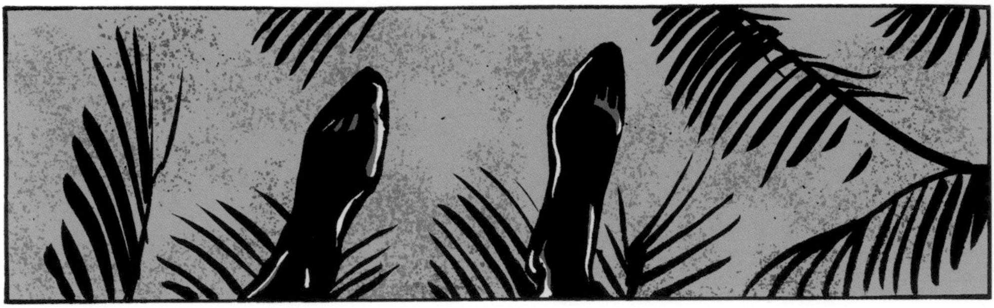

LOOK--
LOOK UP
THERE!

IN THE TREE!

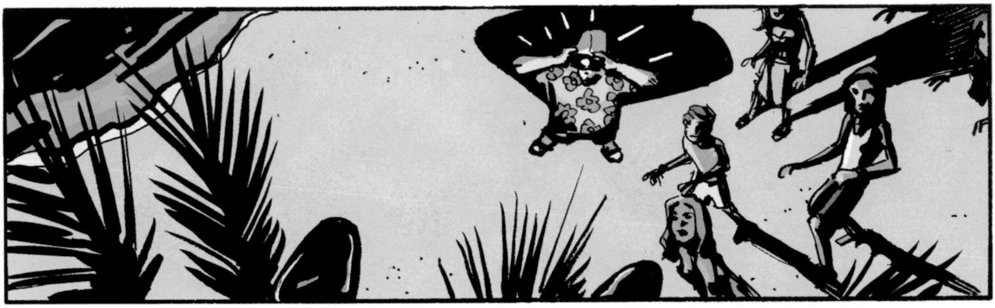

MUST BE ON
A WIRE--CAN'T
BE REAL!

SAW IT GO
DOWN HERE,
HERE--

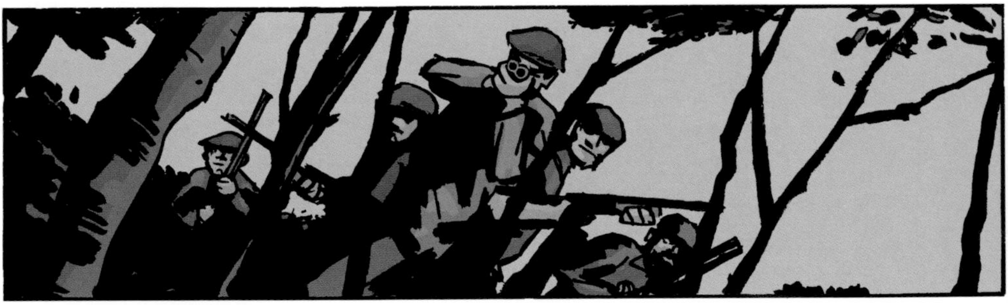

--HELL IAN, IT'S
A MAN, PUT THAT
DOWN--

--AIN'T A MAN,
IT'S ONE OF--
AHHHH!!

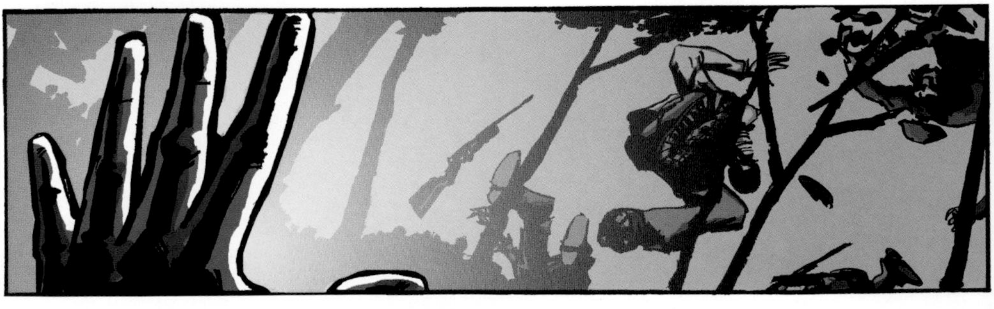

I THOUGHT IT WAS
MY BROTHER--!!

STAY BACK,
STAY AWAY!

ALDEN.
ALDEN. WAKE
UP...

I
KNOW THIS
IS UNUSUAL,
BUT--

MICHAEL
IS IN TROUBLE.
WE NEED TO
GO HELP
HIM!

WE
DO...?

DR.
CAMDEN?

YES. GET
DRESSED,
HURRY!

"I'LL EXPLAIN ON THE WAY."

THAT
METEOR HAS BEEN
THE BIGGEST THING TO
HAPPEN TO MICHAEL'S
DEPARTMENT SINCE
THE APOLLO
MISSIONS.

AFTER
YEARS OF BUDGET
CUTS, HE'S NOT
GOING TO LET GO OF
SOMETHING LIKE
THIS WITHOUT A
FIGHT.

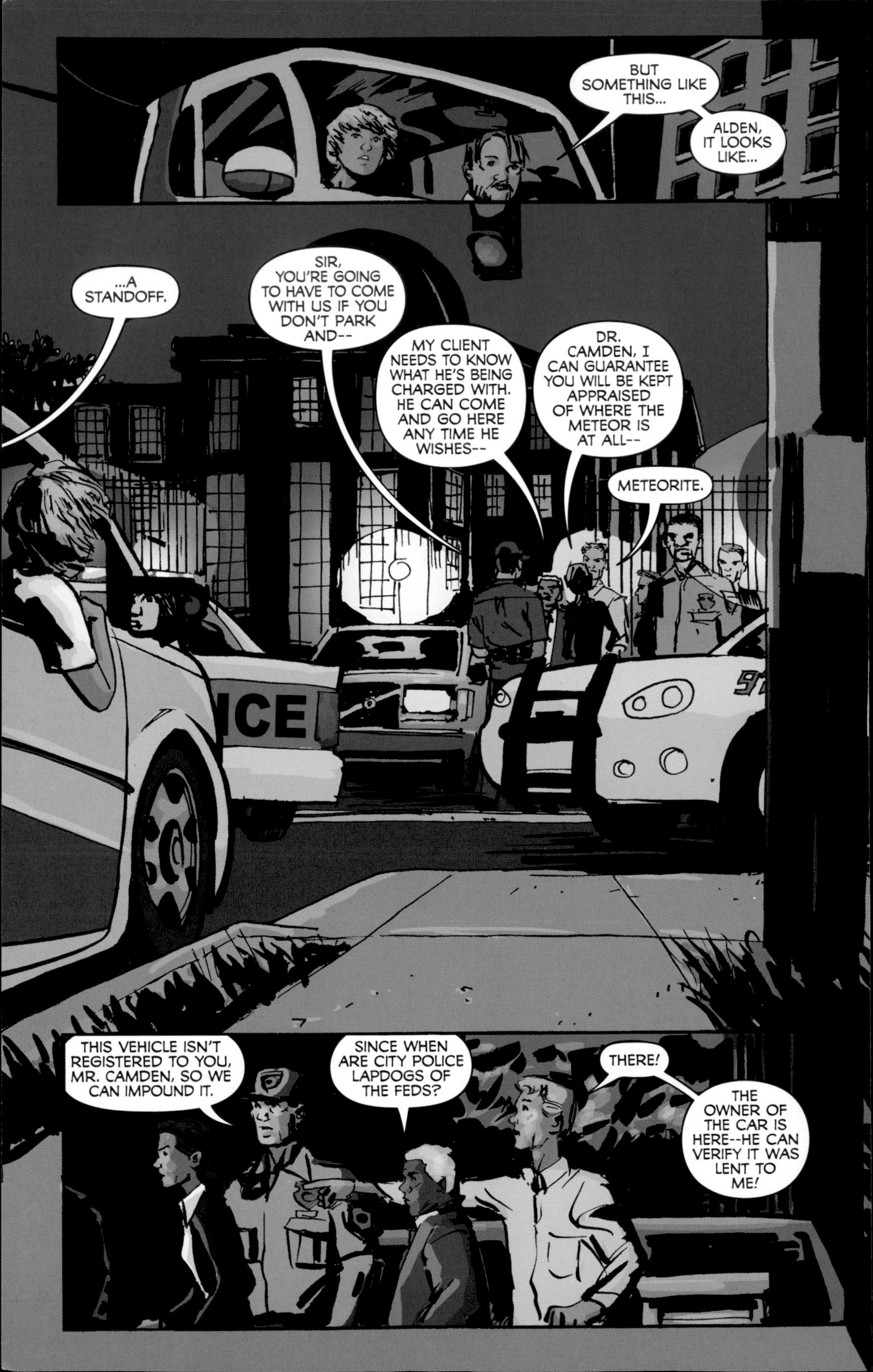
BUT SOMETHING LIKE THIS...
ALDEN, IT LOOKS LIKE...
...A STANDOFF.
SIR, YOU'RE GOING TO HAVE TO COME WITH US IF YOU DON'T PARK AND--
MY CLIENT NEEDS TO KNOW WHAT HE'S BEING CHARGED WITH. HE CAN COME AND GO HERE ANY TIME HE WISHES--
DR. CAMDEN, I CAN GUARANTEE YOU WILL BE KEPT APPRAISED OF WHERE THE METEOR IS AT ALL--
METEORITE.
ICE
THIS VEHICLE ISN'T REGISTERED TO YOU, MR. CAMDEN, SO WE CAN IMPOUND IT.
SINCE WHEN ARE CITY POLICE LAPDOGS OF THE FEDS?
THERE!
THE OWNER OF THE CAR IS HERE--HE CAN VERIFY IT WAS LENT TO ME!

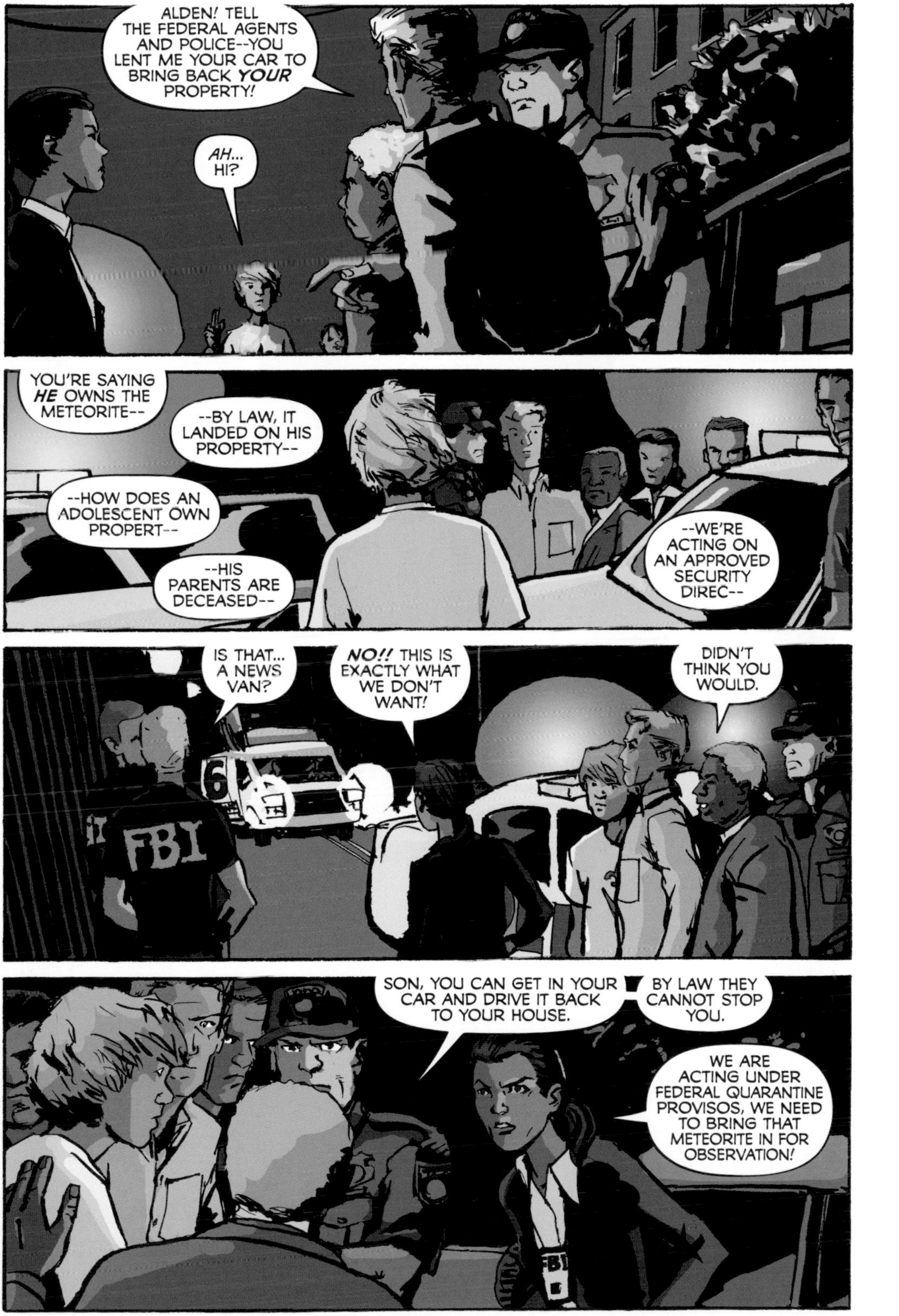
ALDEN! TELL THE FEDERAL AGENTS AND POLICE--YOU LENT ME YOUR CAR TO BRING BACK YOUR PROPERTY!
AH... HI?
YOU'RE SAYING HE OWNS THE METEORITE--
--BY LAW, IT LANDED ON HIS PROPERTY--
--HOW DOES AN ADOLESCENT OWN PROPERT--
--HIS PARENTS ARE DECEASED--
--WE'RE ACTING ON AN APPROVED SECURITY DIREC--
IS THAT... A NEWS VAN?
NO!! THIS IS EXACTLY WHAT WE DON'T WANT!
DIDN'T THINK YOU WOULD.
FBI
SON, YOU CAN GET IN YOUR CAR AND DRIVE IT BACK TO YOUR HOUSE.
BY LAW THEY CANNOT STOP YOU.
WE ARE ACTING UNDER FEDERAL QUARANTINE PROVISOS, WE NEED TO BRING THAT METEORITE IN FOR OBSERVATION!

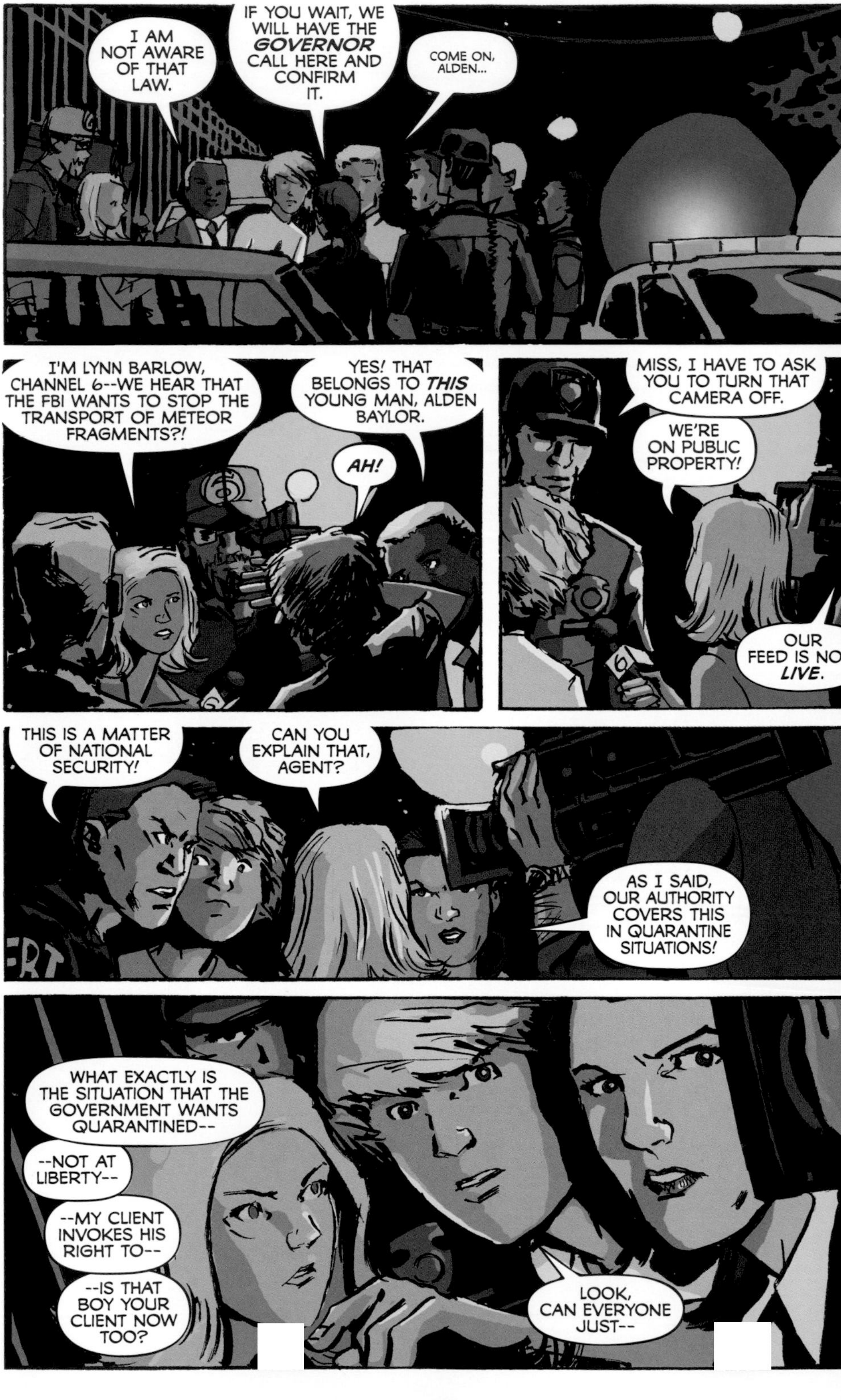
I AM NOT AWARE OF THAT LAW.
IF YOU WAIT, WE WILL HAVE THE *GOVERNOR* CALL HERE AND CONFIRM IT.
COME ON, ALDEN...
I'M LYNN BARLOW, CHANNEL 6--WE HEAR THAT THE FBI WANTS TO STOP THE TRANSPORT OF METEOR FRAGMENTS?!
YES! THAT BELONGS TO *THIS* YOUNG MAN, ALDEN BAYLOR.
AH!
MISS, I HAVE TO ASK YOU TO TURN THAT CAMERA OFF.
WE'RE ON PUBLIC PROPERTY!
OUR FEED IS NOW *LIVE*.
THIS IS A MATTER OF NATIONAL SECURITY!
CAN YOU EXPLAIN THAT, AGENT?
AS I SAID, OUR AUTHORITY COVERS THIS IN QUARANTINE SITUATIONS!
WHAT EXACTLY IS THE SITUATION THAT THE GOVERNMENT WANTS QUARANTINED--
--NOT AT LIBERTY--
--MY CLIENT INVOKES HIS RIGHT TO--
--IS THAT BOY YOUR CLIENT NOW TOO?
LOOK, CAN EVERYONE JUST--

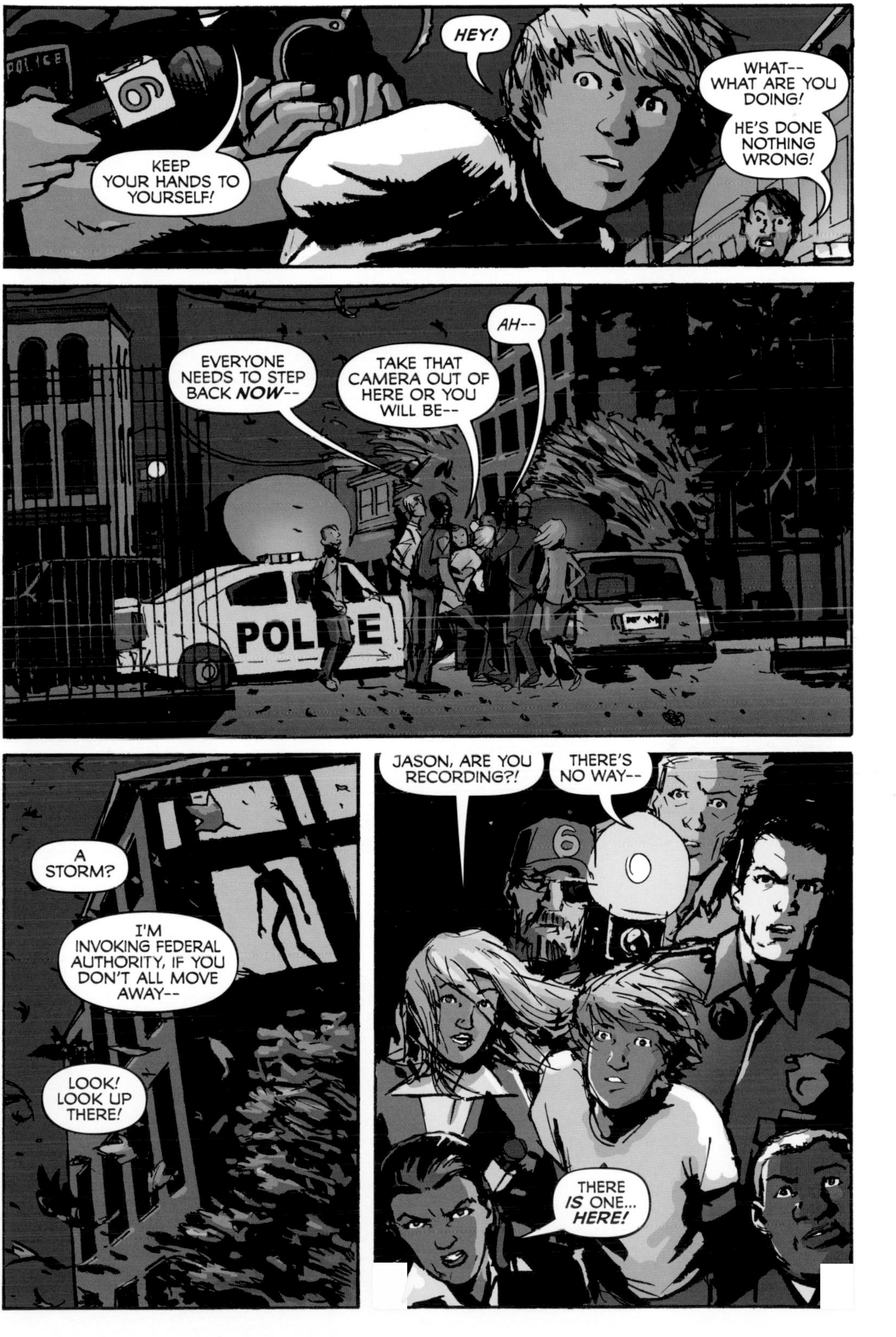
HEY!
KEEP YOUR HANDS TO YOURSELF!
WHAT-- WHAT ARE YOU DOING!
HE'S DONE NOTHING WRONG!
POLICE
EVERYONE NEEDS TO STEP BACK *NOW*--
TAKE THAT CAMERA OUT OF HERE OR YOU WILL BE--
AH--
POLICE
A STORM?
I'M INVOKING FEDERAL AUTHORITY, IF YOU DON'T ALL MOVE AWAY--
LOOK! LOOK UP THERE!
JASON, ARE YOU RECORDING?!
THERE'S NO WAY--
THERE *IS* ONE... *HERE!*

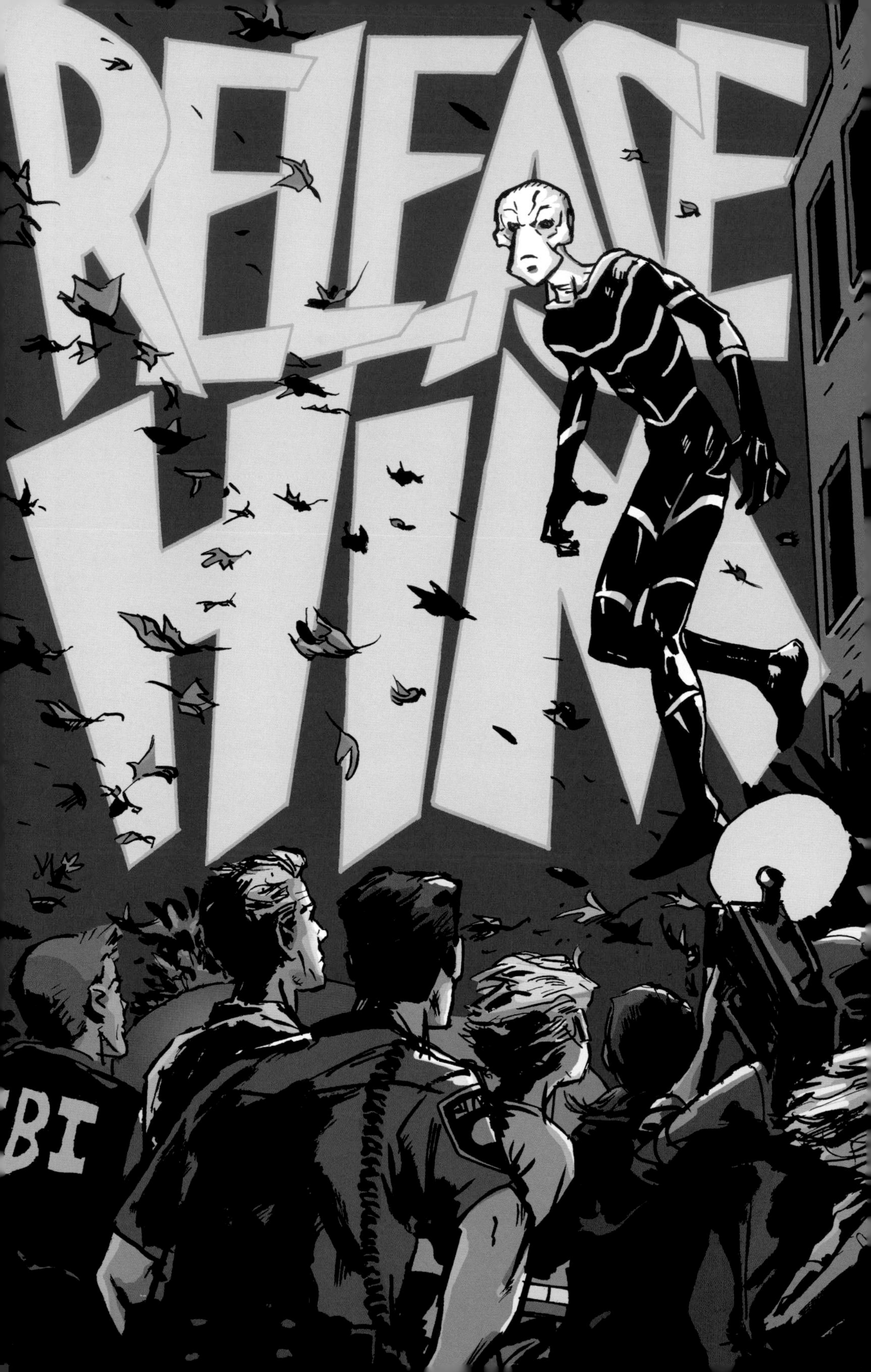
RELEASE HIM

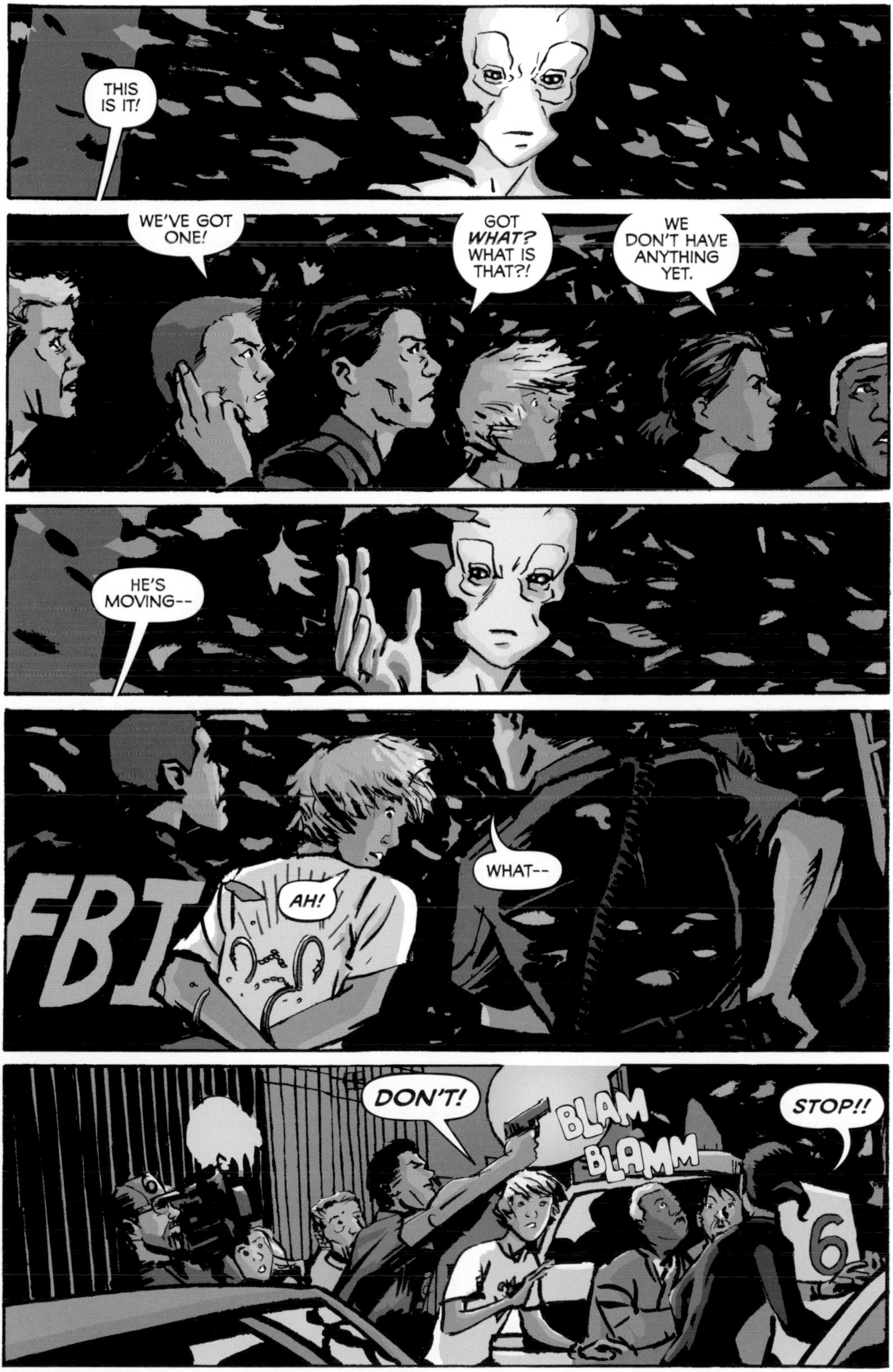
THIS IS IT!
WE'VE GOT ONE!
GOT *WHAT?* WHAT IS THAT?!
WE DON'T HAVE ANYTHING YET.
HE'S MOVING--
FBI
AH!
WHAT--
DON'T!
BLAM
BLAMM
STOP!!
6

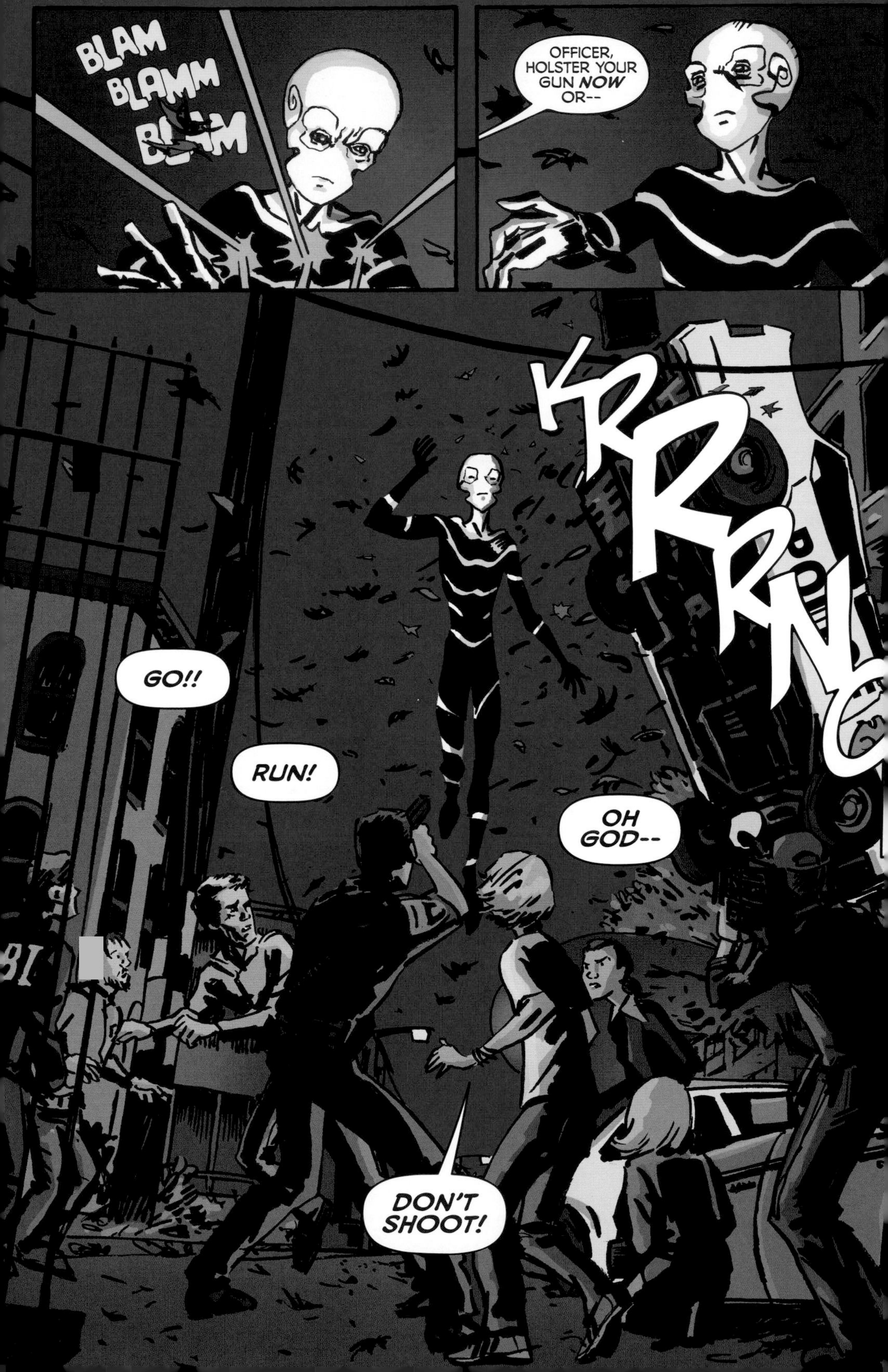
BLAM
BLAMM
BLAM
OFFICER, HOLSTER YOUR GUN *NOW* OR--
K'RRRNG
GO!!
RUN!
OH GOD--
DON'T SHOOT!

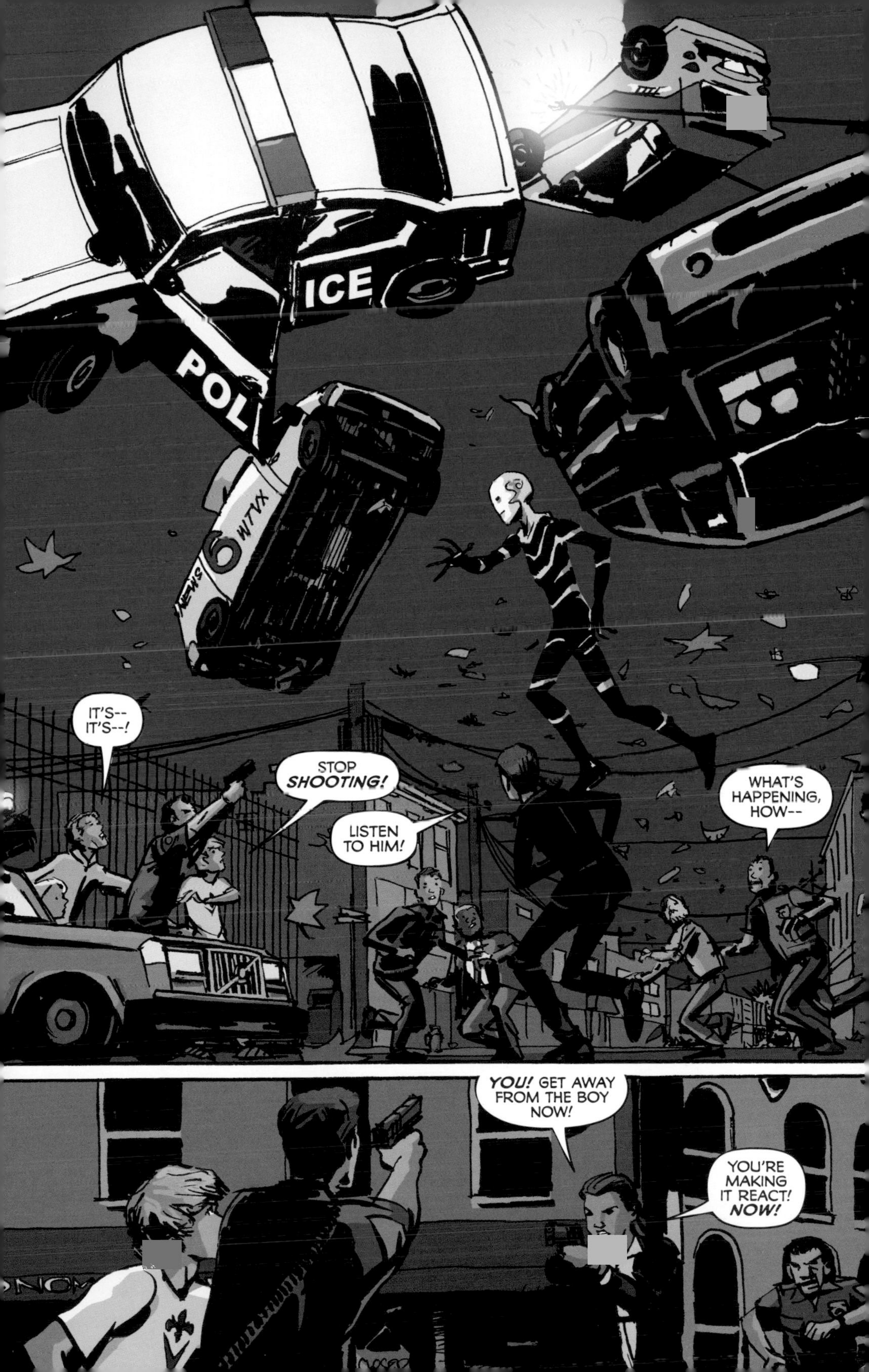
POLICE
WTVX
NEWS 6
IT'S-- IT'S--!
STOP SHOOTING!
LISTEN TO HIM!
WHAT'S HAPPENING, HOW--
YOU! GET AWAY FROM THE BOY NOW!
YOU'RE MAKING IT REACT! NOW!

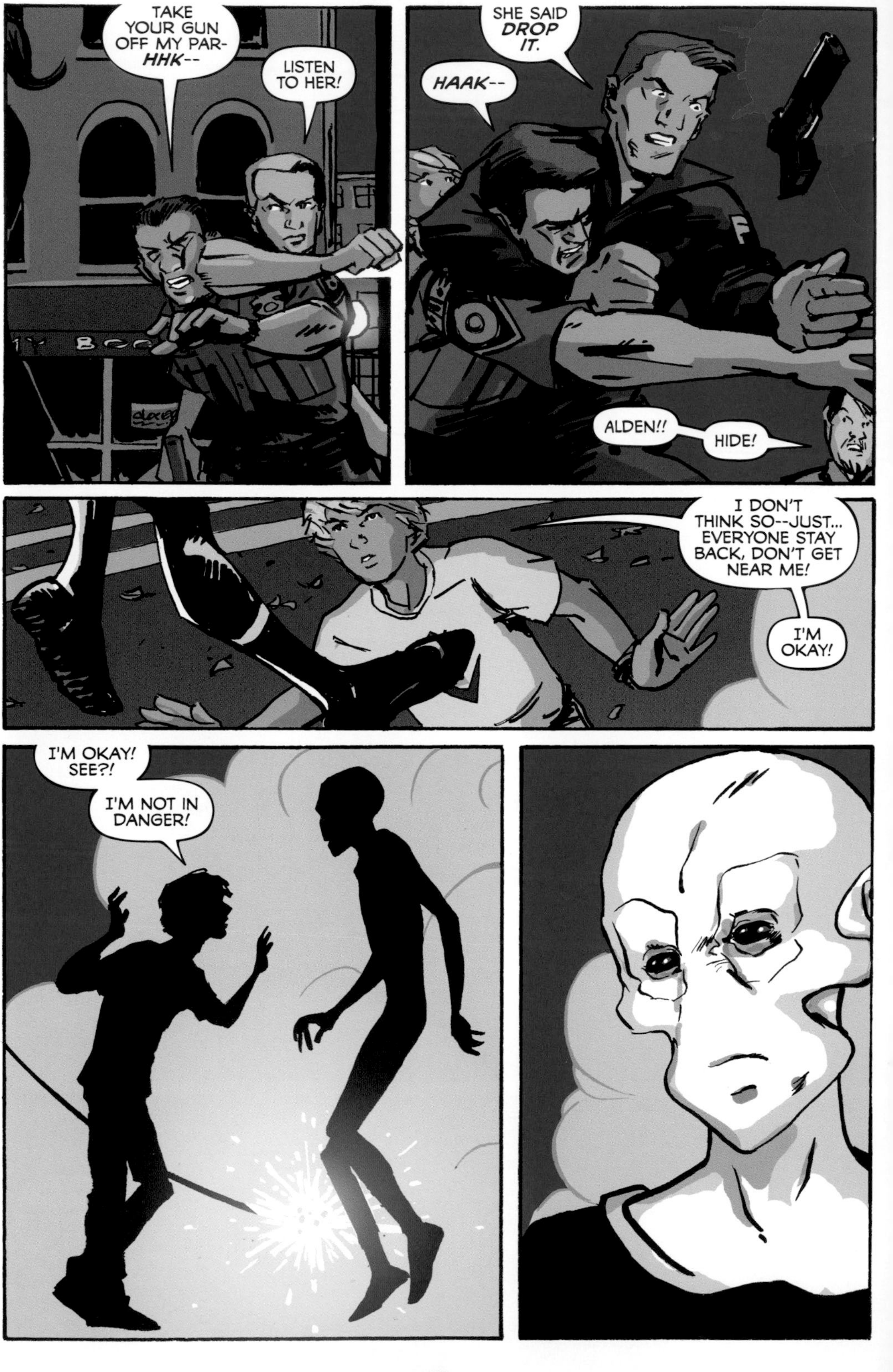
TAKE YOUR GUN OFF MY PAR-HHK--
LISTEN TO HER!
SHE SAID DROP IT.
HAAK--
ALDEN!!
HIDE!
I DON'T THINK SO--JUST... EVERYONE STAY BACK, DON'T GET NEAR ME!
I'M OKAY!
I'M OKAY! SEE?!
I'M NOT IN DANGER!

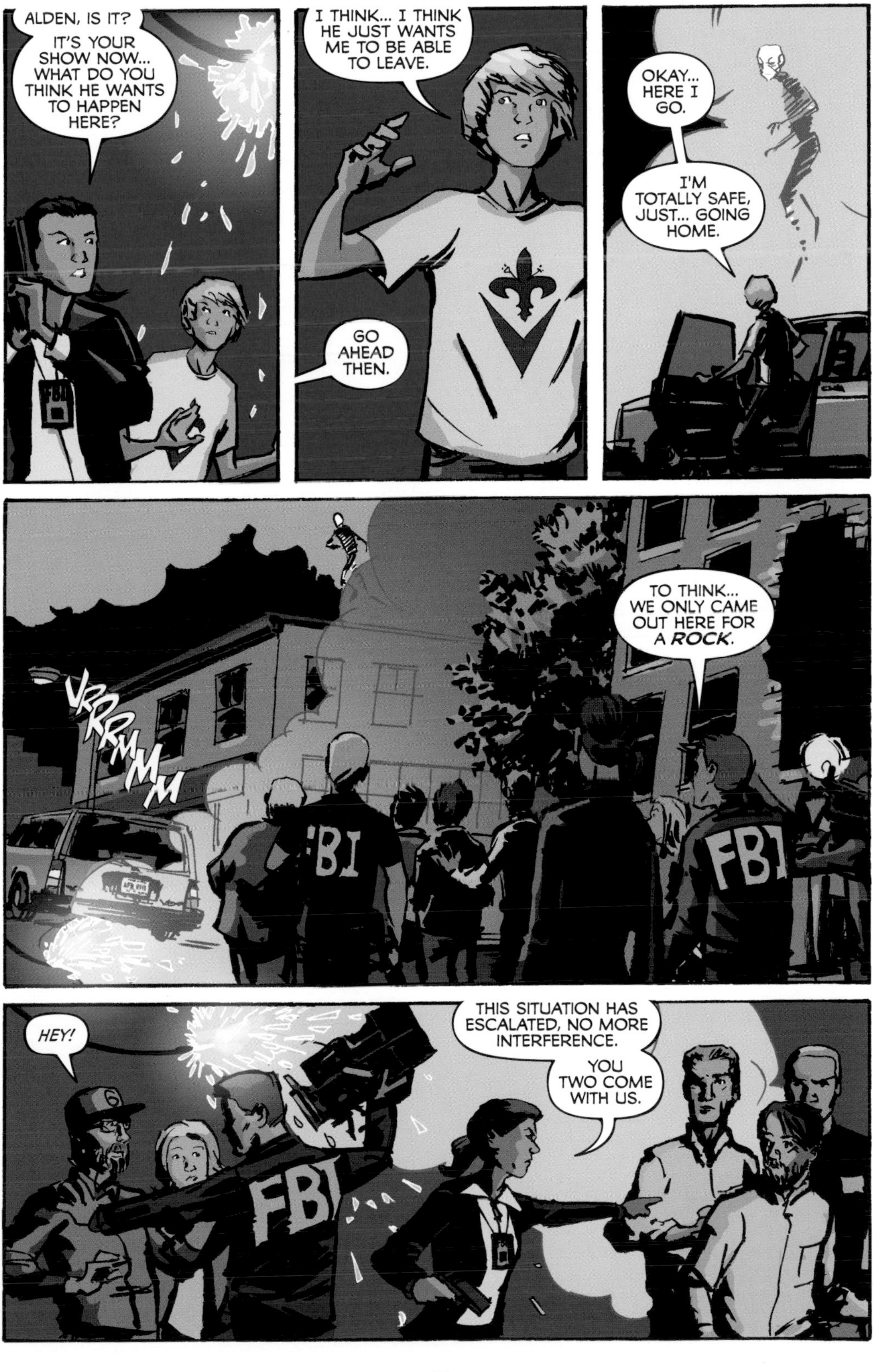
ALDEN, IS IT?
IT'S YOUR SHOW NOW... WHAT DO YOU THINK HE WANTS TO HAPPEN HERE?
I THINK... I THINK HE JUST WANTS ME TO BE ABLE TO LEAVE.
GO AHEAD THEN.
OKAY... HERE I GO.
I'M TOTALLY SAFE, JUST... GOING HOME.
VRRRMMMM
TO THINK... WE ONLY CAME OUT HERE FOR A *ROCK*.
FBI
FBI
HEY!
THIS SITUATION HAS ESCALATED, NO MORE INTERFERENCE.
YOU TWO COME WITH US.
FBI

NO, THEY BROUGHT US TO AN FBI OFFICE FOR QUESTIONING ALL NIGHT--I DIDN'T EVEN KNOW WE HAD AN FBI OFFICE IN THIS COUNTY!

THEY'VE KEPT MICHAEL AND ME SEPARATE, PROBABLY TO MAKE SURE OUR "STORIES" LINE UP. FINALLY LETTING ME MAKE A CALL.

BEEDEEDEEDEEDEEDEEDEEDEE

ALDEN? ARE YOU UP?

YEAH-- ≥COFF≤ YEAH I'M UP, PHILIP.

DID YOU GO TO DR. CAMDEN'S?

AH... N-- DO YOU THINK THEY'LL LET YOU GO SOON?

I THINK SO. I'VE JUST BEEN LEFT IN HERE TO WAIT FOR THE PAST TWO HOURS.

NOTHING ON THE NEWS ABOUT LAST NIGHT, THEY TOOK ALL THE VIDEO FROM THE REPORTERS.

SAY THEY DON'T WANT A PANIC, NOT SURE WHAT WE ALL REALLY SAW, BUNCH OF CRAP... DON'T KNOW HOW THEY'RE EXPLAINING THE CARS--

PHILIP? THE NEWS DID GET OUT!

OF OF ALIENS! ACTUAL A-TERRESTRIALS!

MERICA! These pics are from ous to university erp , last night entr s crazy with and things flying where, spinning--and you see right there the ALIEN just he kind they are denying s all around the world after netear shower!!!

ars a kind of black suit but a big head like Roswell aliens

WHAT? WHERE?

ONLINE! PEOPLE WERE GETTING PHONE PICS LAST NIGHT FROM INSIDE THE BUILDINGS!

I WAS STARTING TO THINK I DREAMED IT ALL.

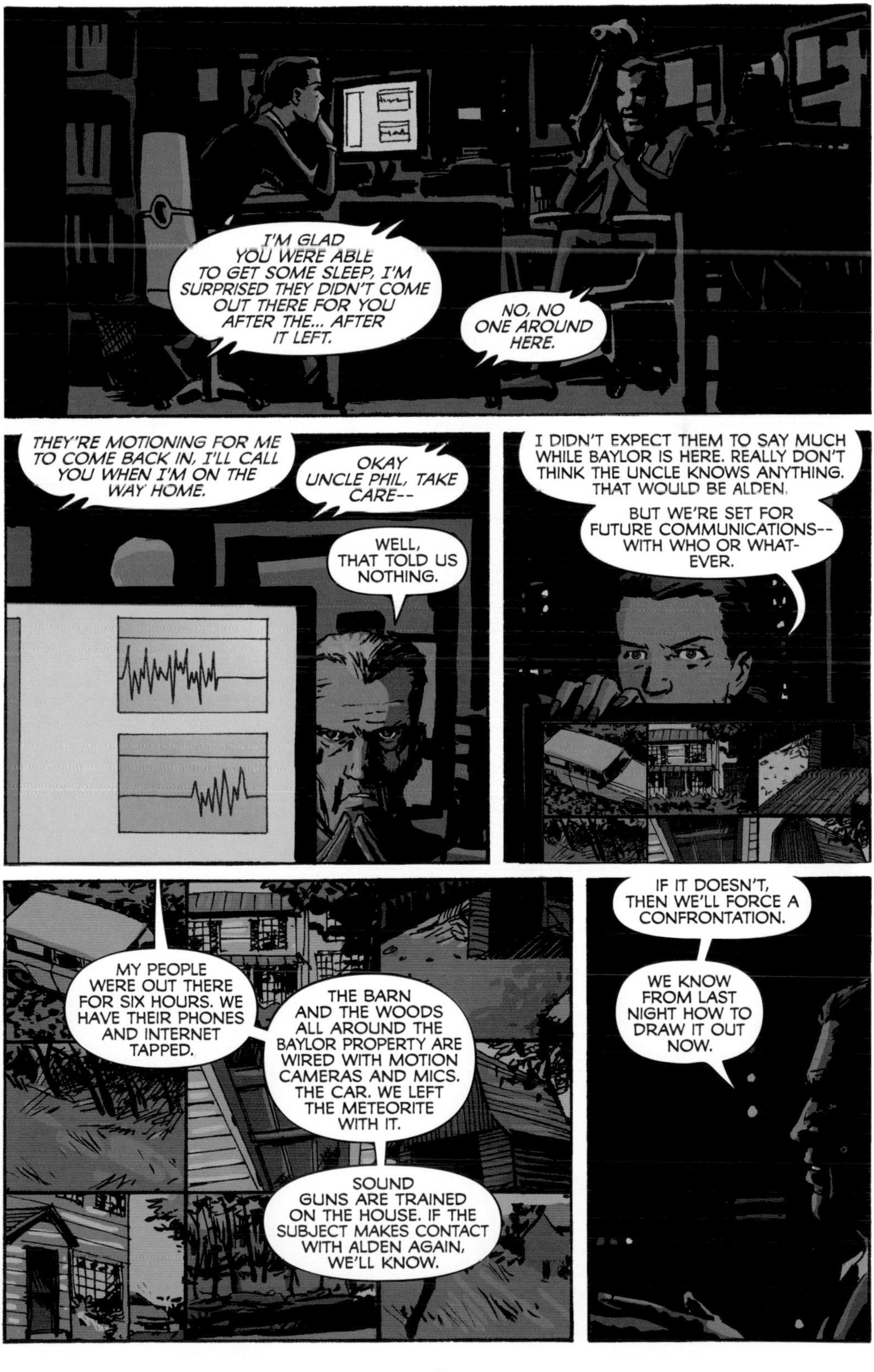
I'M GLAD YOU WERE ABLE TO GET SOME SLEEP, I'M SURPRISED THEY DIDN'T COME OUT THERE FOR YOU AFTER THE... AFTER IT LEFT.
NO, NO ONE AROUND HERE.
THEY'RE MOTIONING FOR ME TO COME BACK IN, I'LL CALL YOU WHEN I'M ON THE WAY HOME.
OKAY UNCLE PHIL, TAKE CARE--
WELL, THAT TOLD US NOTHING.
I DIDN'T EXPECT THEM TO SAY MUCH WHILE BAYLOR IS HERE. REALLY DON'T THINK THE UNCLE KNOWS ANYTHING. THAT WOULD BE ALDEN.
BUT WE'RE SET FOR FUTURE COMMUNICATIONS-- WITH WHO OR WHAT-EVER.
MY PEOPLE WERE OUT THERE FOR SIX HOURS. WE HAVE THEIR PHONES AND INTERNET TAPPED.
THE BARN AND THE WOODS ALL AROUND THE BAYLOR PROPERTY ARE WIRED WITH MOTION CAMERAS AND MICS. THE CAR. WE LEFT THE METEORITE WITH IT.
SOUND GUNS ARE TRAINED ON THE HOUSE. IF THE SUBJECT MAKES CONTACT WITH ALDEN AGAIN, WE'LL KNOW.
IF IT DOESN'T, THEN WE'LL FORCE A CONFRONTATION.
WE KNOW FROM LAST NIGHT HOW TO DRAW IT OUT NOW.

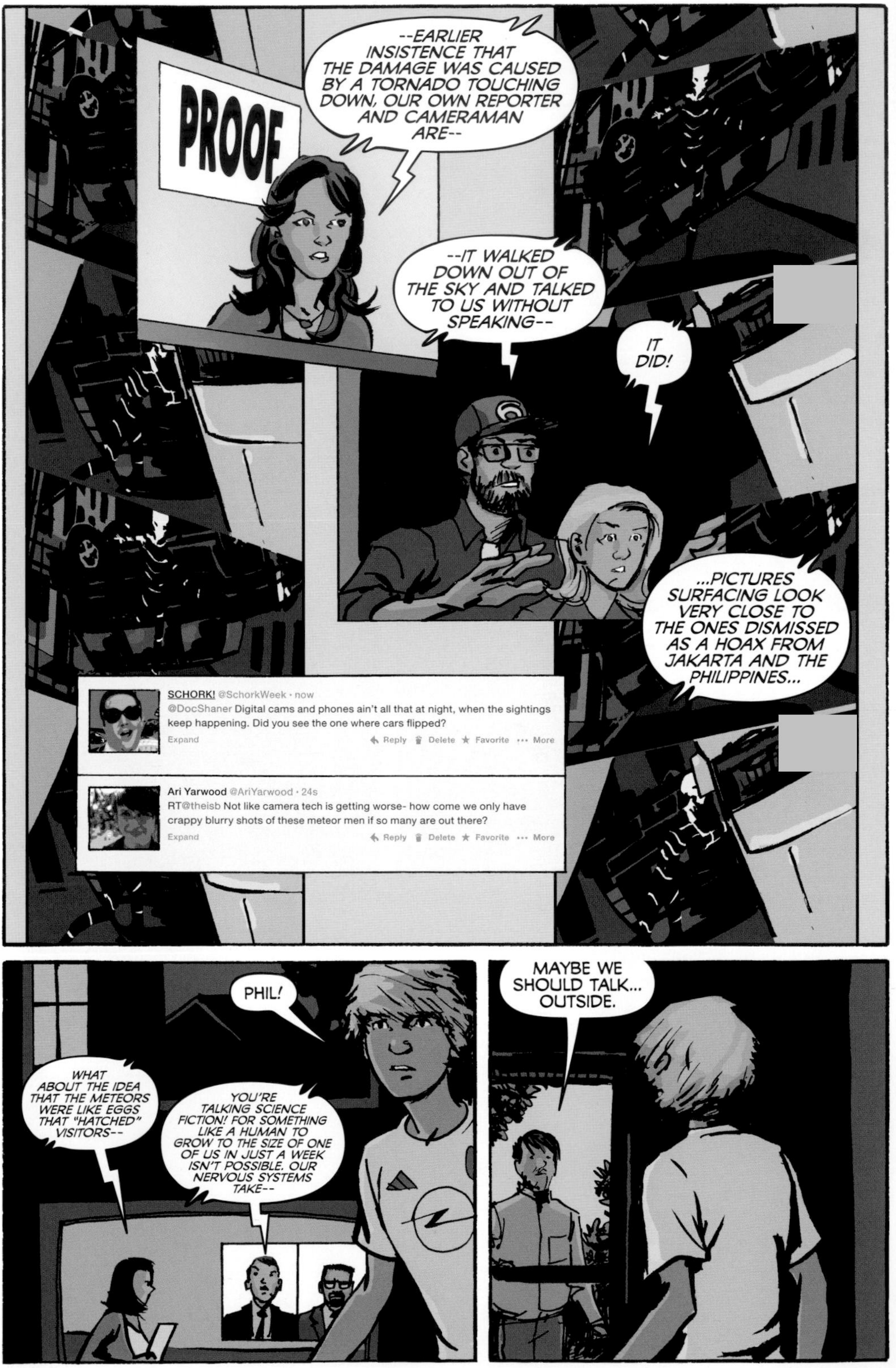
PROOF
--EARLIER INSISTENCE THAT THE DAMAGE WAS CAUSED BY A TORNADO TOUCHING DOWN, OUR OWN REPORTER AND CAMERAMAN ARE--
--IT WALKED DOWN OUT OF THE SKY AND TALKED TO US WITHOUT SPEAKING--
IT DID!
...PICTURES SURFACING LOOK VERY CLOSE TO THE ONES DISMISSED AS A HOAX FROM JAKARTA AND THE PHILIPPINES...
SCHORK! @SchorkWeek · now
@DocShaner Digital cams and phones ain't all that at night, when the sightings keep happening. Did you see the one where cars flipped?
Expand Reply Delete Favorite ··· More
Ari Yarwood @AriYarwood · 24s
RT@theisb Not like camera tech is getting worse- how come we only have crappy blurry shots of these meteor men if so many are out there?
Expand Reply Delete Favorite ··· More
PHIL!
WHAT ABOUT THE IDEA THAT THE METEORS WERE LIKE EGGS THAT "HATCHED" VISITORS--
YOU'RE TALKING SCIENCE FICTION! FOR SOMETHING LIKE A HUMAN TO GROW TO THE SIZE OF ONE OF US IN JUST A WEEK ISN'T POSSIBLE. OUR NERVOUS SYSTEMS TAKE--
MAYBE WE SHOULD TALK... OUTSIDE.

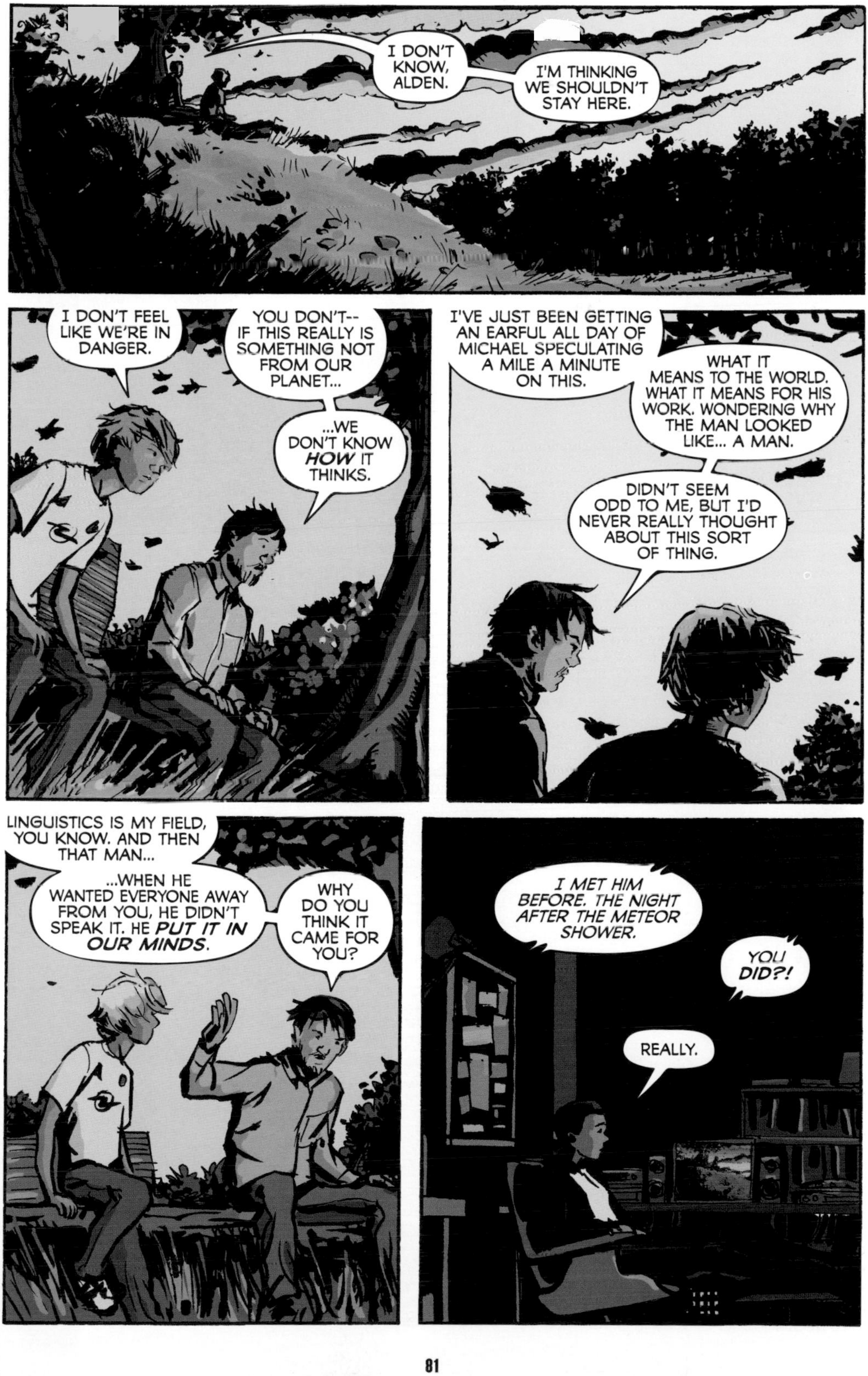
I DON'T KNOW, ALDEN.
I'M THINKING WE SHOULDN'T STAY HERE.
I DON'T FEEL LIKE WE'RE IN DANGER.
YOU DON'T-- IF THIS REALLY IS SOMETHING NOT FROM OUR PLANET...
...WE DON'T KNOW HOW IT THINKS.
I'VE JUST BEEN GETTING AN EARFUL ALL DAY OF MICHAEL SPECULATING A MILE A MINUTE ON THIS.
WHAT IT MEANS TO THE WORLD. WHAT IT MEANS FOR HIS WORK. WONDERING WHY THE MAN LOOKED LIKE... A MAN.
DIDN'T SEEM ODD TO ME, BUT I'D NEVER REALLY THOUGHT ABOUT THIS SORT OF THING.
LINGUISTICS IS MY FIELD, YOU KNOW. AND THEN THAT MAN...
...WHEN HE WANTED EVERYONE AWAY FROM YOU, HE DIDN'T SPEAK IT. HE PUT IT IN OUR MINDS.
WHY DO YOU THINK IT CAME FOR YOU?
I MET HIM BEFORE. THE NIGHT AFTER THE METEOR SHOWER.
YOU DID?!
REALLY.

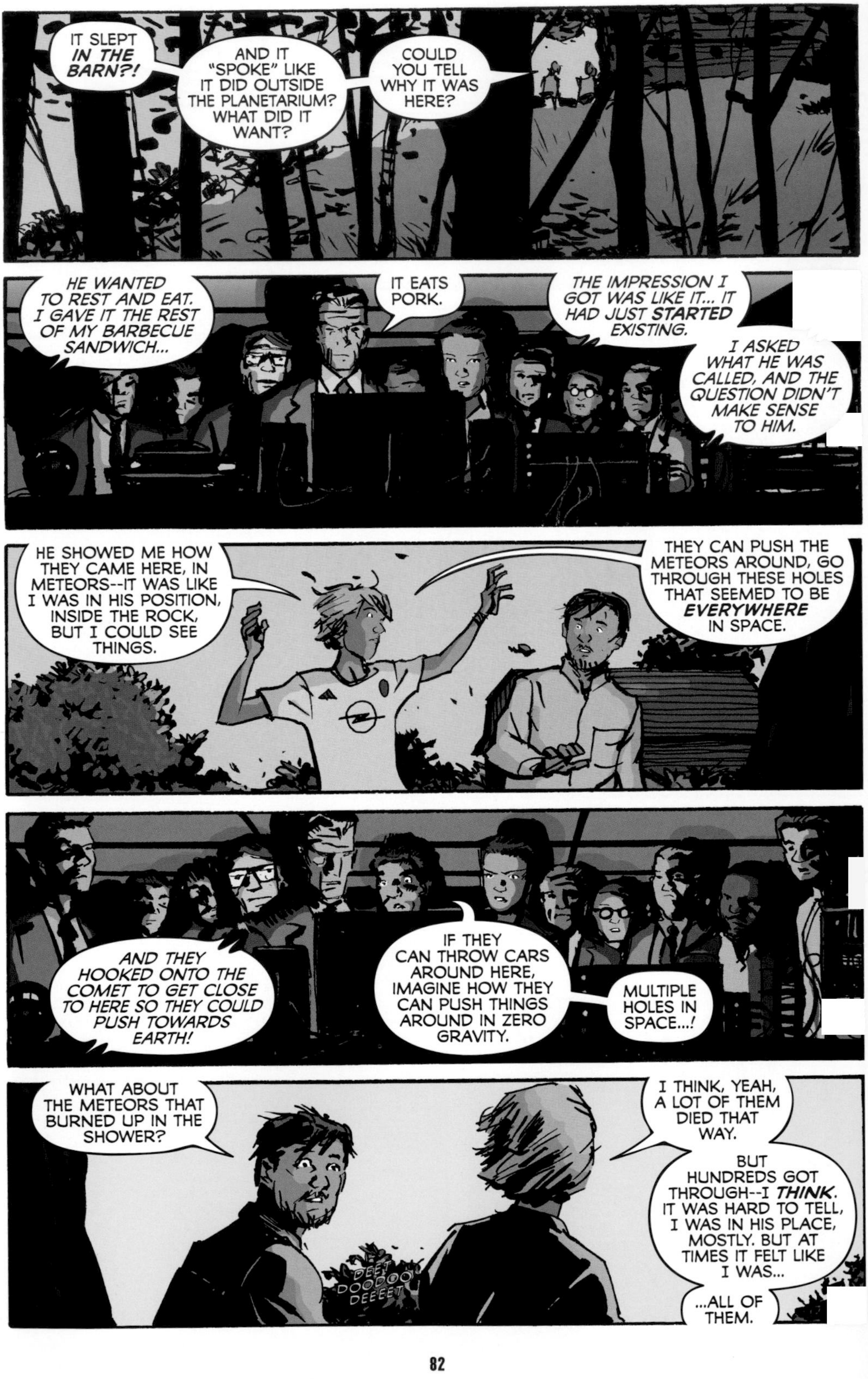
IT SLEPT *IN THE BARN?!*
AND IT "SPOKE" LIKE IT DID OUTSIDE THE PLANETARIUM? WHAT DID IT WANT?
COULD YOU TELL WHY IT WAS HERE?
HE WANTED TO REST AND EAT. I GAVE IT THE REST OF MY BARBECUE SANDWICH...
IT EATS PORK.
*THE IMPRESSION I GOT WAS LIKE IT... IT HAD JUST **STARTED** EXISTING.*
I ASKED WHAT HE WAS CALLED, AND THE QUESTION DIDN'T MAKE SENSE TO HIM.
HE SHOWED ME HOW THEY CAME HERE, IN METEORS--IT WAS LIKE I WAS IN HIS POSITION, INSIDE THE ROCK, BUT I COULD SEE THINGS.
THEY CAN PUSH THE METEORS AROUND, GO THROUGH THESE HOLES THAT SEEMED TO BE ***EVERYWHERE*** IN SPACE.
AND THEY HOOKED ONTO THE COMET TO GET CLOSE TO HERE SO THEY COULD PUSH TOWARDS EARTH!
IF THEY CAN THROW CARS AROUND HERE, IMAGINE HOW THEY CAN PUSH THINGS AROUND IN ZERO GRAVITY.
MULTIPLE HOLES IN SPACE...!
WHAT ABOUT THE METEORS THAT BURNED UP IN THE SHOWER?
I THINK, YEAH, A LOT OF THEM DIED THAT WAY.
BUT HUNDREDS GOT THROUGH--I ***THINK***. IT WAS HARD TO TELL, I WAS IN HIS PLACE, MOSTLY. BUT AT TIMES IT FELT LIKE I WAS...
DEET DOODOO DEEEET
...ALL OF THEM.

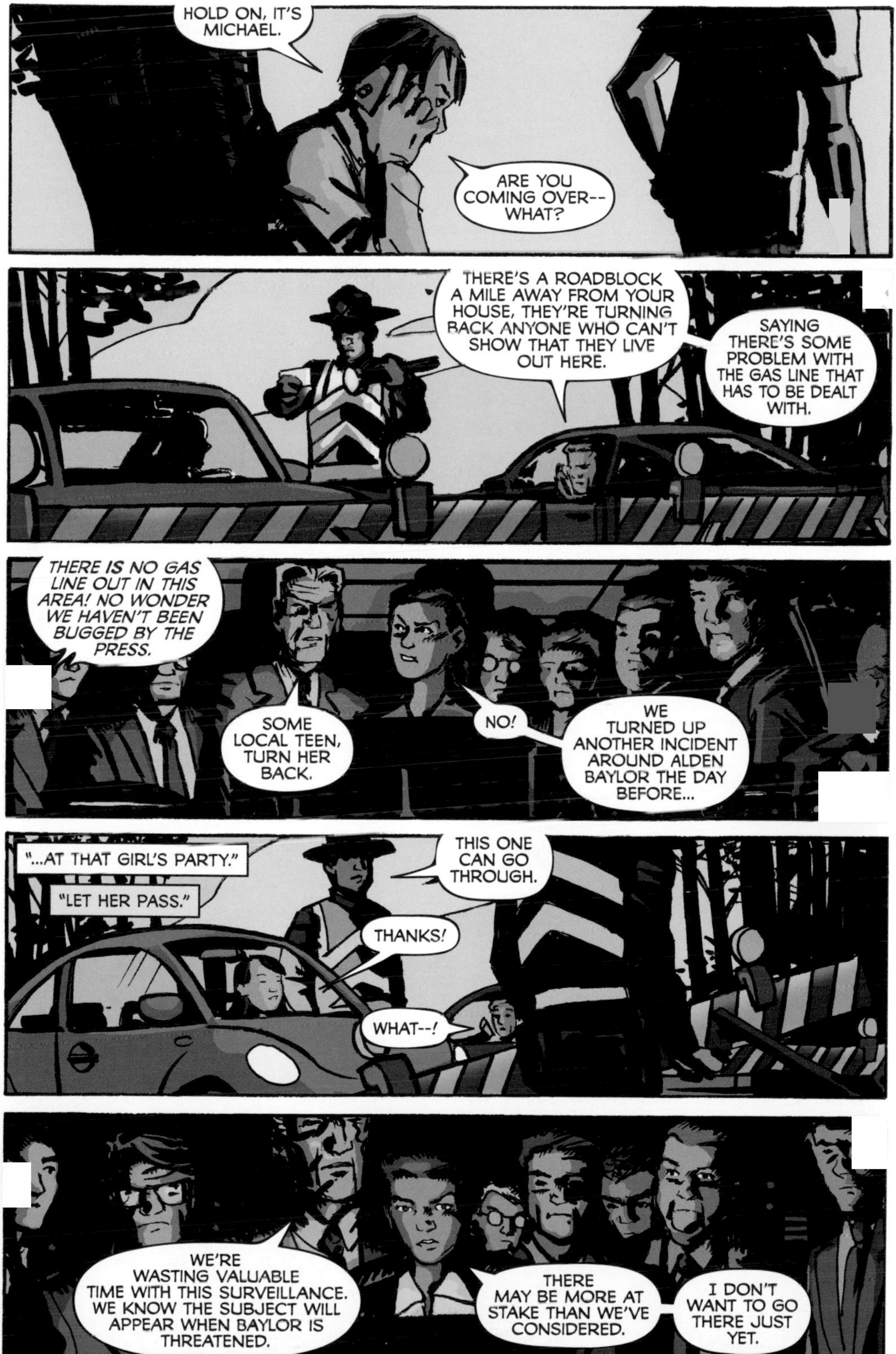
HOLD ON, IT'S MICHAEL.
ARE YOU COMING OVER-- WHAT?
THERE'S A ROADBLOCK A MILE AWAY FROM YOUR HOUSE, THEY'RE TURNING BACK ANYONE WHO CAN'T SHOW THAT THEY LIVE OUT HERE.
SAYING THERE'S SOME PROBLEM WITH THE GAS LINE THAT HAS TO BE DEALT WITH.
THERE *IS* NO GAS LINE OUT IN THIS AREA! NO WONDER WE HAVEN'T BEEN BUGGED BY THE PRESS.
SOME LOCAL TEEN, TURN HER BACK.
NO!
WE TURNED UP ANOTHER INCIDENT AROUND ALDEN BAYLOR THE DAY BEFORE...
"...AT THAT GIRL'S PARTY."
"LET HER PASS."
THIS ONE CAN GO THROUGH.
THANKS!
WHAT--!
WE'RE WASTING VALUABLE TIME WITH THIS SURVEILLANCE. WE KNOW THE SUBJECT WILL APPEAR WHEN BAYLOR IS THREATENED.
THERE MAY BE MORE AT STAKE THAN WE'VE CONSIDERED.
I DON'T WANT TO GO THERE JUST YET.

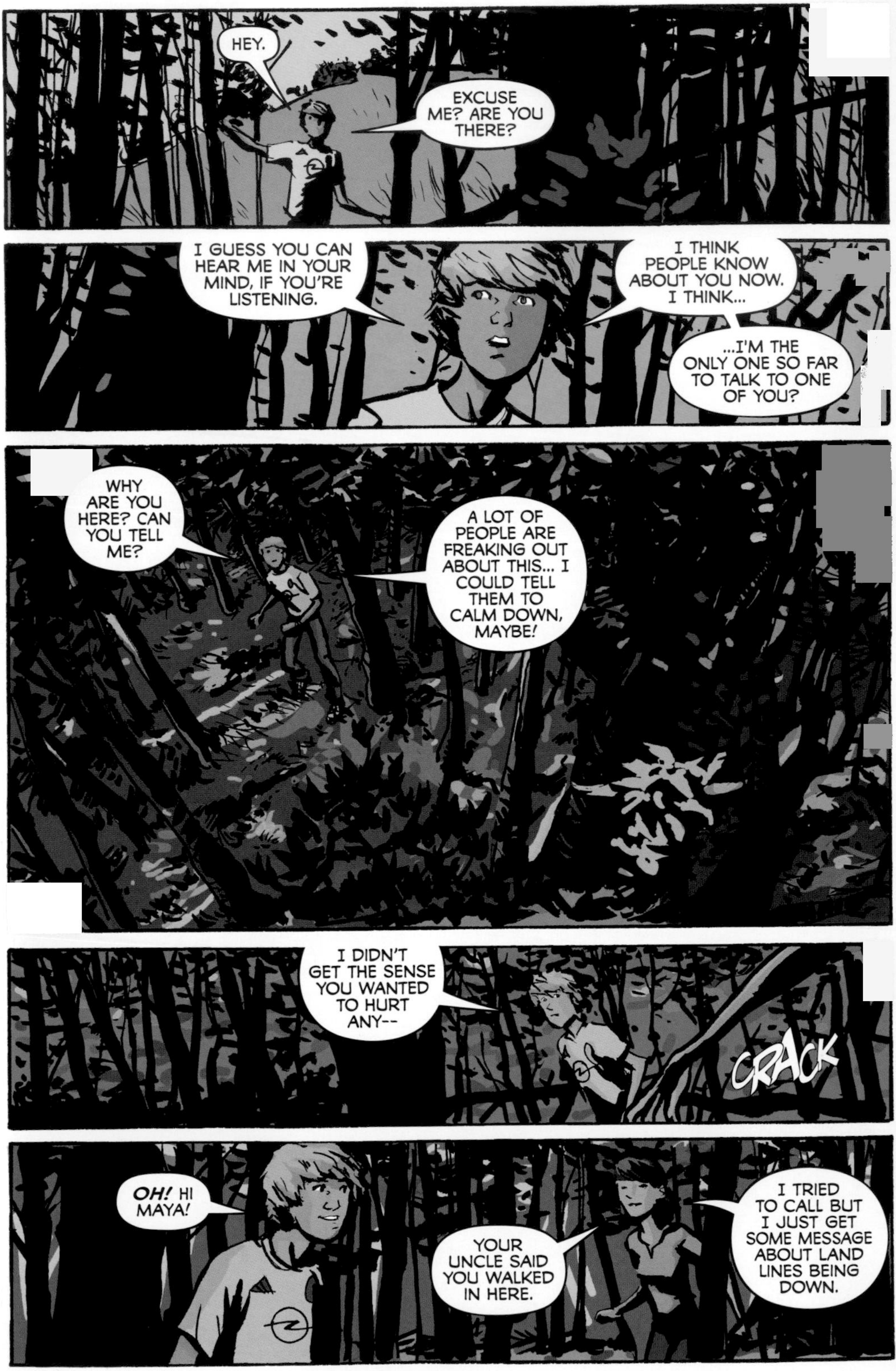
HEY.
EXCUSE ME? ARE YOU THERE?
I GUESS YOU CAN HEAR ME IN YOUR MIND, IF YOU'RE LISTENING.
I THINK PEOPLE KNOW ABOUT YOU NOW. I THINK...
...I'M THE ONLY ONE SO FAR TO TALK TO ONE OF YOU?
WHY ARE YOU HERE? CAN YOU TELL ME?
A LOT OF PEOPLE ARE FREAKING OUT ABOUT THIS... I COULD TELL THEM TO CALM DOWN, MAYBE!
I DIDN'T GET THE SENSE YOU WANTED TO HURT ANY--
CRACK
OH! HI MAYA!
YOUR UNCLE SAID YOU WALKED IN HERE.
I TRIED TO CALL BUT I JUST GET SOME MESSAGE ABOUT LAND LINES BEING DOWN.

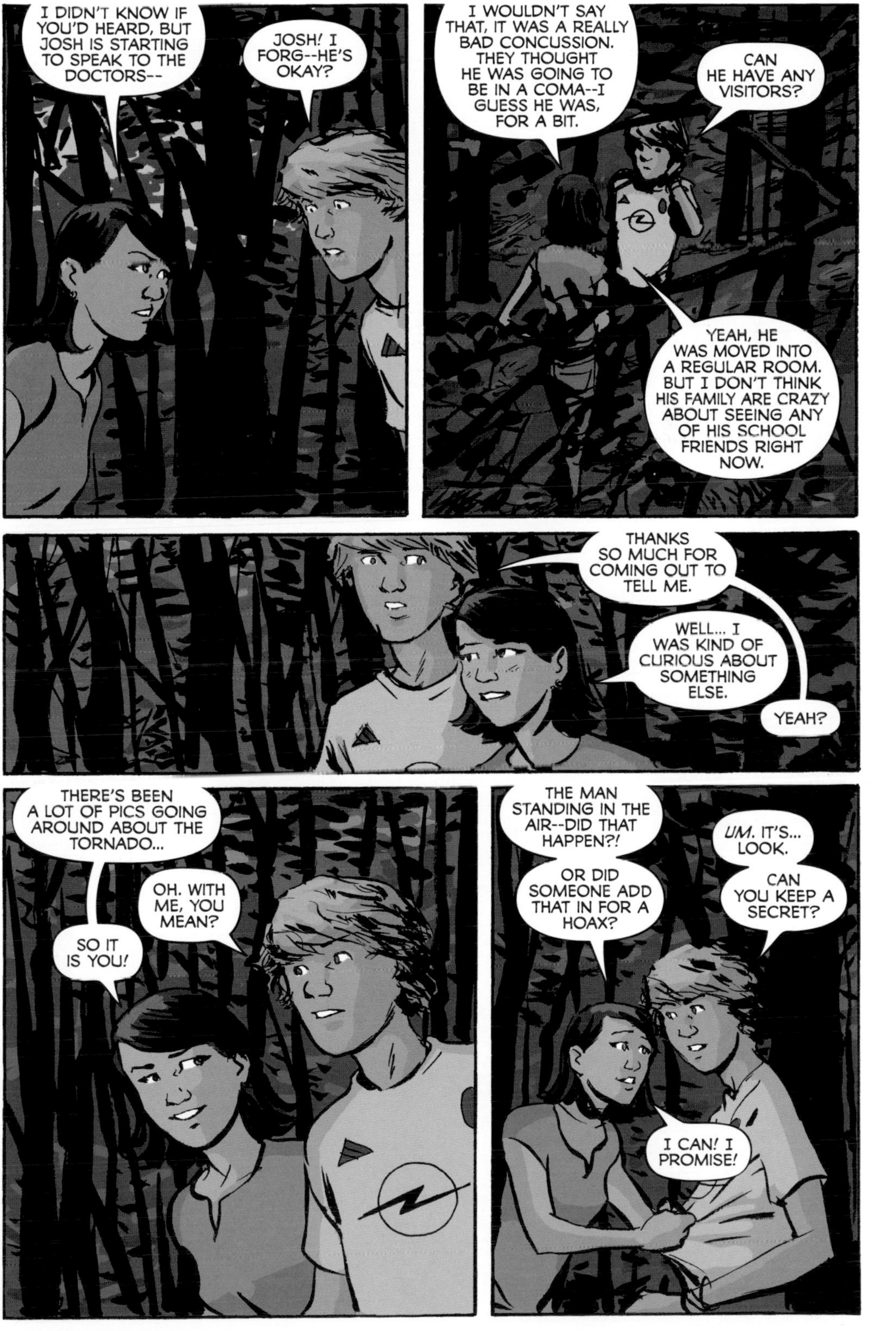
I DIDN'T KNOW IF YOU'D HEARD, BUT JOSH IS STARTING TO SPEAK TO THE DOCTORS--
JOSH! I FORG--HE'S OKAY?
I WOULDN'T SAY THAT, IT WAS A REALLY BAD CONCUSSION. THEY THOUGHT HE WAS GOING TO BE IN A COMA--I GUESS HE WAS, FOR A BIT.
CAN HE HAVE ANY VISITORS?
YEAH, HE WAS MOVED INTO A REGULAR ROOM. BUT I DON'T THINK HIS FAMILY ARE CRAZY ABOUT SEEING ANY OF HIS SCHOOL FRIENDS RIGHT NOW.
THANKS SO MUCH FOR COMING OUT TO TELL ME.
WELL... I WAS KIND OF CURIOUS ABOUT SOMETHING ELSE.
YEAH?
THERE'S BEEN A LOT OF PICS GOING AROUND ABOUT THE TORNADO...
OH. WITH ME, YOU MEAN?
SO IT IS YOU!
THE MAN STANDING IN THE AIR--DID THAT HAPPEN?!
OR DID SOMEONE ADD THAT IN FOR A HOAX?
UM. IT'S... LOOK.
CAN YOU KEEP A SECRET?
I CAN! I PROMISE!

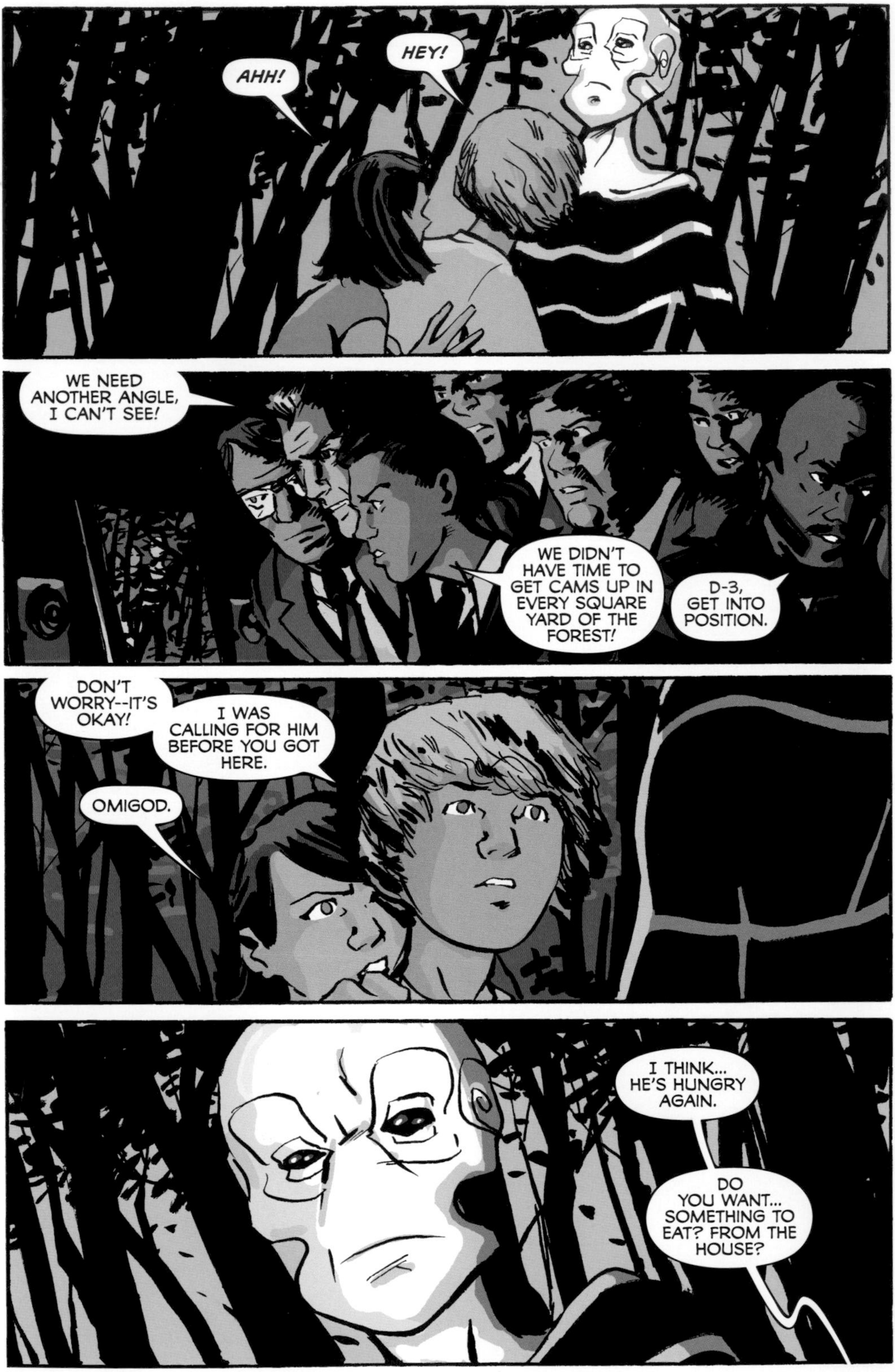
AHH!
HEY!
WE NEED ANOTHER ANGLE, I CAN'T SEE!
WE DIDN'T HAVE TIME TO GET CAMS UP IN EVERY SQUARE YARD OF THE FOREST!
D-3, GET INTO POSITION.
DON'T WORRY--IT'S OKAY!
I WAS CALLING FOR HIM BEFORE YOU GOT HERE.
OMIGOD.
I THINK... HE'S HUNGRY AGAIN.
DO YOU WANT... SOMETHING TO EAT? FROM THE HOUSE?

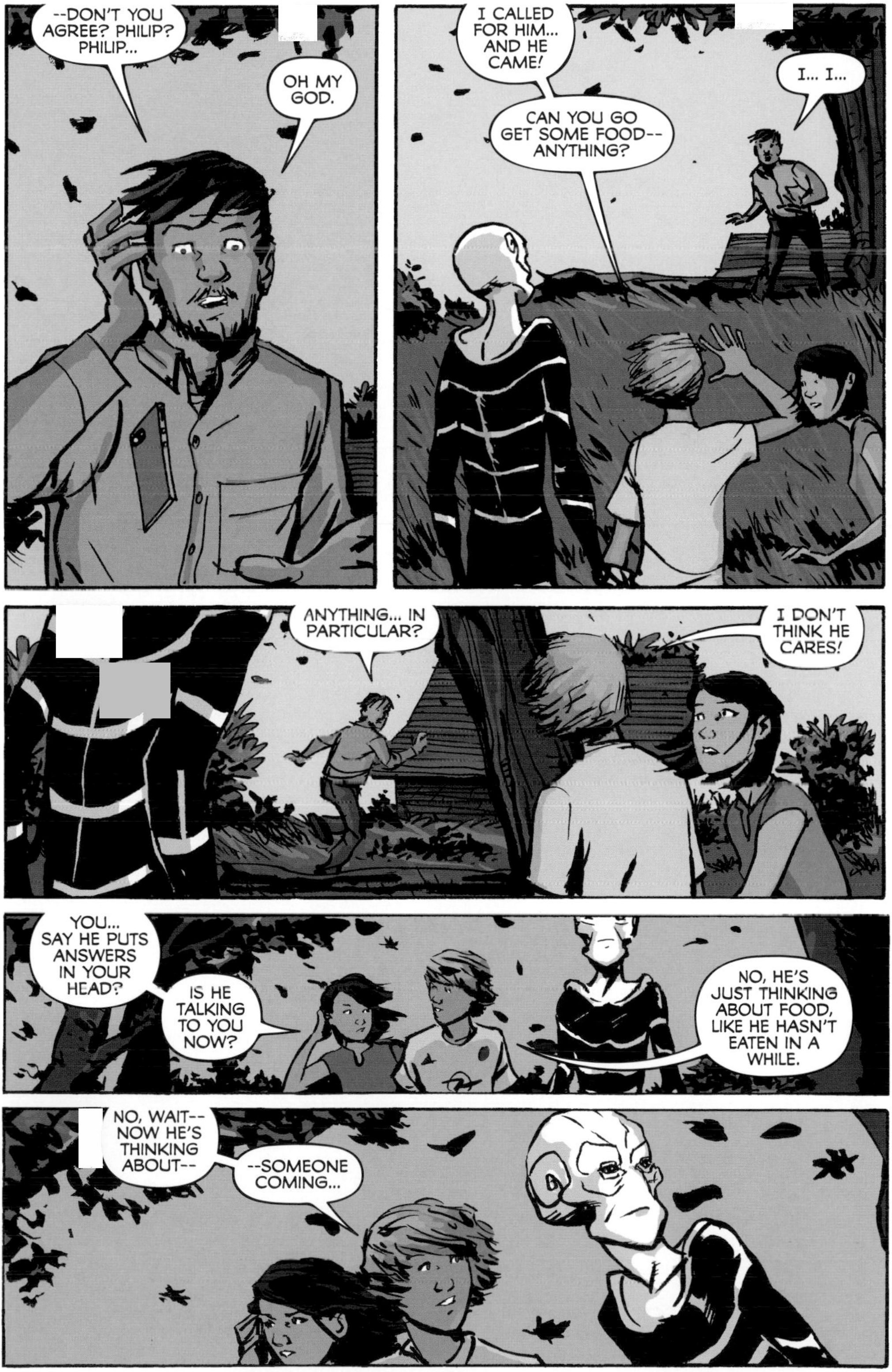
--DON'T YOU AGREE? PHILIP? PHILIP...
OH MY GOD.
I CALLED FOR HIM... AND HE CAME!
CAN YOU GO GET SOME FOOD-- ANYTHING?
I... I...
ANYTHING... IN PARTICULAR?
I DON'T THINK HE CARES!
YOU... SAY HE PUTS ANSWERS IN YOUR HEAD?
IS HE TALKING TO YOU NOW?
NO, HE'S JUST THINKING ABOUT FOOD, LIKE HE HASN'T EATEN IN A WHILE.
NO, WAIT-- NOW HE'S THINKING ABOUT--
--SOMEONE COMING...

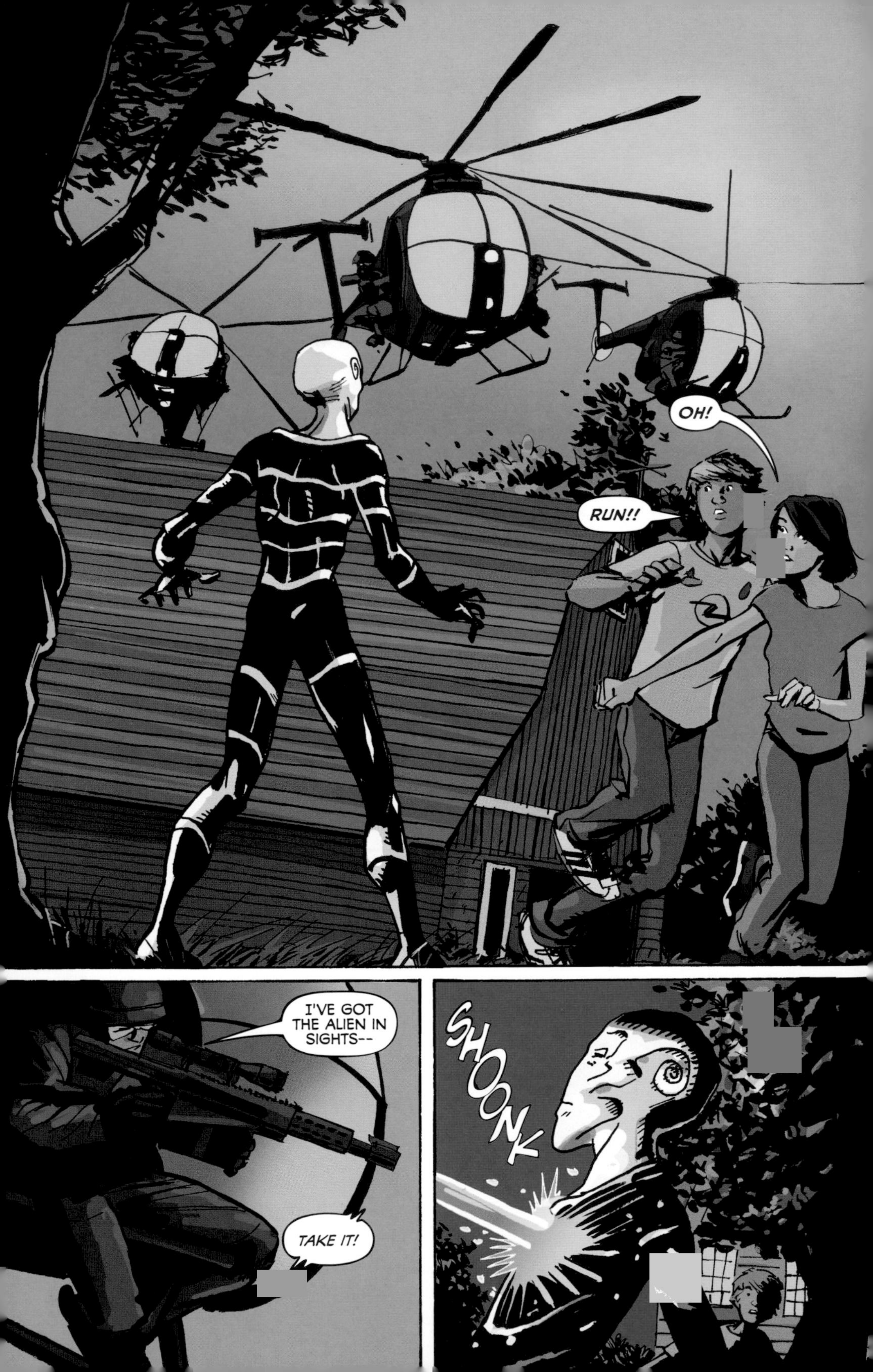
OH!
RUN!!
I'VE GOT THE ALIEN IN SIGHTS--
TAKE IT!
SHOONK

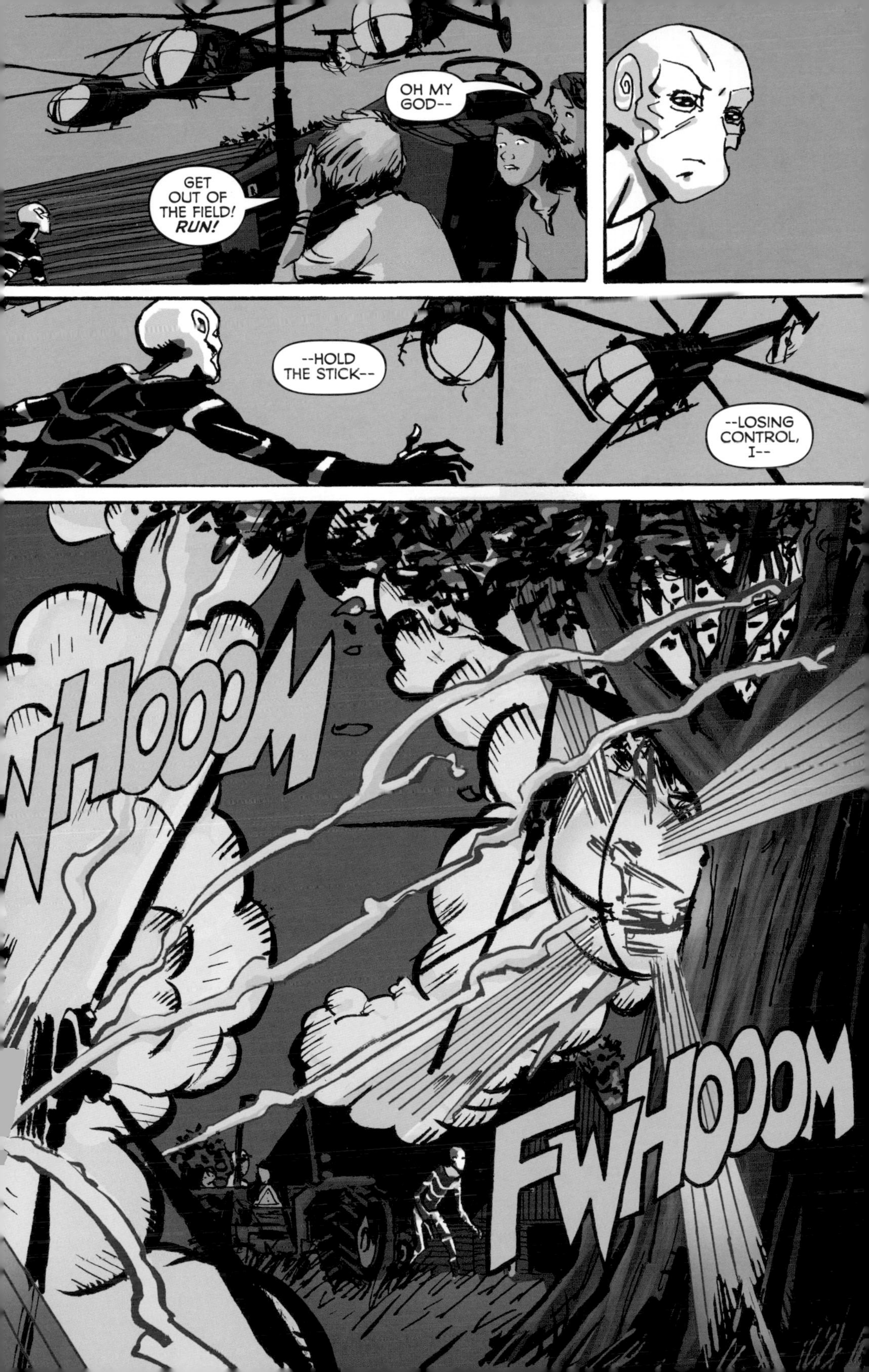

OH MY GOD--
GET OUT OF THE FIELD! *RUN!*
--HOLD THE STICK--
--LOSING CONTROL, I--
WHOOOM
FWHOOOM

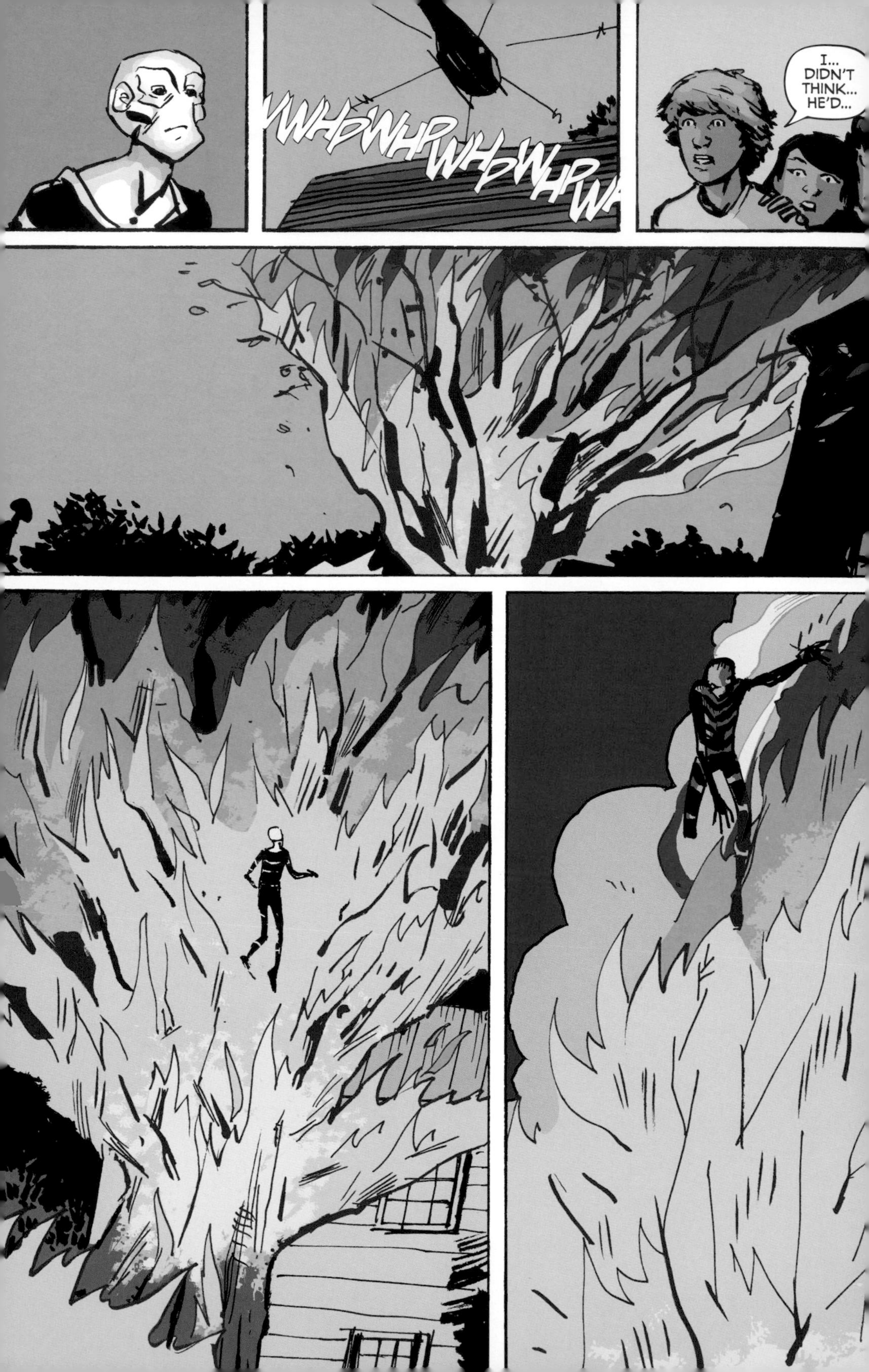
WHPWHPWHPWHPWA
I... DIDN'T THINK... HE'D...

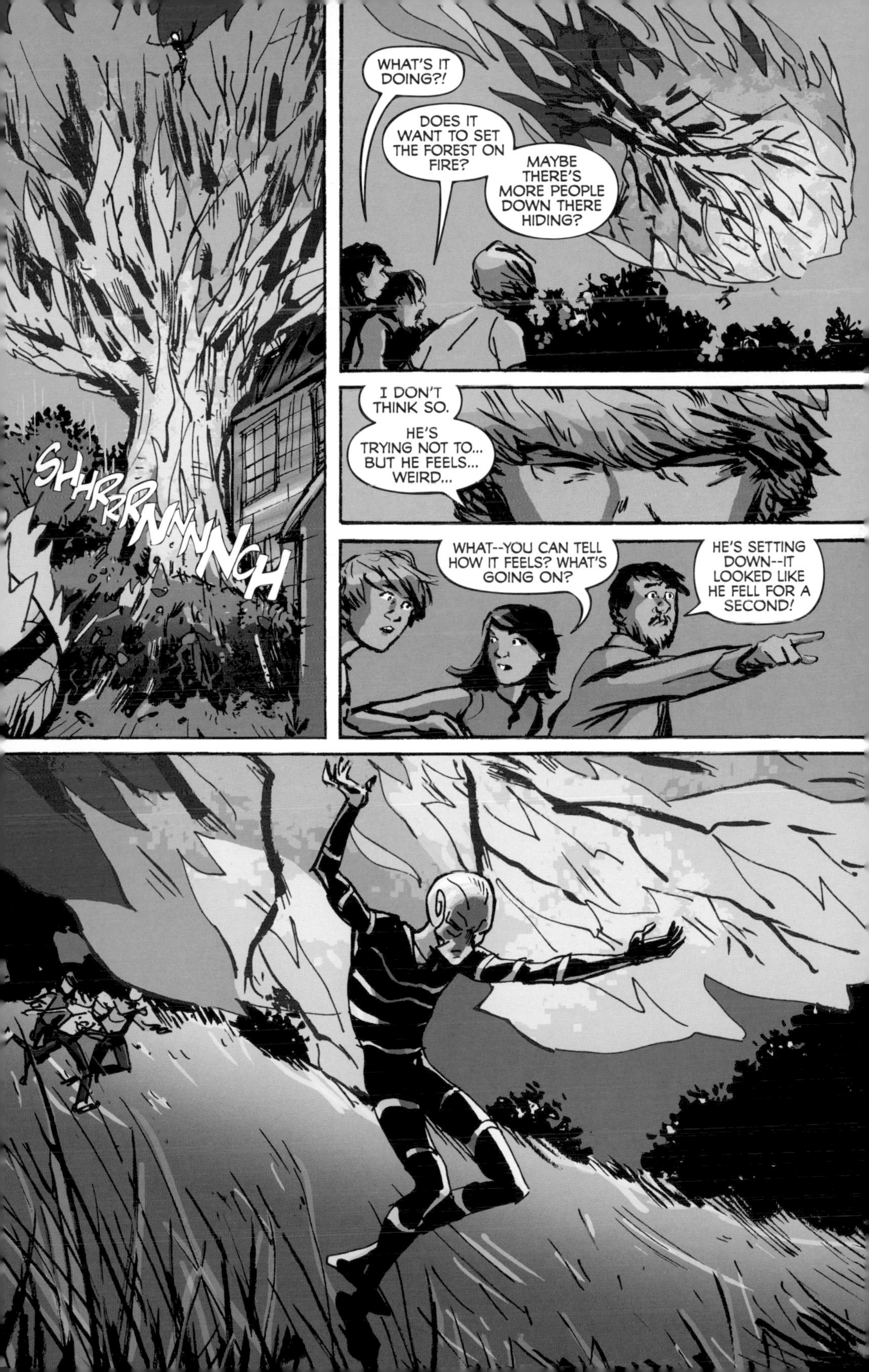
SHHRRRNNNNCH
WHAT'S IT DOING?!
DOES IT WANT TO SET THE FOREST ON FIRE?
MAYBE THERE'S MORE PEOPLE DOWN THERE HIDING?
I DON'T THINK SO.
HE'S TRYING NOT TO... BUT HE FEELS... WEIRD...
WHAT--YOU CAN TELL HOW IT FEELS? WHAT'S GOING ON?
HE'S SETTING DOWN--IT LOOKED LIKE HE FELL FOR A SECOND!

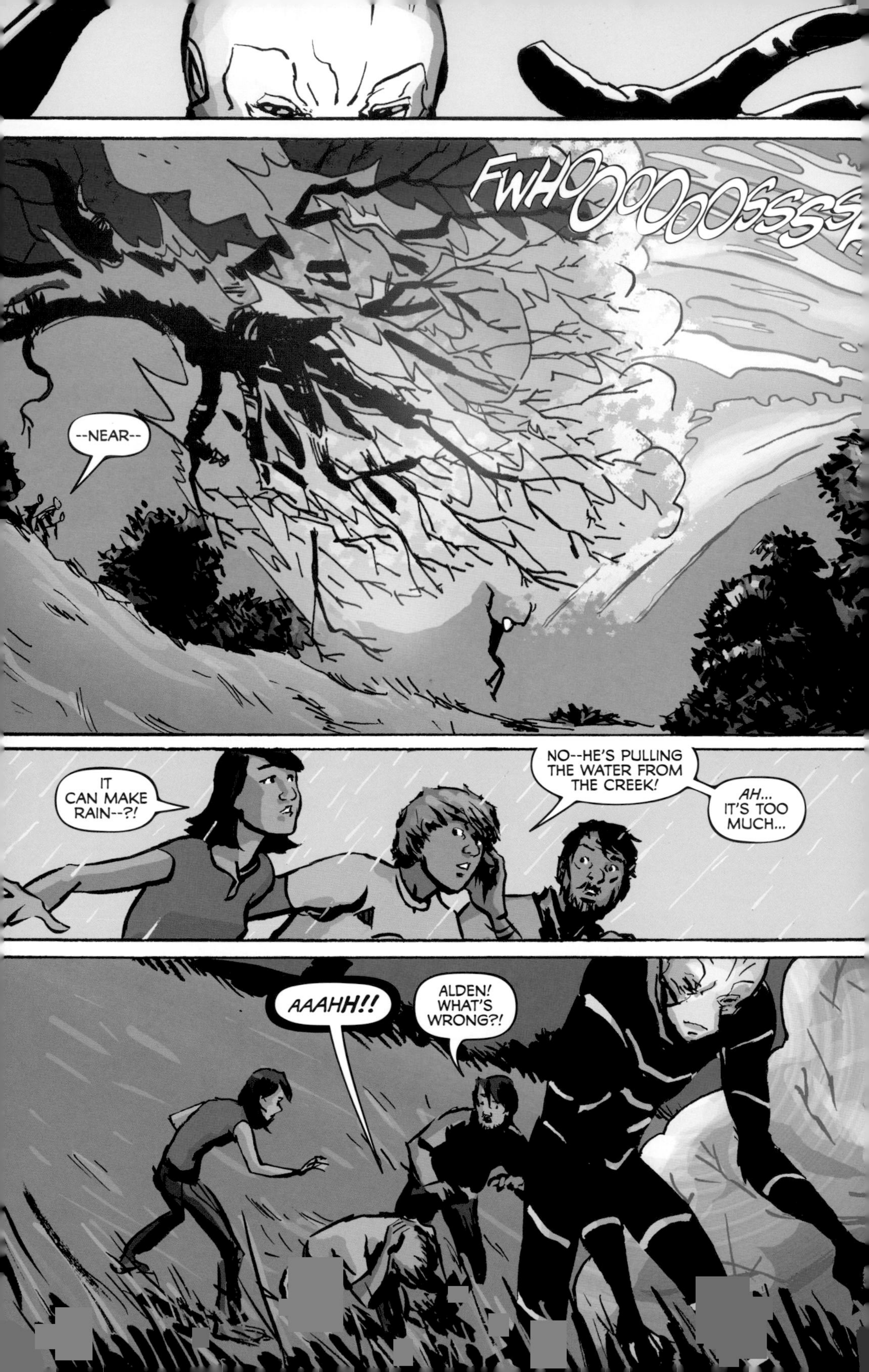
FWHOOOOOOSSSSH
--NEAR--
IT CAN MAKE RAIN--?!
NO--HE'S PULLING THE WATER FROM THE CREEK!
AH... IT'S TOO MUCH...
AAAHH!!
ALDEN! WHAT'S WRONG?!

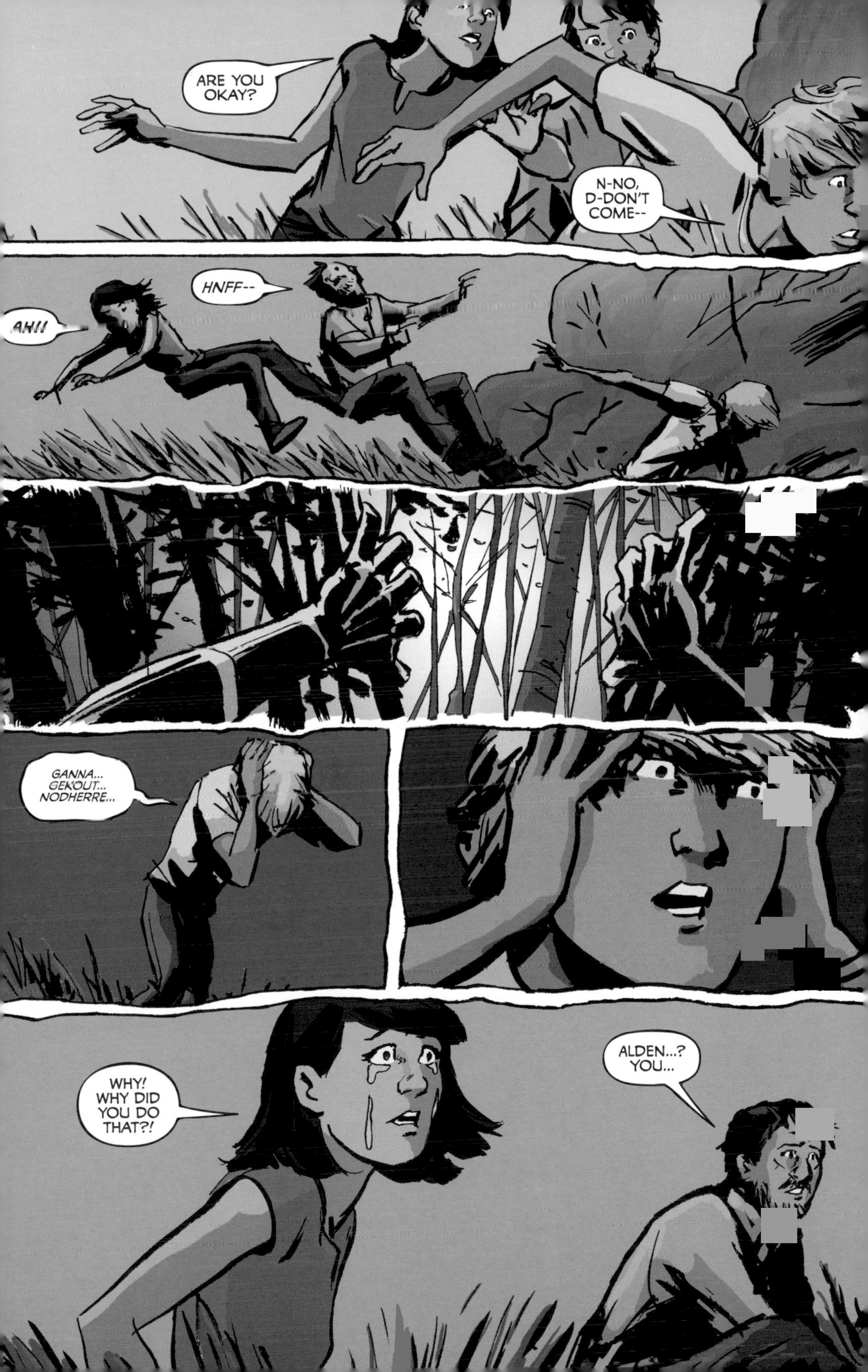
ARE YOU OKAY?
N-NO, D-DON'T COME--
HNFF--
AHH!
GANNA... GEKOUT... NODHERRE...
WHY! WHY DID YOU DO THAT?!
ALDEN...? YOU...

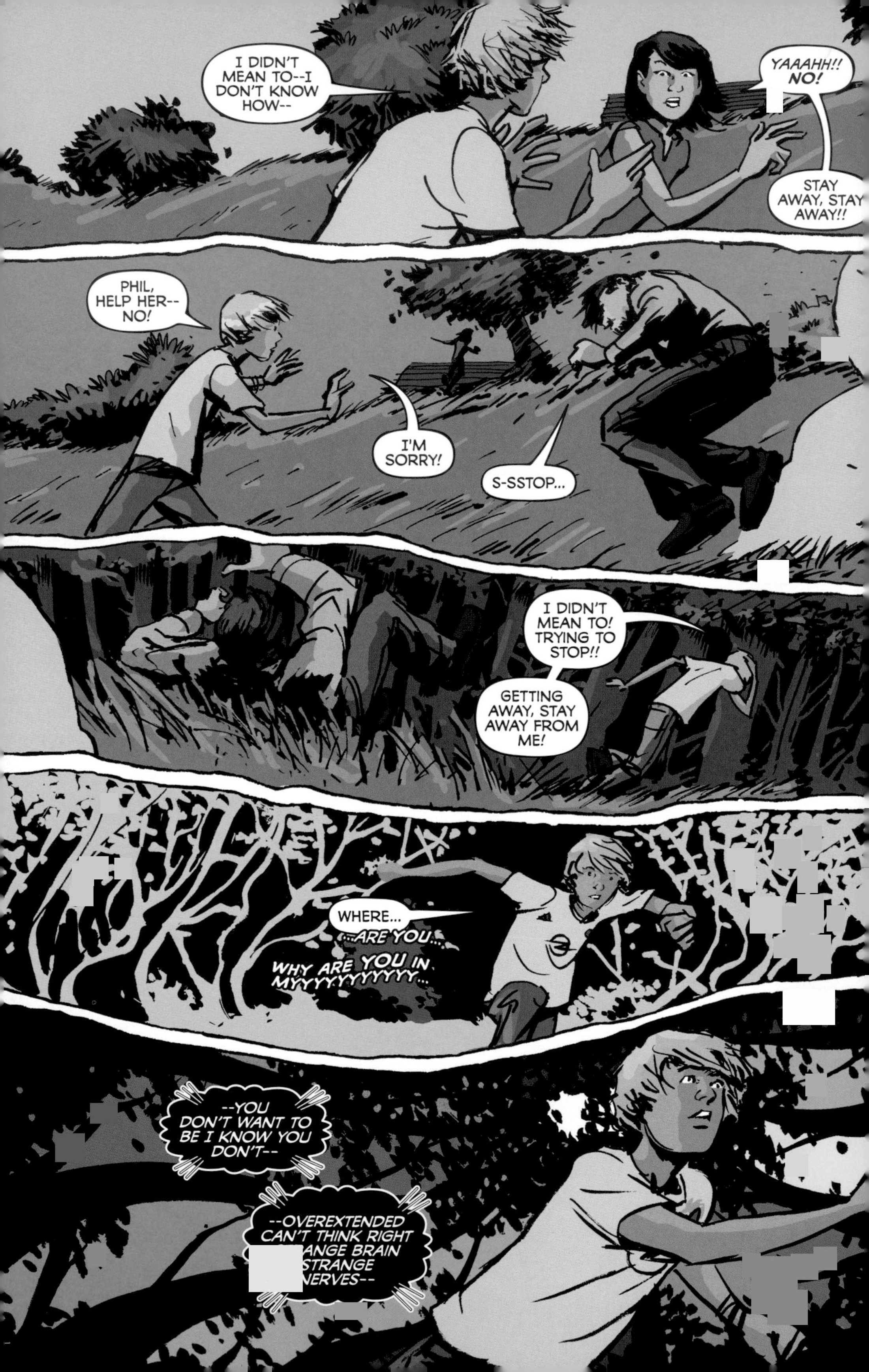

I DIDN'T MEAN TO--I DON'T KNOW HOW--
YAAAHH!! NO!
STAY AWAY, STAY AWAY!!
PHIL, HELP HER-- NO!
I'M SORRY!
S-SSTOP...
I DIDN'T MEAN TO! TRYING TO STOP!!
GETTING AWAY, STAY AWAY FROM ME!
WHERE...
...ARE YOU...
WHY ARE YOU IN MYYYYYYYYYY...
--YOU DON'T WANT TO BE I KNOW YOU DON'T--
--OVEREXTENDED CAN'T THINK RIGHT

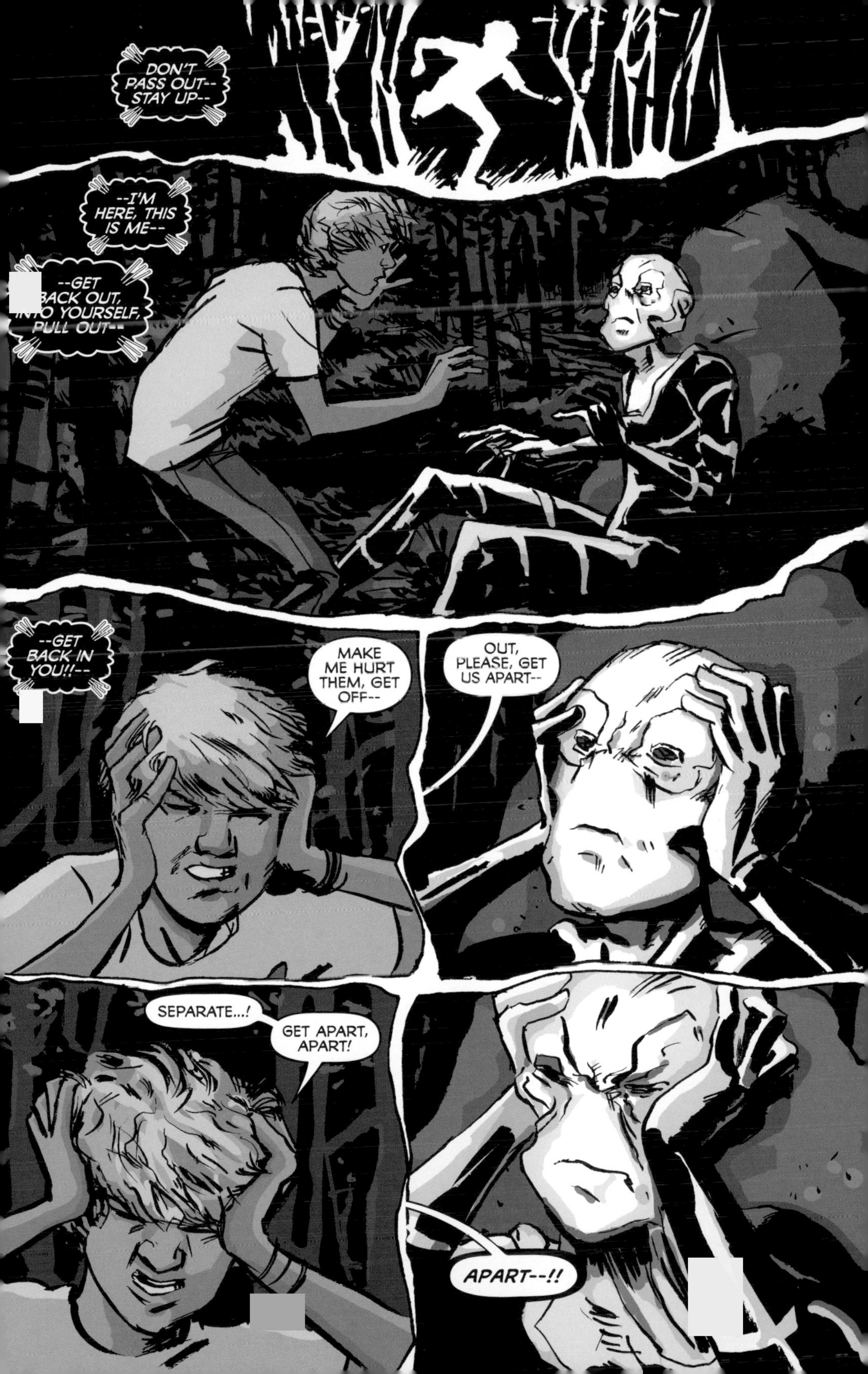
DON'T PASS OUT-- STAY UP--
--I'M HERE, THIS IS ME--
--GET BACK OUT, INTO YOURSELF, PULL OUT--
--GET BACK IN YOU!!--
MAKE ME HURT THEM, GET OFF--
OUT, PLEASE, GET US APART--
SEPARATE...!
GET APART, APART!
APART--!!

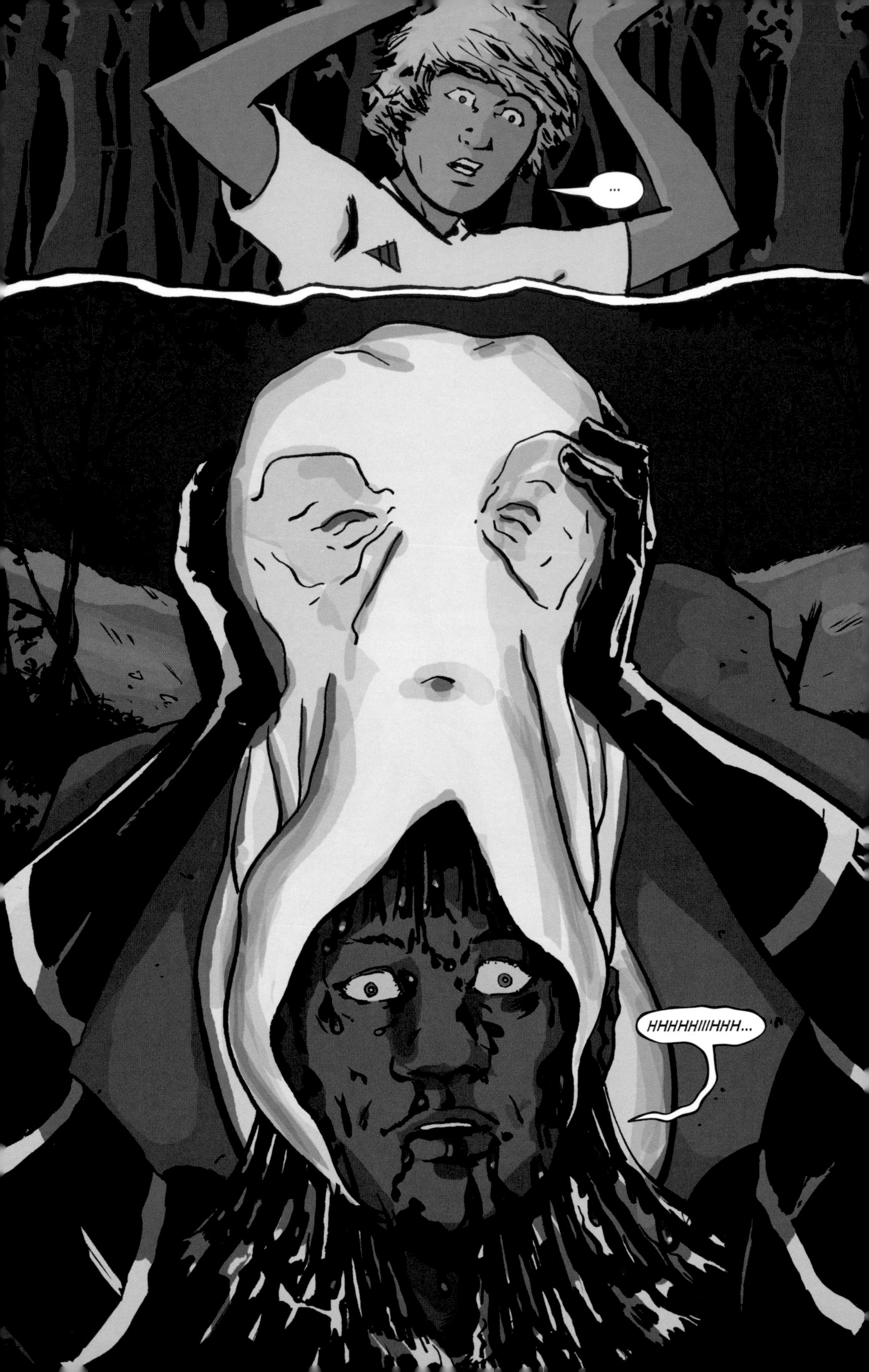
...
HHHHHIIIIHHH...

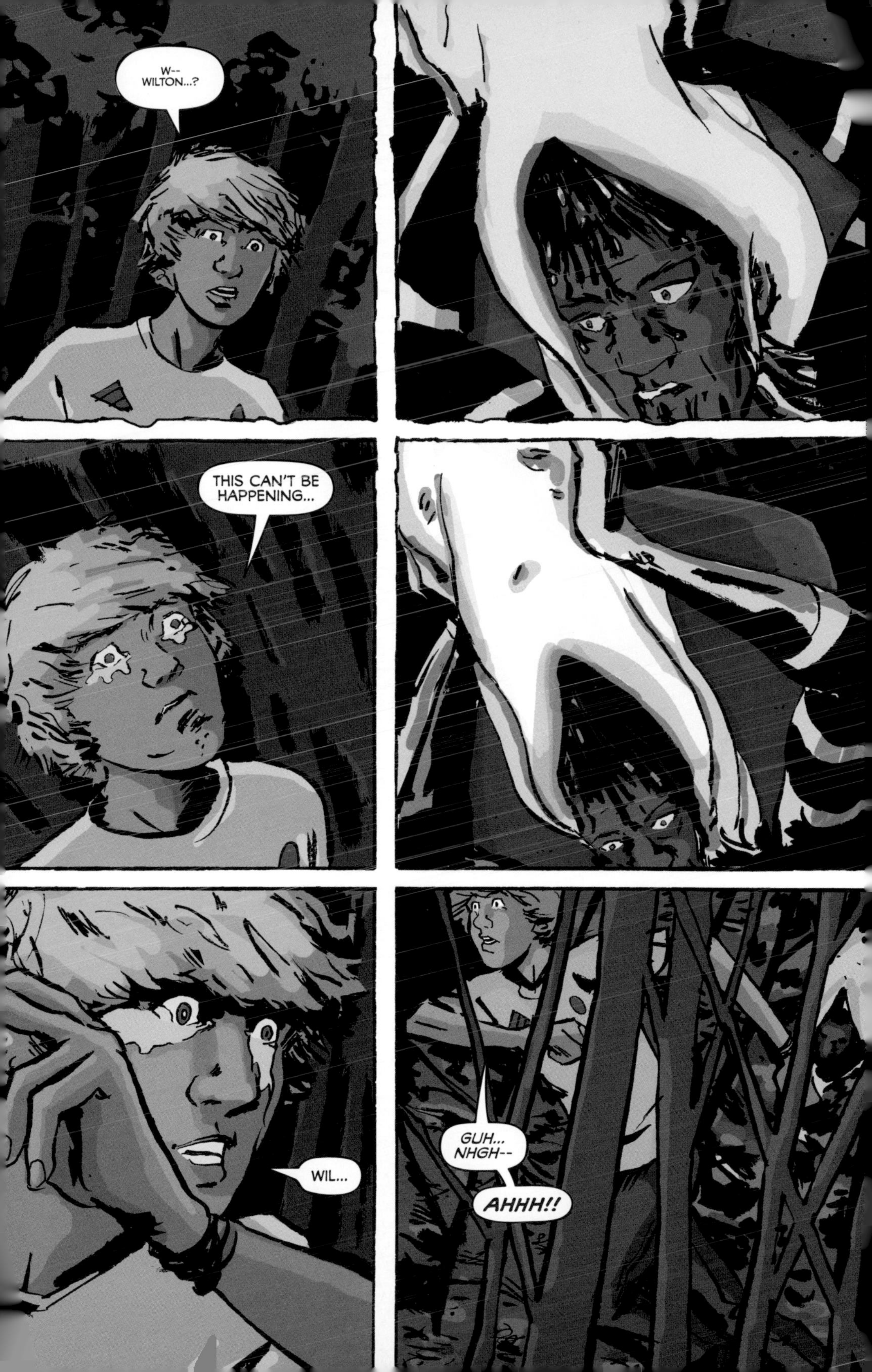
W-- WILTON...?
THIS CAN'T BE HAPPENING...
WIL...
GUH... NHGH--
AHHH!!

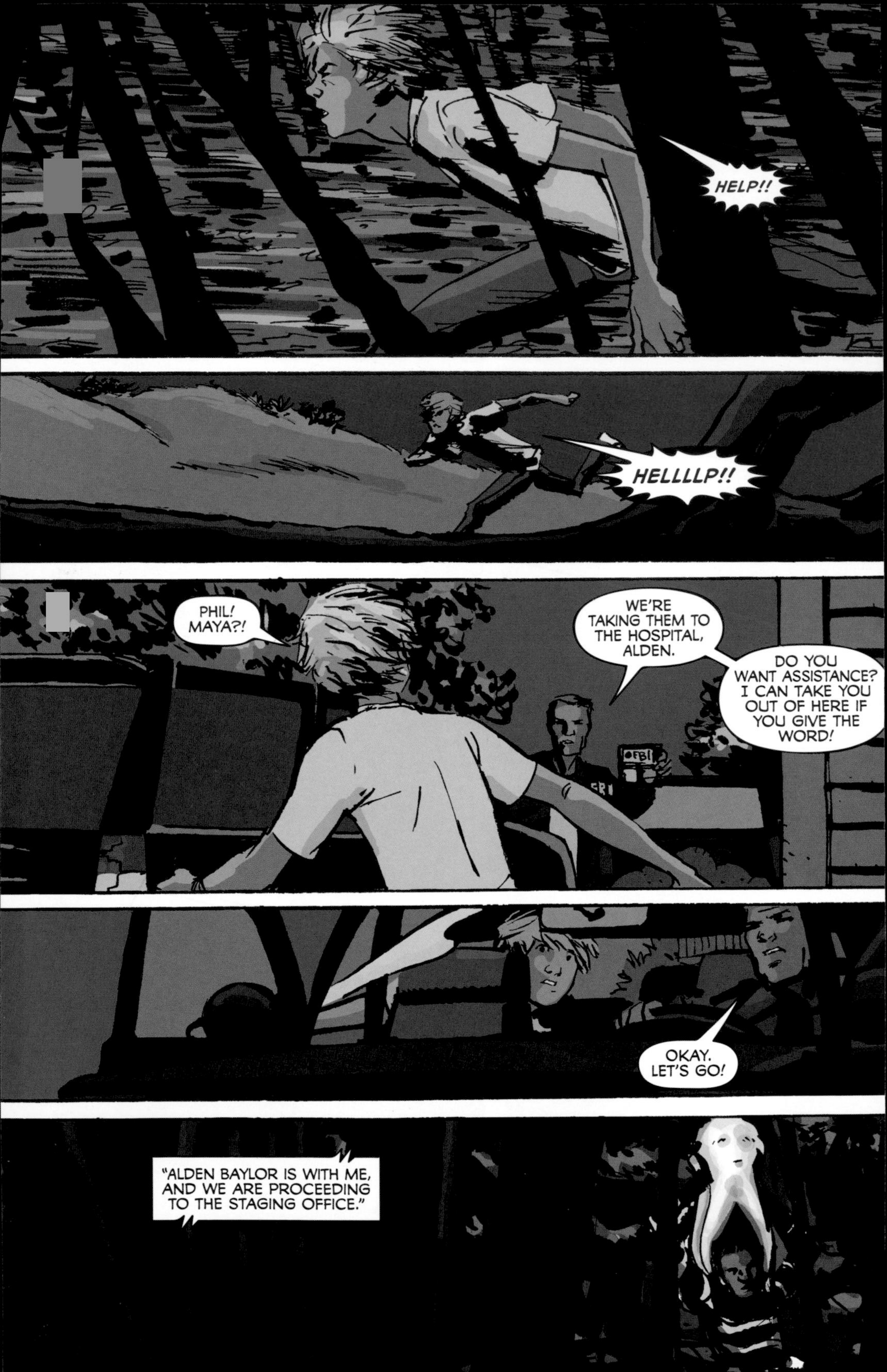
HELP!!
HELLLLP!!
PHIL! MAYA?!
WE'RE TAKING THEM TO THE HOSPITAL, ALDEN.
DO YOU WANT ASSISTANCE? I CAN TAKE YOU OUT OF HERE IF YOU GIVE THE WORD!
FBI
OKAY. LET'S GO!
"ALDEN BAYLOR IS WITH ME, AND WE ARE PROCEEDING TO THE STAGING OFFICE."

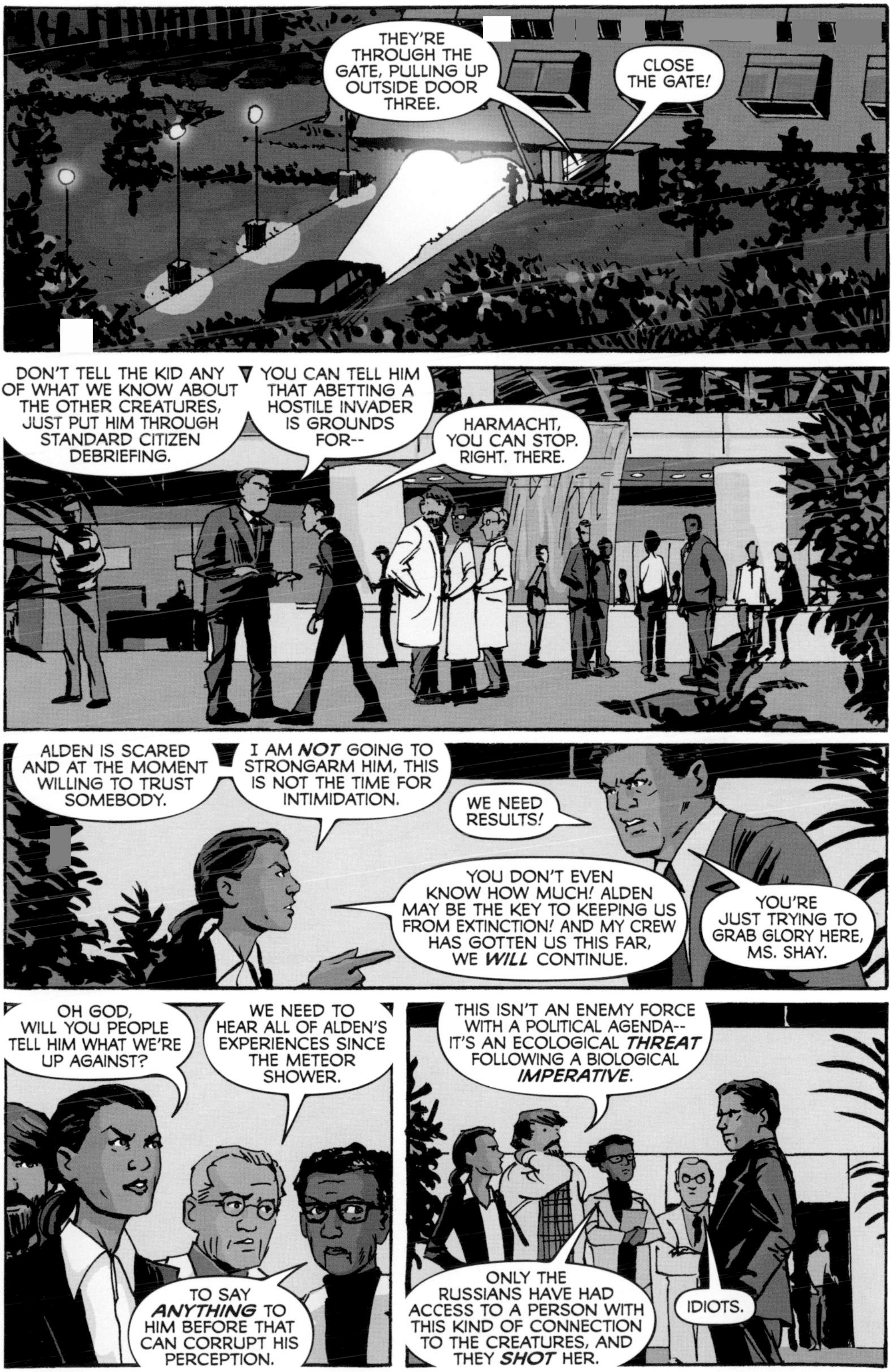
THEY'RE THROUGH THE GATE, PULLING UP OUTSIDE DOOR THREE.
CLOSE THE GATE!
DON'T TELL THE KID ANY OF WHAT WE KNOW ABOUT THE OTHER CREATURES, JUST PUT HIM THROUGH STANDARD CITIZEN DEBRIEFING.
YOU CAN TELL HIM THAT ABETTING A HOSTILE INVADER IS GROUNDS FOR--
HARMACHT, YOU CAN STOP. RIGHT. THERE.
ALDEN IS SCARED AND AT THE MOMENT WILLING TO TRUST SOMEBODY.
I AM ***NOT*** GOING TO STRONGARM HIM, THIS IS NOT THE TIME FOR INTIMIDATION.
WE NEED RESULTS!
YOU'RE JUST TRYING TO GRAB GLORY HERE, MS. SHAY.
YOU DON'T EVEN KNOW HOW MUCH! ALDEN MAY BE THE KEY TO KEEPING US FROM EXTINCTION! AND MY CREW HAS GOTTEN US THIS FAR, WE ***WILL*** CONTINUE.
OH GOD, WILL YOU PEOPLE TELL HIM WHAT WE'RE UP AGAINST?
WE NEED TO HEAR ALL OF ALDEN'S EXPERIENCES SINCE THE METEOR SHOWER.
TO SAY ***ANYTHING*** TO HIM BEFORE THAT CAN CORRUPT HIS PERCEPTION.
THIS ISN'T AN ENEMY FORCE WITH A POLITICAL AGENDA-- IT'S AN ECOLOGICAL ***THREAT*** FOLLOWING A BIOLOGICAL ***IMPERATIVE***.
ONLY THE RUSSIANS HAVE HAD ACCESS TO A PERSON WITH THIS KIND OF CONNECTION TO THE CREATURES, AND THEY ***SHOT*** HER.
IDIOTS.

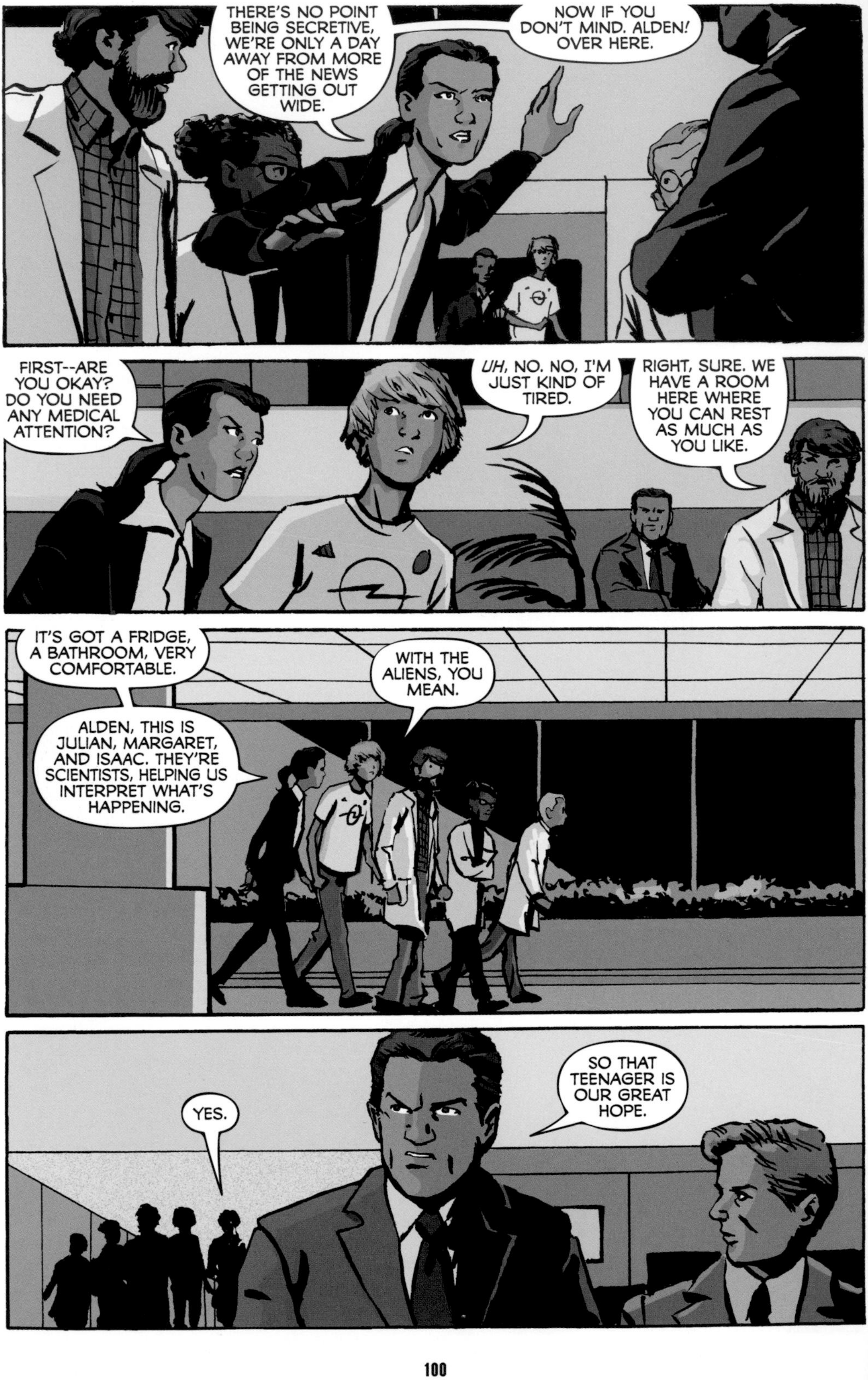
THERE'S NO POINT BEING SECRETIVE, WE'RE ONLY A DAY AWAY FROM MORE OF THE NEWS GETTING OUT WIDE.
NOW IF YOU DON'T MIND. ALDEN! OVER HERE.
FIRST--ARE YOU OKAY? DO YOU NEED ANY MEDICAL ATTENTION?
UH, NO. NO, I'M JUST KIND OF TIRED.
RIGHT, SURE. WE HAVE A ROOM HERE WHERE YOU CAN REST AS MUCH AS YOU LIKE.
IT'S GOT A FRIDGE, A BATHROOM, VERY COMFORTABLE.
ALDEN, THIS IS JULIAN, MARGARET, AND ISAAC. THEY'RE SCIENTISTS, HELPING US INTERPRET WHAT'S HAPPENING.
WITH THE ALIENS, YOU MEAN.
YES.
SO THAT TEENAGER IS OUR GREAT HOPE.

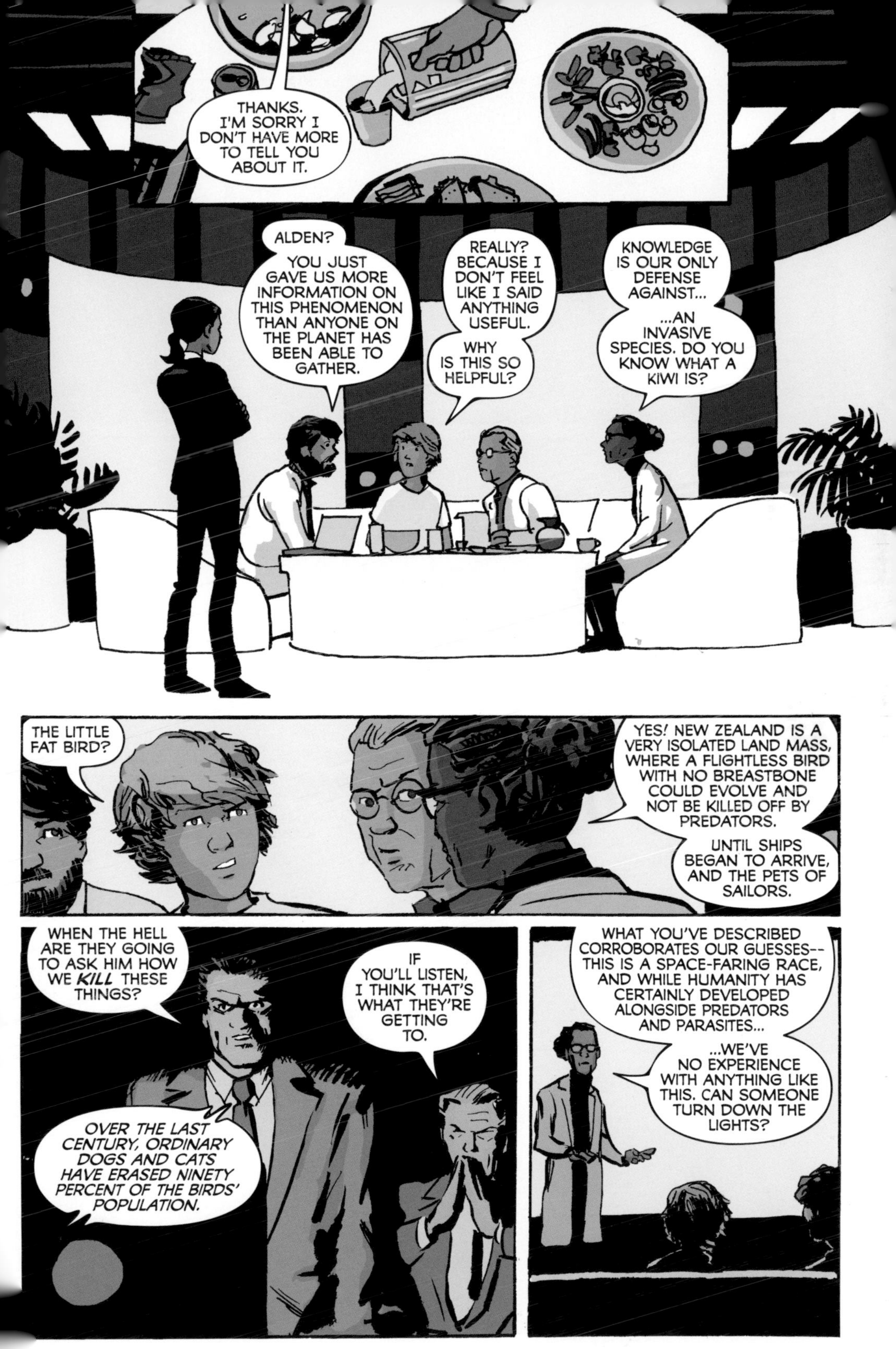
THANKS. I'M SORRY I DON'T HAVE MORE TO TELL YOU ABOUT IT.
ALDEN?
YOU JUST GAVE US MORE INFORMATION ON THIS PHENOMENON THAN ANYONE ON THE PLANET HAS BEEN ABLE TO GATHER.
REALLY? BECAUSE I DON'T FEEL LIKE I SAID ANYTHING USEFUL.
WHY IS THIS SO HELPFUL?
KNOWLEDGE IS OUR ONLY DEFENSE AGAINST...
...AN INVASIVE SPECIES. DO YOU KNOW WHAT A KIWI IS?
THE LITTLE FAT BIRD?
YES! NEW ZEALAND IS A VERY ISOLATED LAND MASS, WHERE A FLIGHTLESS BIRD WITH NO BREASTBONE COULD EVOLVE AND NOT BE KILLED OFF BY PREDATORS.
UNTIL SHIPS BEGAN TO ARRIVE, AND THE PETS OF SAILORS.
WHEN THE HELL ARE THEY GOING TO ASK HIM HOW WE *KILL* THESE THINGS?
IF YOU'LL LISTEN, I THINK THAT'S WHAT THEY'RE GETTING TO.
OVER THE LAST CENTURY, ORDINARY DOGS AND CATS HAVE ERASED NINETY PERCENT OF THE BIRDS' POPULATION.
WHAT YOU'VE DESCRIBED CORROBORATES OUR GUESSES-- THIS IS A SPACE-FARING RACE, AND WHILE HUMANITY HAS CERTAINLY DEVELOPED ALONGSIDE PREDATORS AND PARASITES...
...WE'VE NO EXPERIENCE WITH ANYTHING LIKE THIS. CAN SOMEONE TURN DOWN THE LIGHTS?

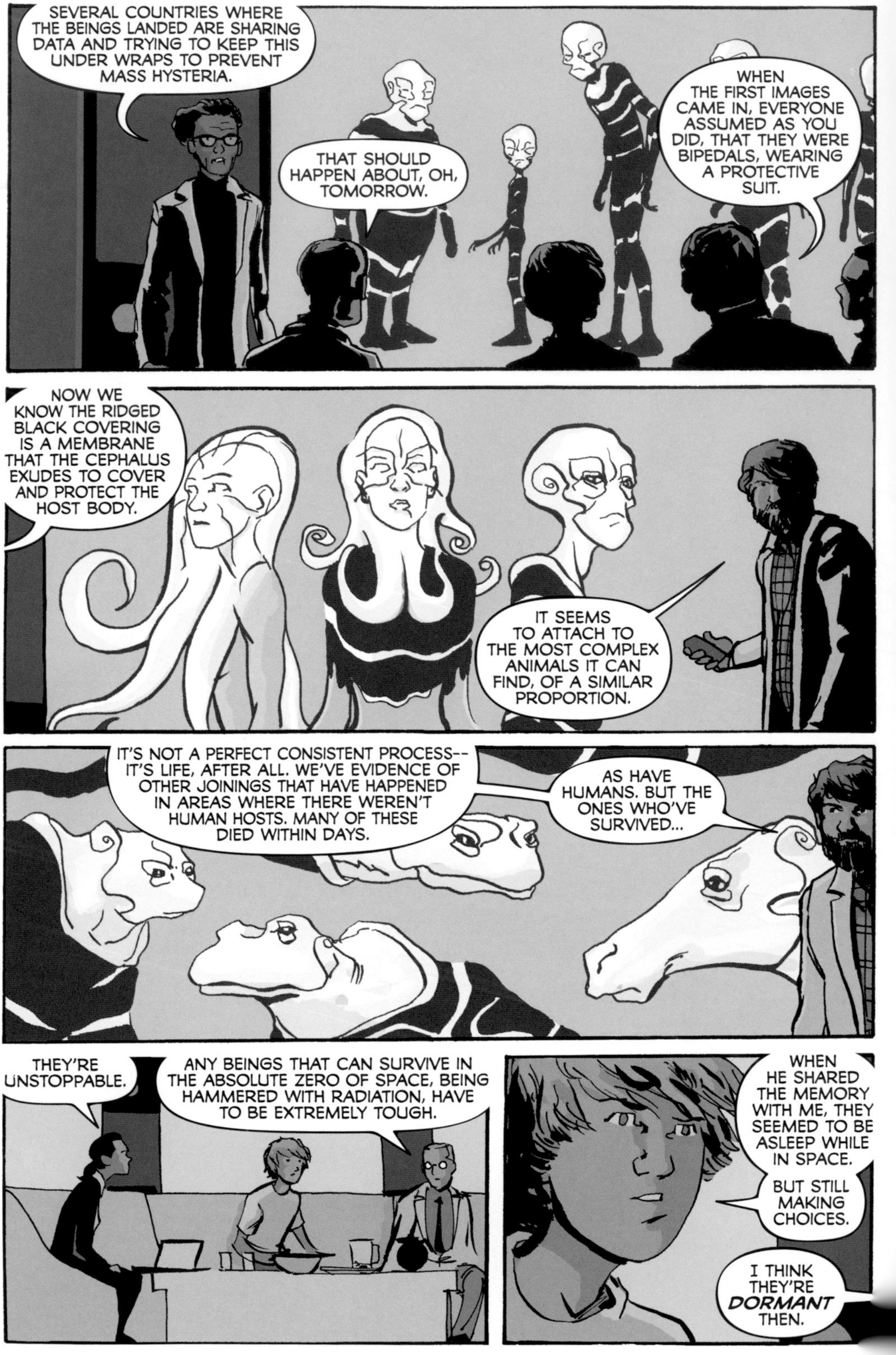
SEVERAL COUNTRIES WHERE THE BEINGS LANDED ARE SHARING DATA AND TRYING TO KEEP THIS UNDER WRAPS TO PREVENT MASS HYSTERIA.
THAT SHOULD HAPPEN ABOUT, OH, TOMORROW.
WHEN THE FIRST IMAGES CAME IN, EVERYONE ASSUMED AS YOU DID, THAT THEY WERE BIPEDALS, WEARING A PROTECTIVE SUIT.
NOW WE KNOW THE RIDGED BLACK COVERING IS A MEMBRANE THAT THE CEPHALUS EXUDES TO COVER AND PROTECT THE HOST BODY.
IT SEEMS TO ATTACH TO THE MOST COMPLEX ANIMALS IT CAN FIND, OF A SIMILAR PROPORTION.
IT'S NOT A PERFECT CONSISTENT PROCESS-- IT'S LIFE, AFTER ALL. WE'VE EVIDENCE OF OTHER JOININGS THAT HAVE HAPPENED IN AREAS WHERE THERE WEREN'T HUMAN HOSTS. MANY OF THESE DIED WITHIN DAYS.
AS HAVE HUMANS. BUT THE ONES WHO'VE SURVIVED...
THEY'RE UNSTOPPABLE.
ANY BEINGS THAT CAN SURVIVE IN THE ABSOLUTE ZERO OF SPACE, BEING HAMMERED WITH RADIATION, HAVE TO BE EXTREMELY TOUGH.
WHEN HE SHARED THE MEMORY WITH ME, THEY SEEMED TO BE ASLEEP WHILE IN SPACE.
BUT STILL MAKING CHOICES.
I THINK THEY'RE ***DORMANT*** THEN.

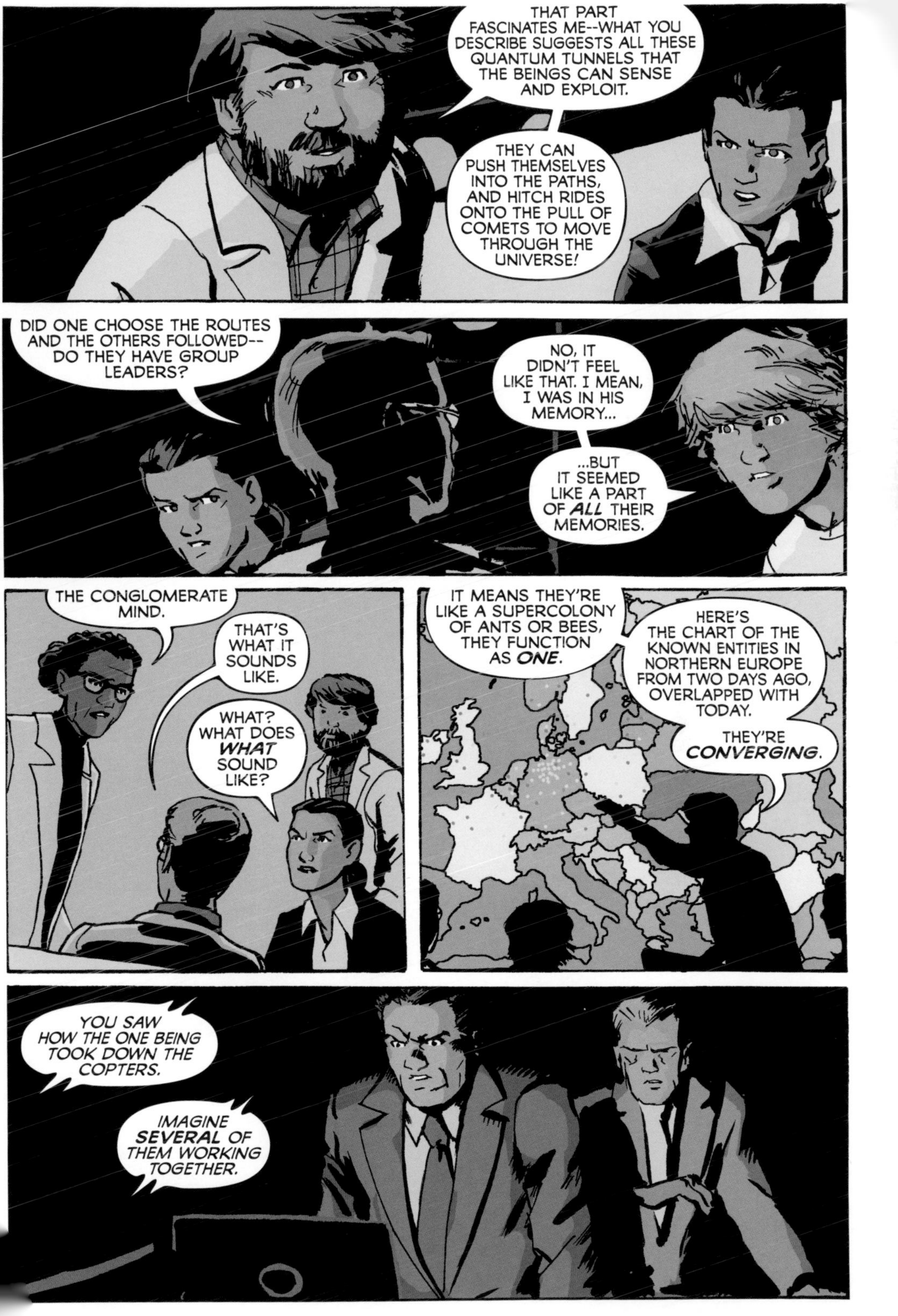
THAT PART FASCINATES ME--WHAT YOU DESCRIBE SUGGESTS ALL THESE QUANTUM TUNNELS THAT THE BEINGS CAN SENSE AND EXPLOIT.
THEY CAN PUSH THEMSELVES INTO THE PATHS, AND HITCH RIDES ONTO THE PULL OF COMETS TO MOVE THROUGH THE UNIVERSE!
DID ONE CHOOSE THE ROUTES AND THE OTHERS FOLLOWED-- DO THEY HAVE GROUP LEADERS?
NO, IT DIDN'T FEEL LIKE THAT. I MEAN, I WAS IN HIS MEMORY...
...BUT IT SEEMED LIKE A PART OF *ALL* THEIR MEMORIES.
THE CONGLOMERATE MIND.
THAT'S WHAT IT SOUNDS LIKE.
WHAT? WHAT DOES *WHAT* SOUND LIKE?
IT MEANS THEY'RE LIKE A SUPERCOLONY OF ANTS OR BEES, THEY FUNCTION AS *ONE*.
HERE'S THE CHART OF THE KNOWN ENTITIES IN NORTHERN EUROPE FROM TWO DAYS AGO, OVERLAPPED WITH TODAY.
THEY'RE *CONVERGING*.
YOU SAW HOW THE ONE BEING TOOK DOWN THE COPTERS.
IMAGINE ***SEVERAL*** *OF THEM WORKING TOGETHER.*

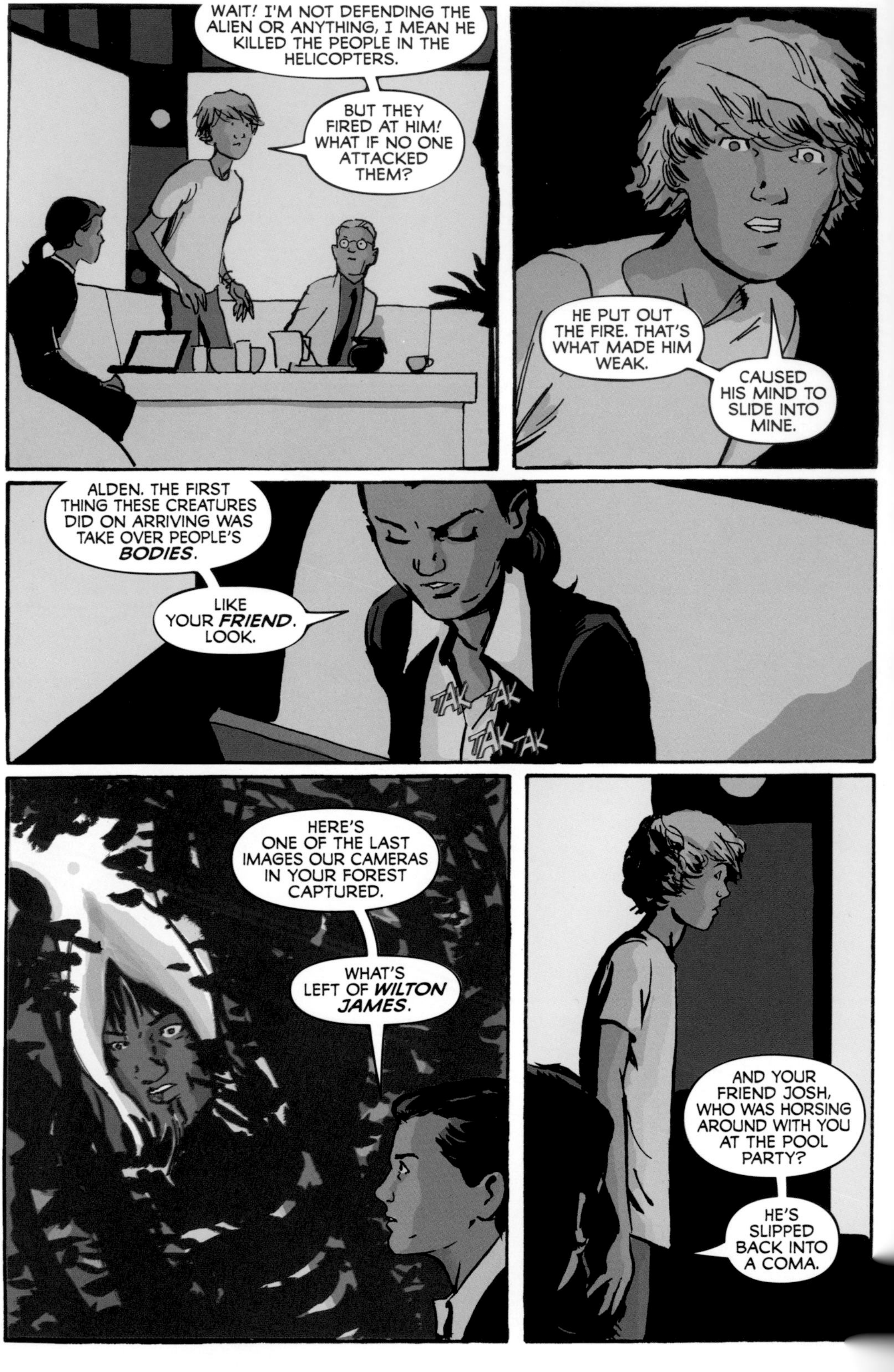
WAIT! I'M NOT DEFENDING THE ALIEN OR ANYTHING, I MEAN HE KILLED THE PEOPLE IN THE HELICOPTERS.
BUT THEY FIRED AT HIM! WHAT IF NO ONE ATTACKED THEM?
HE PUT OUT THE FIRE. THAT'S WHAT MADE HIM WEAK.
CAUSED HIS MIND TO SLIDE INTO MINE.
ALDEN. THE FIRST THING THESE CREATURES DID ON ARRIVING WAS TAKE OVER PEOPLE'S ***BODIES***.
LIKE YOUR ***FRIEND***. LOOK.
TAK TAK
TAK TAK
HERE'S ONE OF THE LAST IMAGES OUR CAMERAS IN YOUR FOREST CAPTURED.
WHAT'S LEFT OF ***WILTON JAMES***.
AND YOUR FRIEND JOSH, WHO WAS HORSING AROUND WITH YOU AT THE POOL PARTY?
HE'S SLIPPED BACK INTO A COMA.

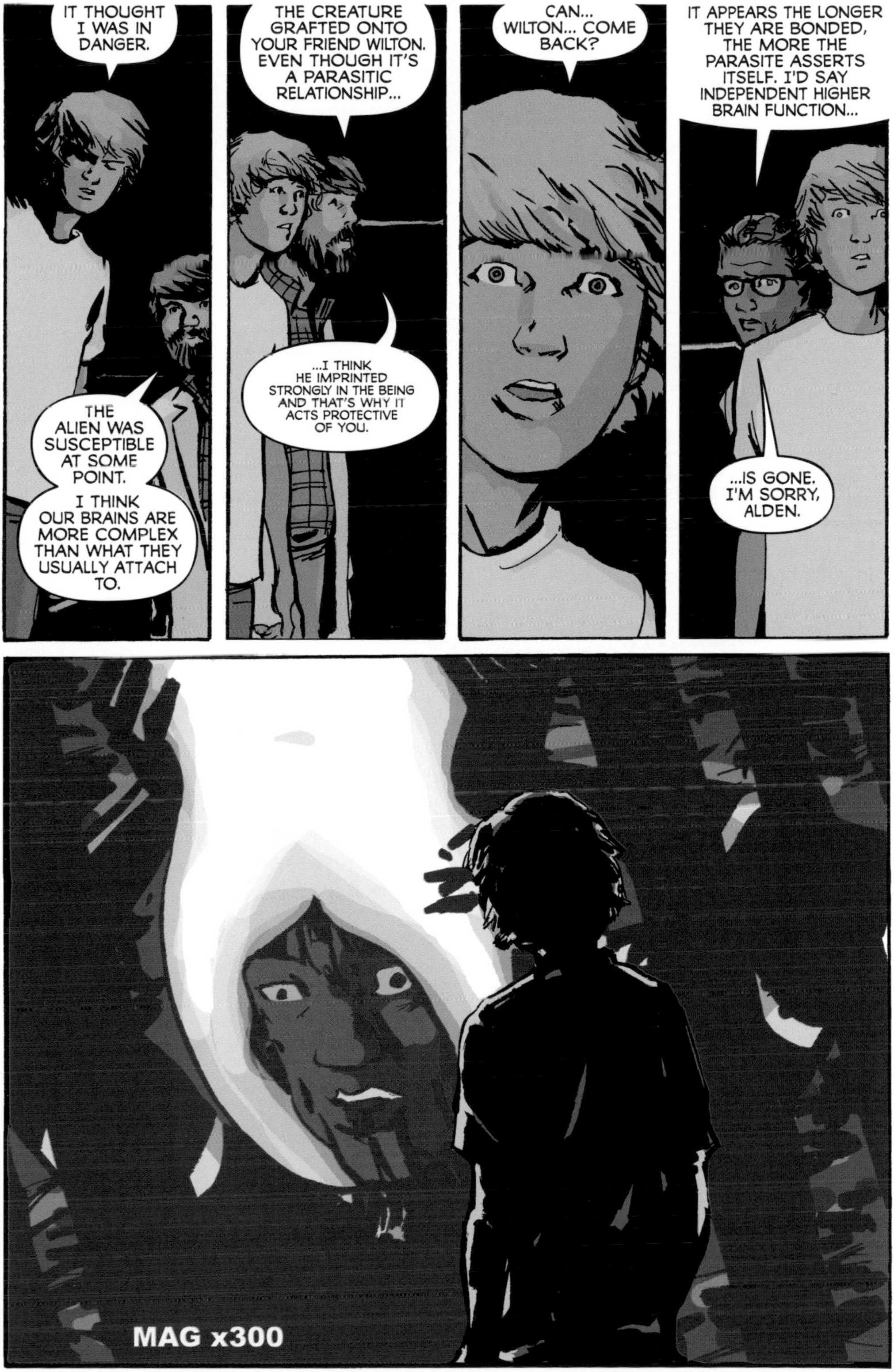
IT THOUGHT I WAS IN DANGER.
THE ALIEN WAS SUSCEPTIBLE AT SOME POINT.
I THINK OUR BRAINS ARE MORE COMPLEX THAN WHAT THEY USUALLY ATTACH TO.
THE CREATURE GRAFTED ONTO YOUR FRIEND WILTON. EVEN THOUGH IT'S A PARASITIC RELATIONSHIP...
...I THINK HE IMPRINTED STRONGLY IN THE BEING AND THAT'S WHY IT ACTS PROTECTIVE OF YOU.
CAN... WILTON... COME BACK?
IT APPEARS THE LONGER THEY ARE BONDED, THE MORE THE PARASITE ASSERTS ITSELF. I'D SAY INDEPENDENT HIGHER BRAIN FUNCTION...
...IS GONE. I'M SORRY, ALDEN.
MAG x300

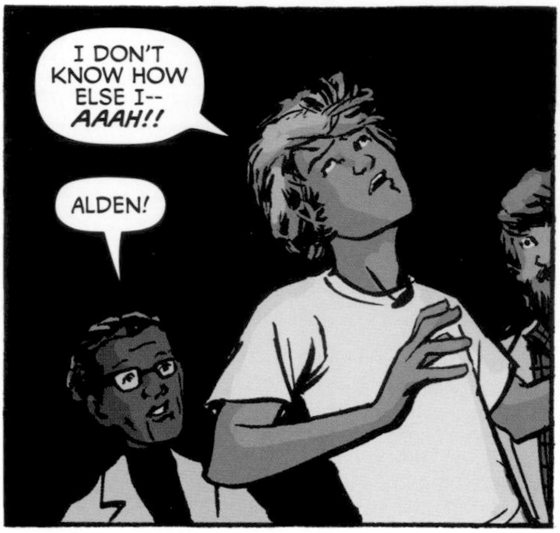
I DON'T KNOW HOW ELSE I-- ***AAAH!!***
ALDEN!

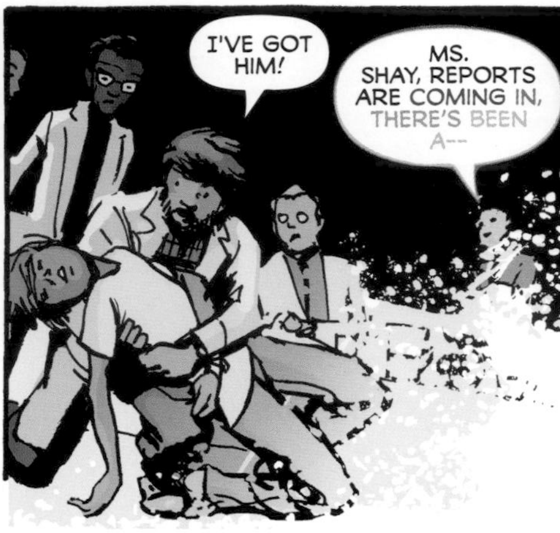
I'VE GOT HIM!
MS. SHAY, REPORTS ARE COMING IN, THERE'S BEEN A--

--UCLEAR EXPLOSION IN INDIA FROM ONE OF--

--ALL INVADERS BEING TRACKED ARE NOW CONVERGING AT--

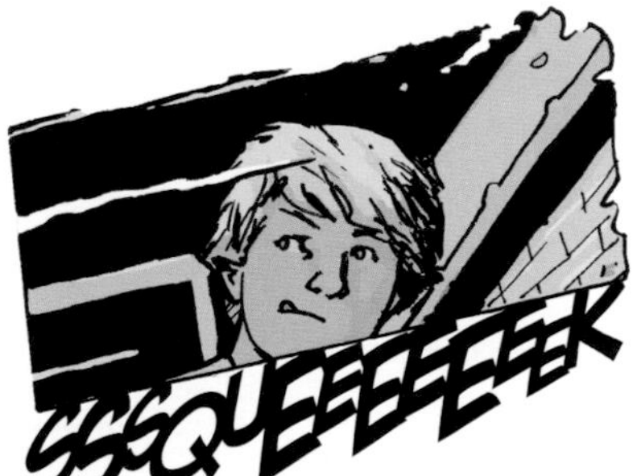
SSSQUEEEEEEEK

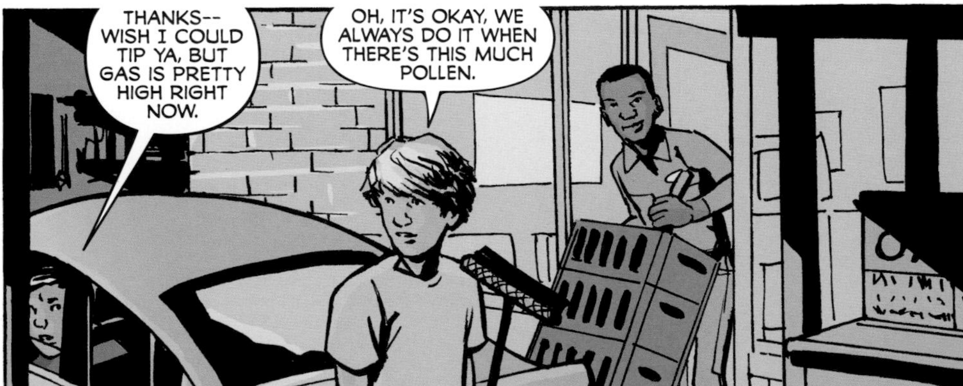
THANKS-- WISH I COULD TIP YA, BUT GAS IS PRETTY HIGH RIGHT NOW.
OH, IT'S OKAY, WE ALWAYS DO IT WHEN THERE'S THIS MUCH POLLEN.

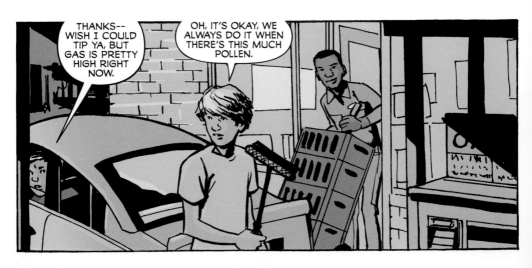

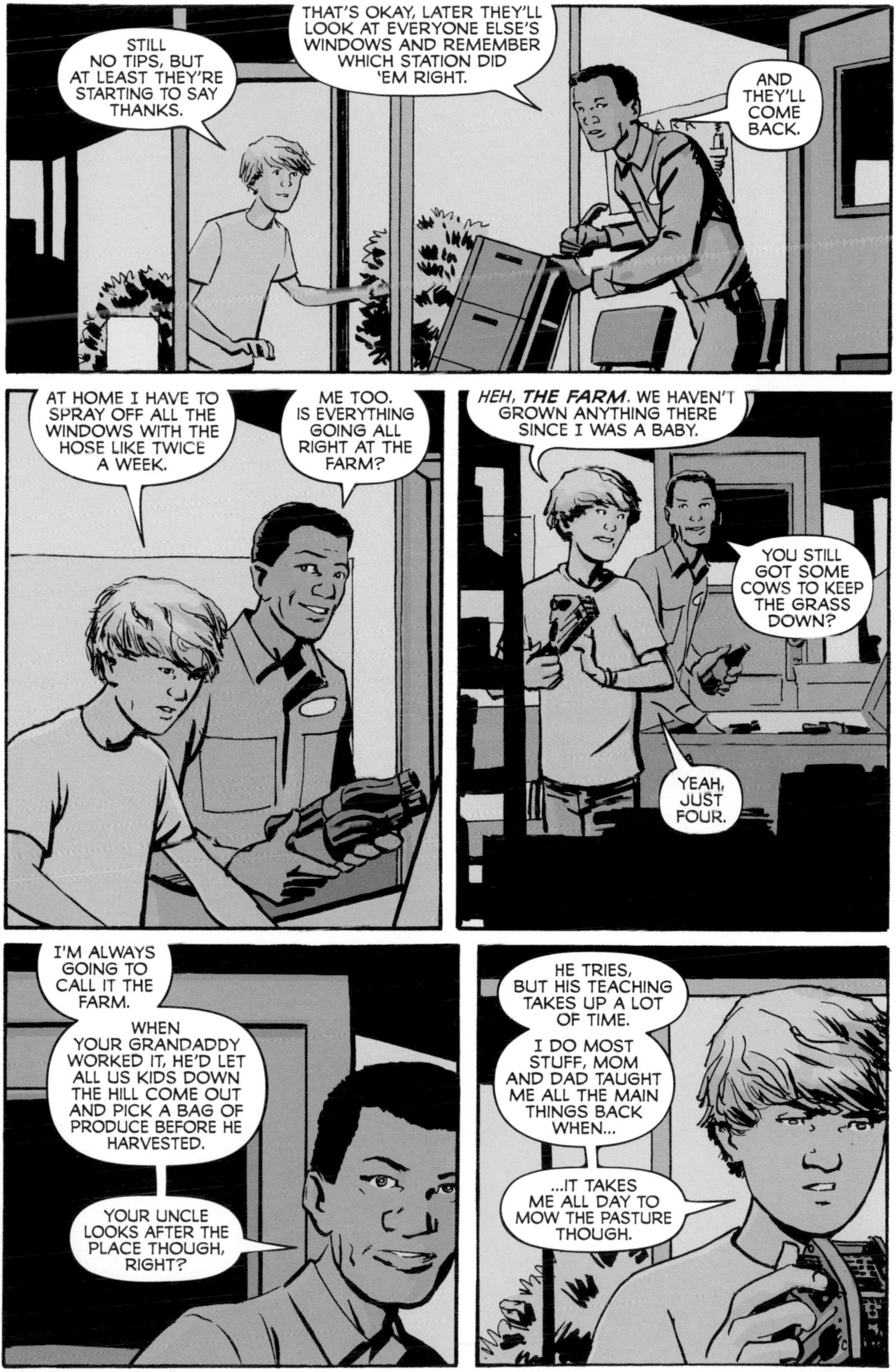
STILL NO TIPS, BUT AT LEAST THEY'RE STARTING TO SAY THANKS.
THAT'S OKAY, LATER THEY'LL LOOK AT EVERYONE ELSE'S WINDOWS AND REMEMBER WHICH STATION DID 'EM RIGHT.
AND THEY'LL COME BACK.
AT HOME I HAVE TO SPRAY OFF ALL THE WINDOWS WITH THE HOSE LIKE TWICE A WEEK.
ME TOO. IS EVERYTHING GOING ALL RIGHT AT THE FARM?
HEH, THE FARM. WE HAVEN'T GROWN ANYTHING THERE SINCE I WAS A BABY.
YOU STILL GOT SOME COWS TO KEEP THE GRASS DOWN?
YEAH, JUST FOUR.
I'M ALWAYS GOING TO CALL IT THE FARM.
WHEN YOUR GRANDADDY WORKED IT, HE'D LET ALL US KIDS DOWN THE HILL COME OUT AND PICK A BAG OF PRODUCE BEFORE HE HARVESTED.
YOUR UNCLE LOOKS AFTER THE PLACE THOUGH, RIGHT?
HE TRIES, BUT HIS TEACHING TAKES UP A LOT OF TIME.
I DO MOST STUFF, MOM AND DAD TAUGHT ME ALL THE MAIN THINGS BACK WHEN...
...IT TAKES ME ALL DAY TO MOW THE PASTURE THOUGH.

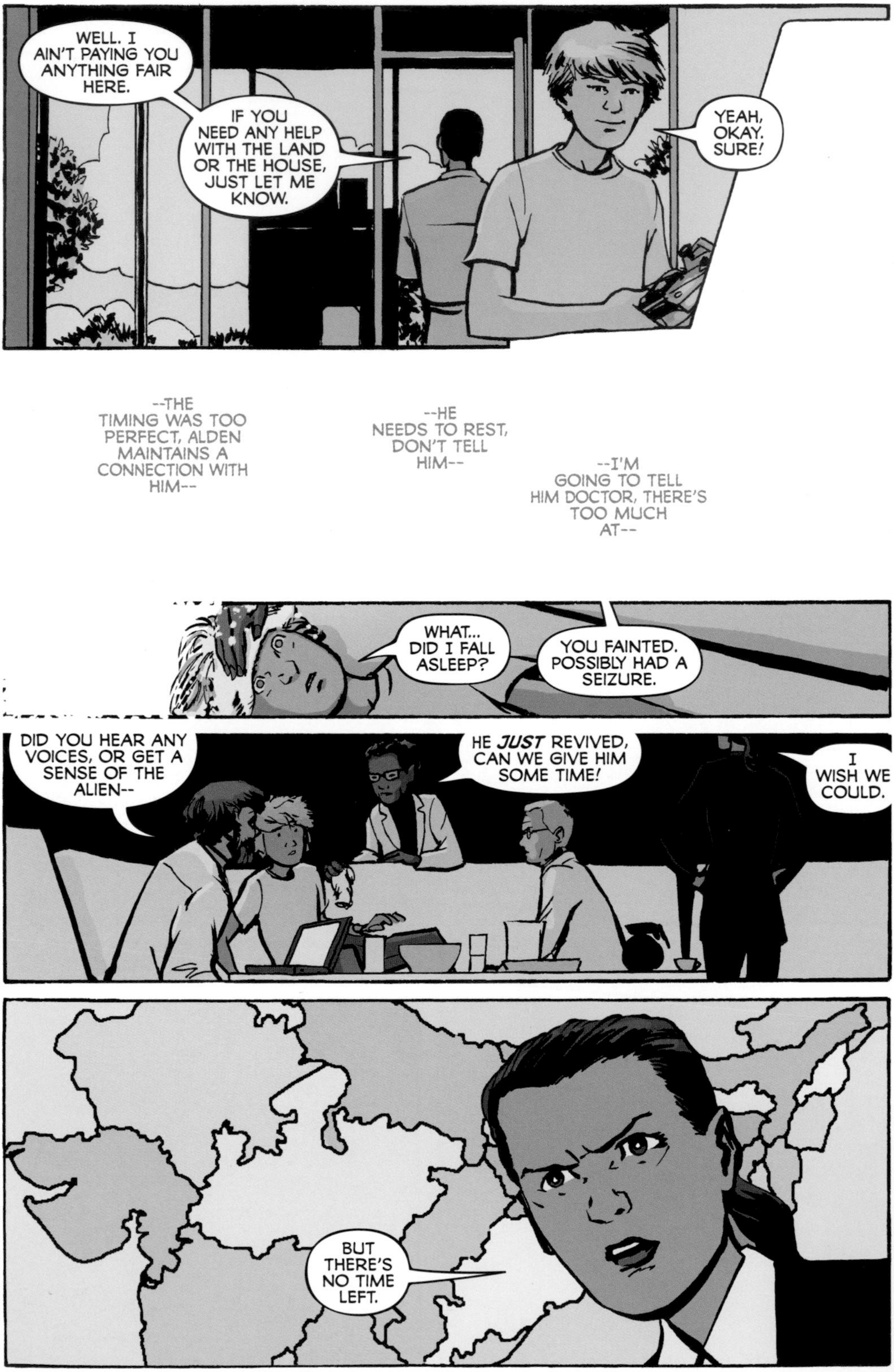
WELL. I AIN'T PAYING YOU ANYTHING FAIR HERE.
IF YOU NEED ANY HELP WITH THE LAND OR THE HOUSE, JUST LET ME KNOW.
YEAH, OKAY. SURE!
--THE TIMING WAS TOO PERFECT, ALDEN MAINTAINS A CONNECTION WITH HIM--
--HE NEEDS TO REST, DON'T TELL HIM--
--I'M GOING TO TELL HIM DOCTOR, THERE'S TOO MUCH AT--
WHAT... DID I FALL ASLEEP?
YOU FAINTED. POSSIBLY HAD A SEIZURE.
DID YOU HEAR ANY VOICES, OR GET A SENSE OF THE ALIEN--
HE *JUST* REVIVED, CAN WE GIVE HIM SOME TIME!
I WISH WE COULD.
BUT THERE'S NO TIME LEFT.

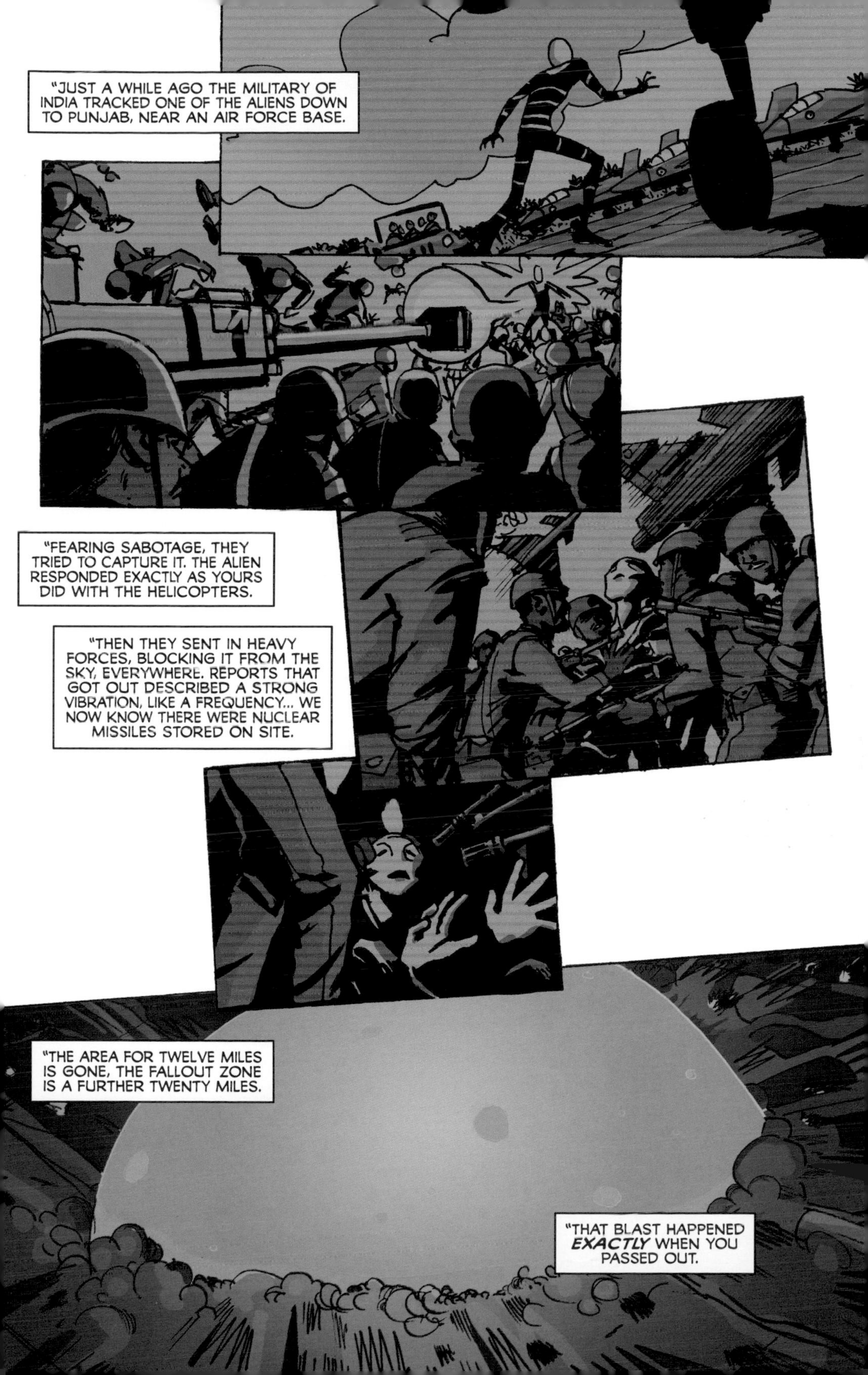
"JUST A WHILE AGO THE MILITARY OF INDIA TRACKED ONE OF THE ALIENS DOWN TO PUNJAB, NEAR AN AIR FORCE BASE.
"FEARING SABOTAGE, THEY TRIED TO CAPTURE IT. THE ALIEN RESPONDED EXACTLY AS YOURS DID WITH THE HELICOPTERS.
"THEN THEY SENT IN HEAVY FORCES, BLOCKING IT FROM THE SKY, EVERYWHERE. REPORTS THAT GOT OUT DESCRIBED A STRONG VIBRATION, LIKE A FREQUENCY... WE NOW KNOW THERE WERE NUCLEAR MISSILES STORED ON SITE.
"THE AREA FOR TWELVE MILES IS GONE, THE FALLOUT ZONE IS A FURTHER TWENTY MILES.
"THAT BLAST HAPPENED *EXACTLY* WHEN YOU PASSED OUT.

FOCUS ON THE POINT IN YOUR MIND, LET NO OTHER THOUGHTS COME NEAR IT.

CAN YOU SENSE HIM?

HE'S MOVING. TOO FAR AWAY, GETTING FAINT.

GOING TO THE OTHERS.

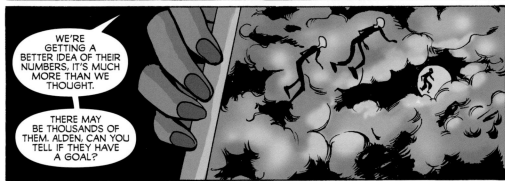

GOOD GOING, ALDEN.

HE'S RIGHT, THEY'RE CONVERGING. THEY MAINLY MOVE AT NIGHT.

REPORTS ARE ROLLING IN FROM EVERYWHERE.

WE'RE GETTING A BETTER IDEA OF THEIR NUMBERS, IT'S MUCH MORE THAN WE THOUGHT.

THERE MAY BE THOUSANDS OF THEM. ALDEN, CAN YOU TELL IF THEY HAVE A GOAL?

NO, THEY JUST... THE DANGER MAKES THEM COME TOGETHER.

THEY DON'T WANT TO BE *OUTNUMBERED* AGAIN.

CAN YOU TAKE ME TO WHERE THEY'RE GOING?

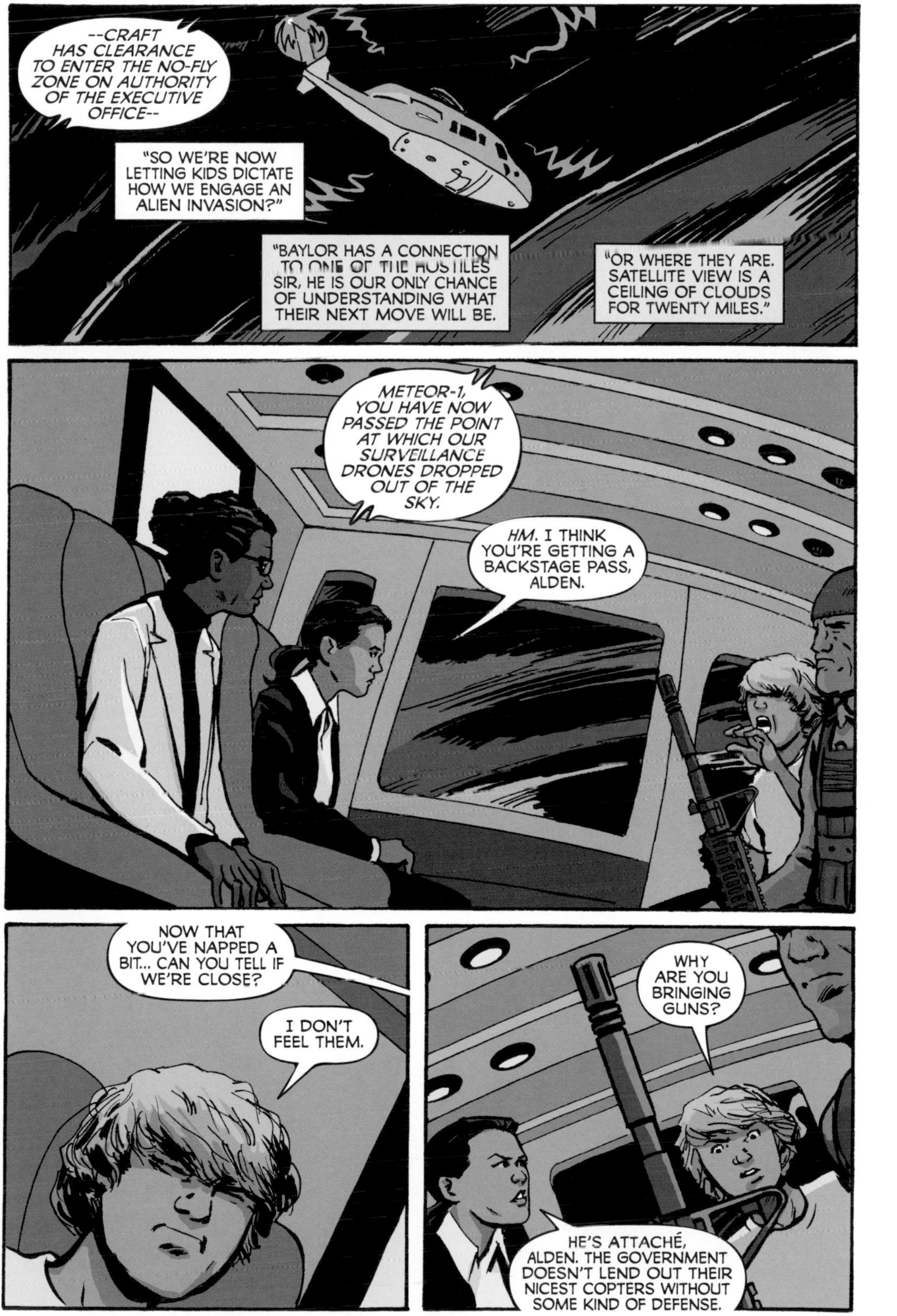
--CRAFT HAS CLEARANCE TO ENTER THE NO-FLY ZONE ON AUTHORITY OF THE EXECUTIVE OFFICE--
"SO WE'RE NOW LETTING KIDS DICTATE HOW WE ENGAGE AN ALIEN INVASION?"
"BAYLOR HAS A CONNECTION TO ONE OF THE HOSTILES SIR, HE IS OUR ONLY CHANCE OF UNDERSTANDING WHAT THEIR NEXT MOVE WILL BE.
"OR WHERE THEY ARE. SATELLITE VIEW IS A CEILING OF CLOUDS FOR TWENTY MILES."
METEOR-1, YOU HAVE NOW PASSED THE POINT AT WHICH OUR SURVEILLANCE DRONES DROPPED OUT OF THE SKY.
HM. I THINK YOU'RE GETTING A BACKSTAGE PASS, ALDEN.
NOW THAT YOU'VE NAPPED A BIT... CAN YOU TELL IF WE'RE CLOSE?
I DON'T FEEL THEM.
WHY ARE YOU BRINGING GUNS?
HE'S ATTACHÉ, ALDEN. THE GOVERNMENT DOESN'T LEND OUT THEIR NICEST COPTERS WITHOUT SOME KIND OF DEFENSE.

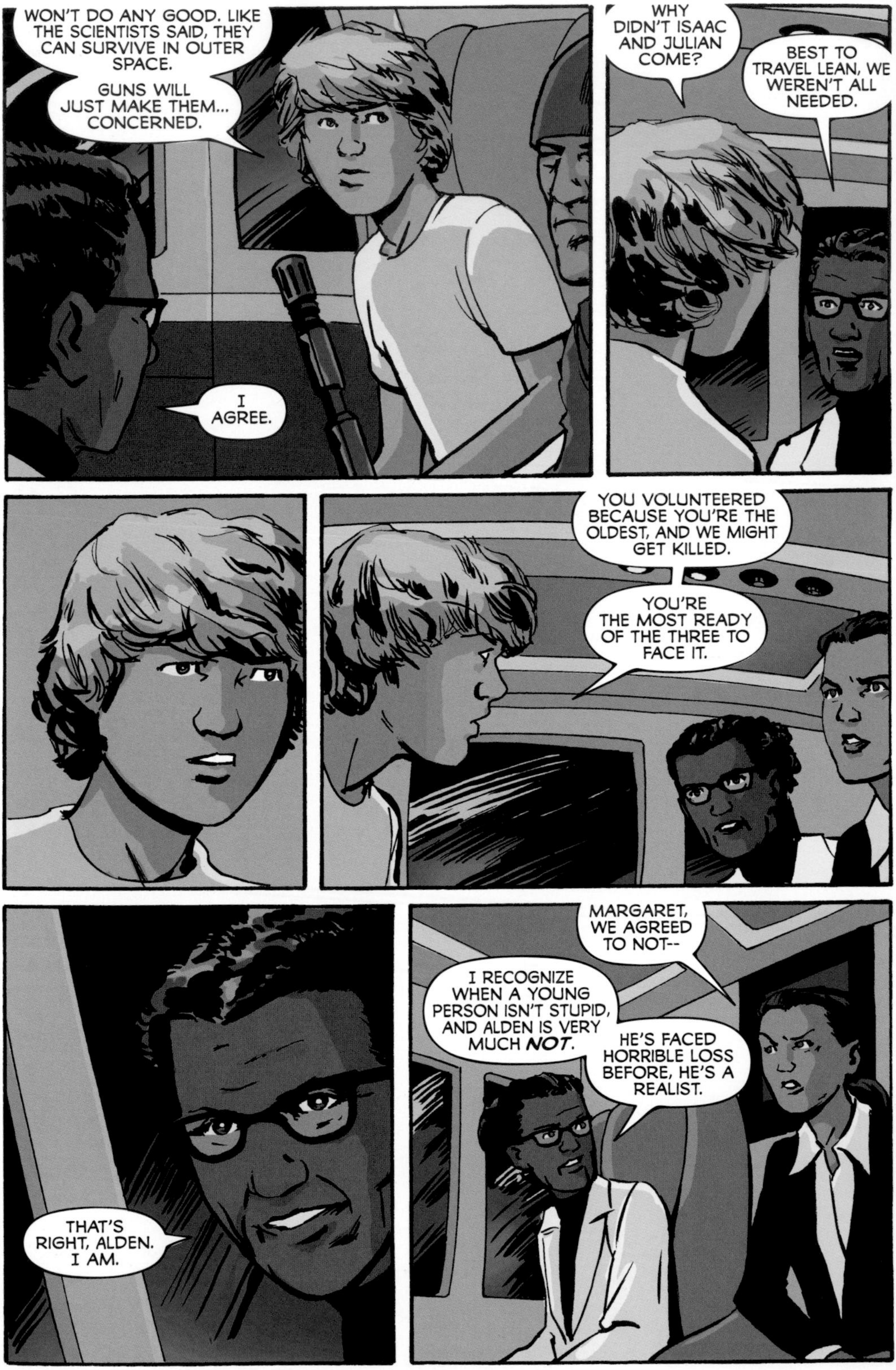
WON'T DO ANY GOOD. LIKE THE SCIENTISTS SAID, THEY CAN SURVIVE IN OUTER SPACE.
GUNS WILL JUST MAKE THEM... CONCERNED.
I AGREE.
WHY DIDN'T ISAAC AND JULIAN COME?
BEST TO TRAVEL LEAN, WE WEREN'T ALL NEEDED.
YOU VOLUNTEERED BECAUSE YOU'RE THE OLDEST, AND WE MIGHT GET KILLED.
YOU'RE THE MOST READY OF THE THREE TO FACE IT.
THAT'S RIGHT, ALDEN. I AM.
MARGARET, WE AGREED TO NOT--
I RECOGNIZE WHEN A YOUNG PERSON ISN'T STUPID, AND ALDEN IS VERY MUCH ***NOT***.
HE'S FACED HORRIBLE LOSS BEFORE, HE'S A REALIST.

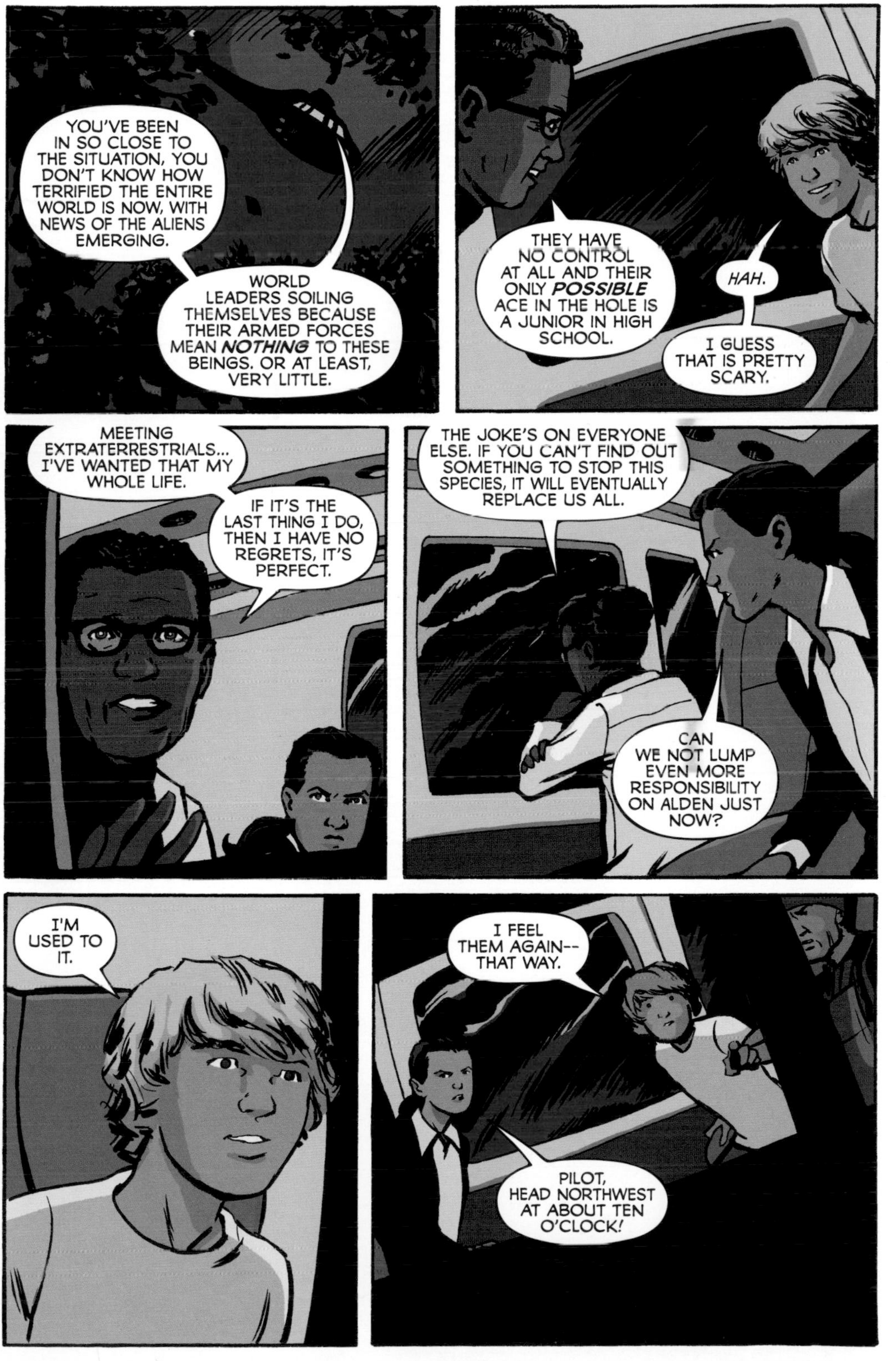
YOU'VE BEEN IN SO CLOSE TO THE SITUATION, YOU DON'T KNOW HOW TERRIFIED THE ENTIRE WORLD IS NOW, WITH NEWS OF THE ALIENS EMERGING.
WORLD LEADERS SOILING THEMSELVES BECAUSE THEIR ARMED FORCES MEAN *NOTHING* TO THESE BEINGS. OR AT LEAST, VERY LITTLE.
THEY HAVE NO CONTROL AT ALL AND THEIR ONLY ***POSSIBLE*** ACE IN THE HOLE IS A JUNIOR IN HIGH SCHOOL.
HAH.
I GUESS THAT IS PRETTY SCARY.
MEETING EXTRATERRESTRIALS... I'VE WANTED THAT MY WHOLE LIFE.
IF IT'S THE LAST THING I DO, THEN I HAVE NO REGRETS, IT'S PERFECT.
THE JOKE'S ON EVERYONE ELSE. IF YOU CAN'T FIND OUT SOMETHING TO STOP THIS SPECIES, IT WILL EVENTUALLY REPLACE US ALL.
CAN WE NOT LUMP EVEN MORE RESPONSIBILITY ON ALDEN JUST NOW?
I'M USED TO IT.
I FEEL THEM AGAIN-- THAT WAY.
PILOT, HEAD NORTHWEST AT ABOUT TEN O'CLOCK!

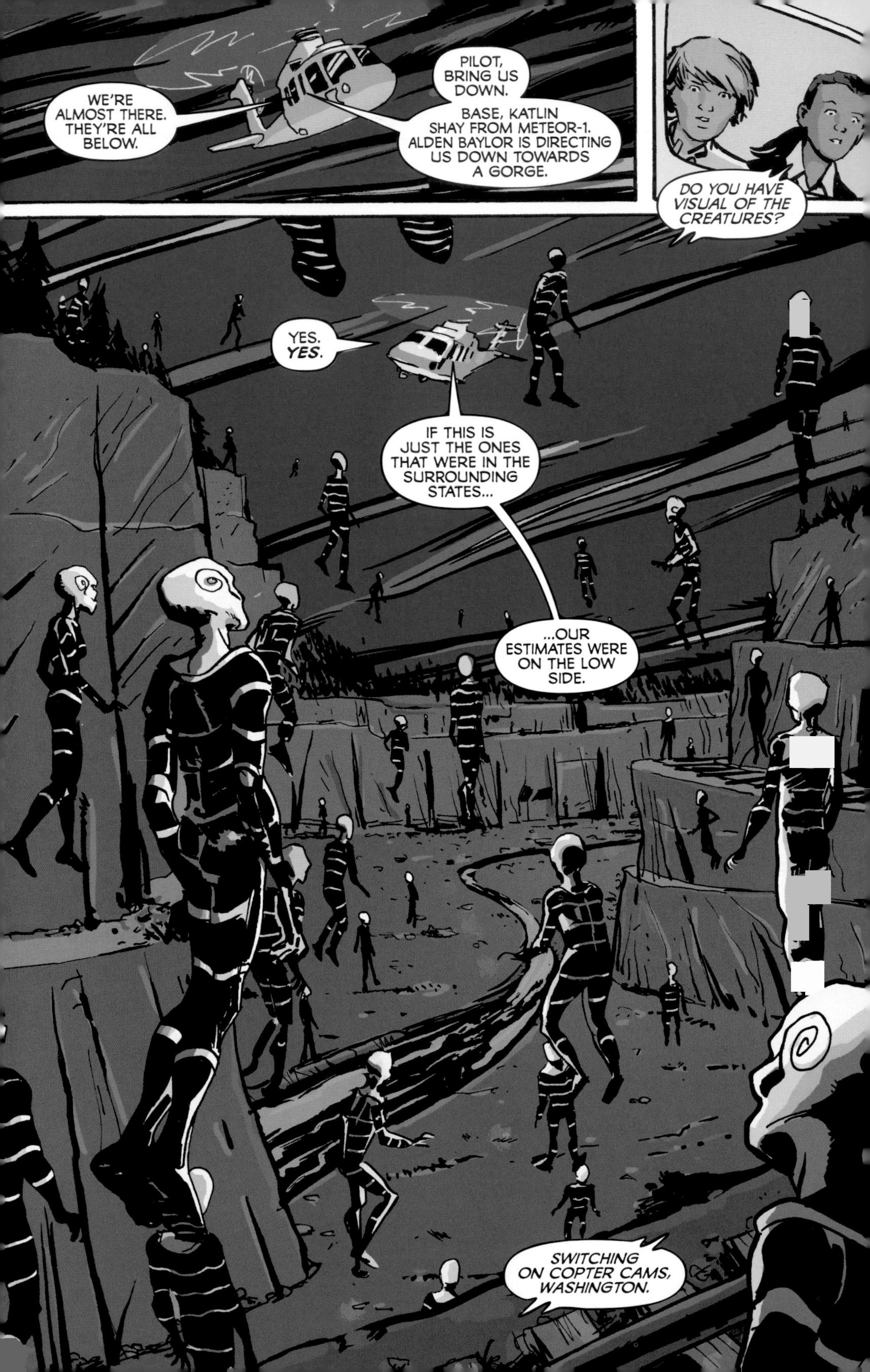
WE'RE ALMOST THERE. THEY'RE ALL BELOW.
PILOT, BRING US DOWN.
BASE, KATLIN SHAY FROM METEOR-1. ALDEN BAYLOR IS DIRECTING US DOWN TOWARDS A GORGE.
DO YOU HAVE VISUAL OF THE CREATURES?
YES. *YES*.
IF THIS IS JUST THE ONES THAT WERE IN THE SURROUNDING STATES...
...OUR ESTIMATES WERE ON THE LOW SIDE.
SWITCHING ON COPTER CAMS, WASHINGTON.

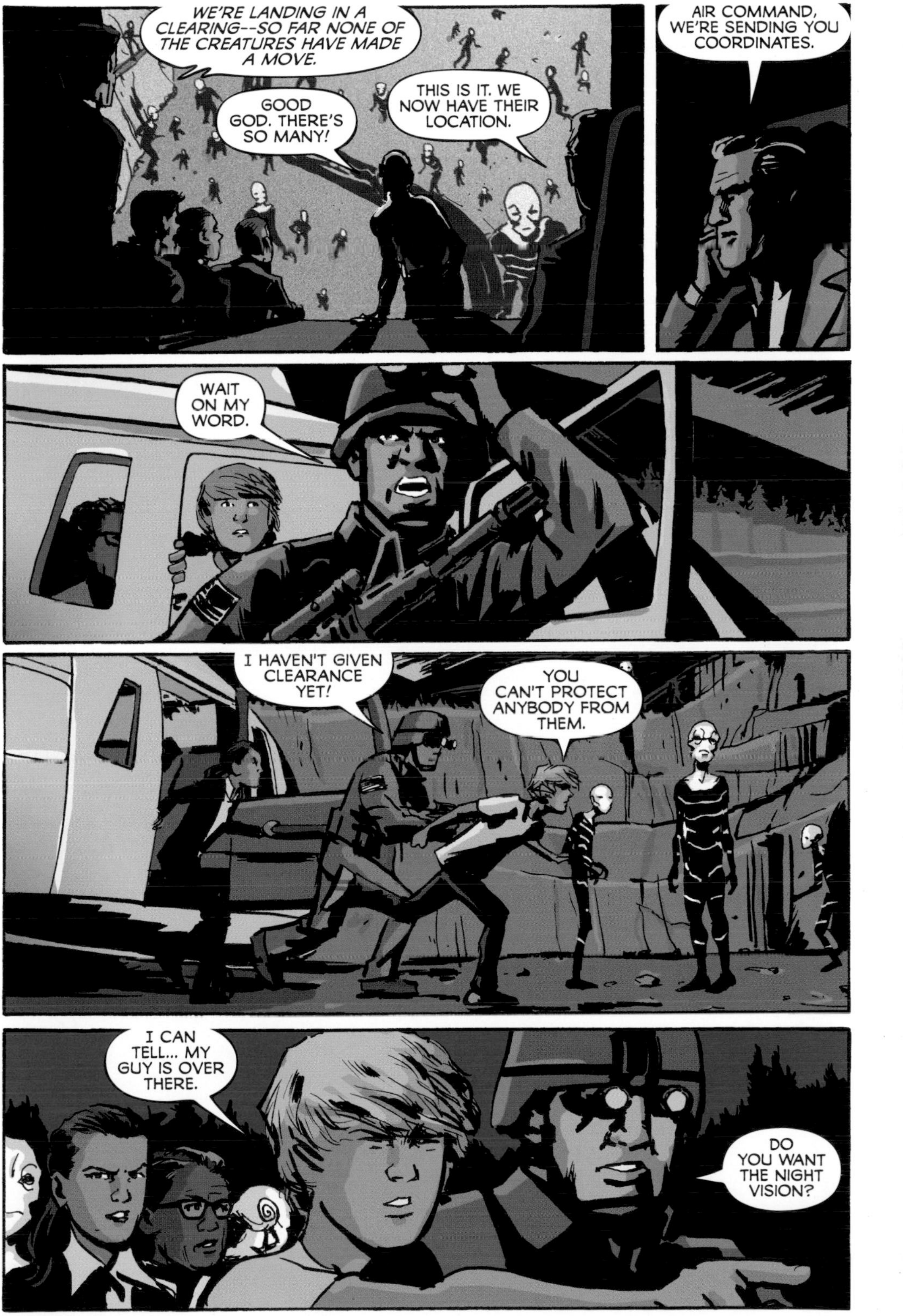
WE'RE LANDING IN A CLEARING--SO FAR NONE OF THE CREATURES HAVE MADE A MOVE.
GOOD GOD. THERE'S SO MANY!
THIS IS IT. WE NOW HAVE THEIR LOCATION.
AIR COMMAND, WE'RE SENDING YOU COORDINATES.
WAIT ON MY WORD.
I HAVEN'T GIVEN CLEARANCE YET!
YOU CAN'T PROTECT ANYBODY FROM THEM.
I CAN TELL... MY GUY IS OVER THERE.
DO YOU WANT THE NIGHT VISION?

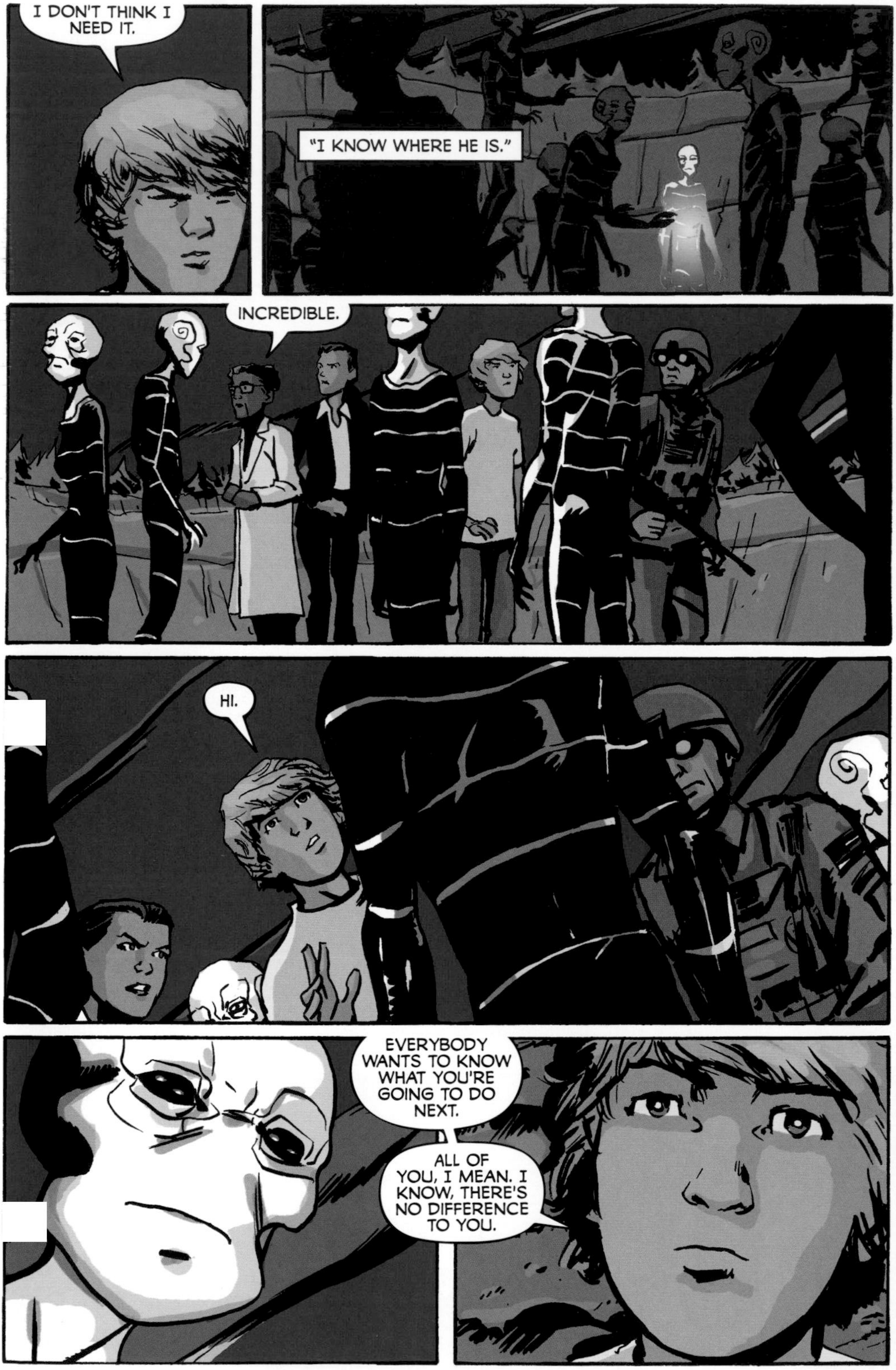
I DON'T THINK I NEED IT.
"I KNOW WHERE HE IS."
INCREDIBLE.
HI.
EVERYBODY WANTS TO KNOW WHAT YOU'RE GOING TO DO NEXT.
ALL OF YOU, I MEAN. I KNOW, THERE'S NO DIFFERENCE TO YOU.

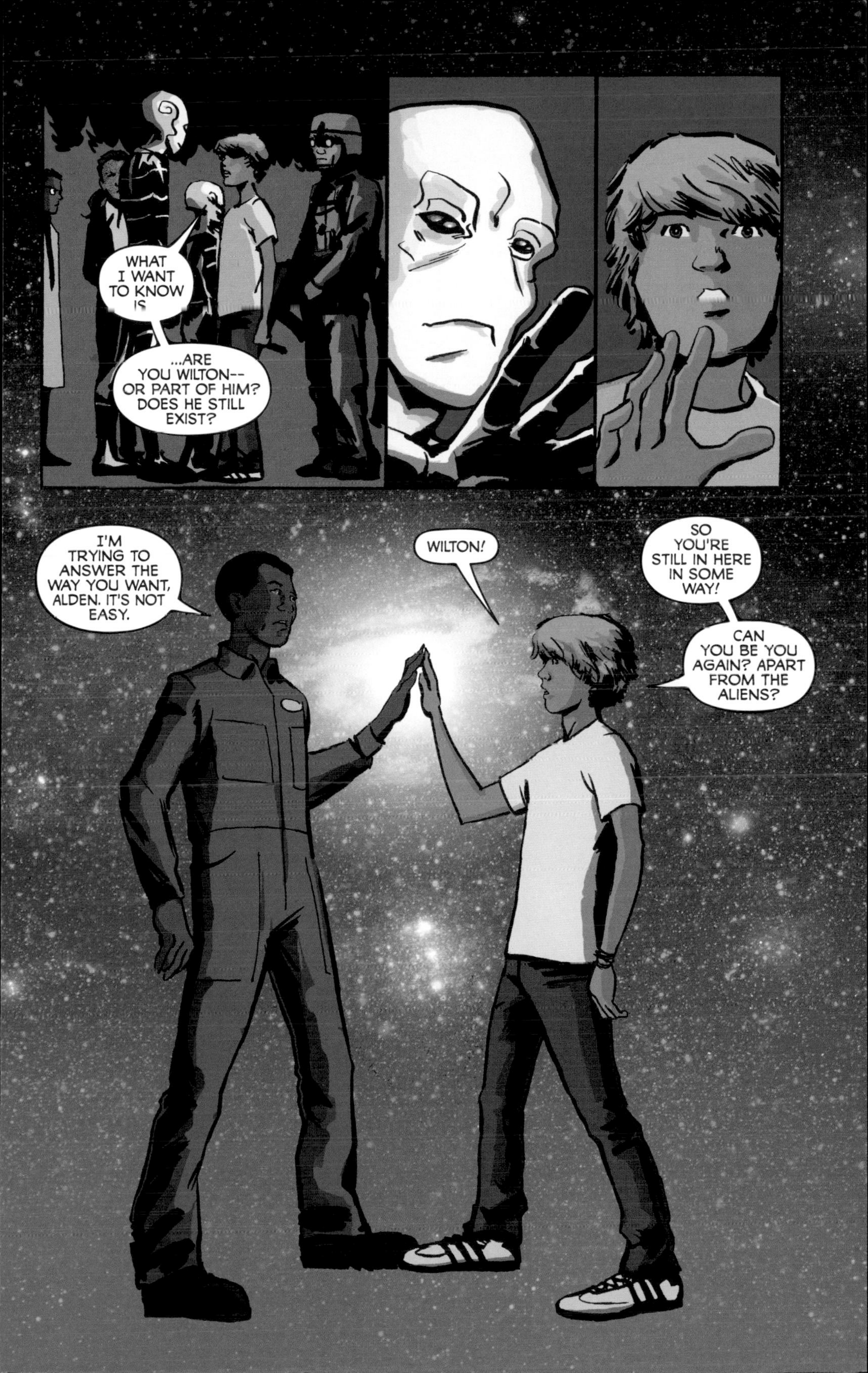
WHAT I WANT TO KNOW IS
...ARE YOU WILTON-- OR PART OF HIM? DOES HE STILL EXIST?
I'M TRYING TO ANSWER THE WAY YOU WANT, ALDEN. IT'S NOT EASY.
WILTON!
SO YOU'RE STILL IN HERE IN SOME WAY!
CAN YOU BE YOU AGAIN? APART FROM THE ALIENS?

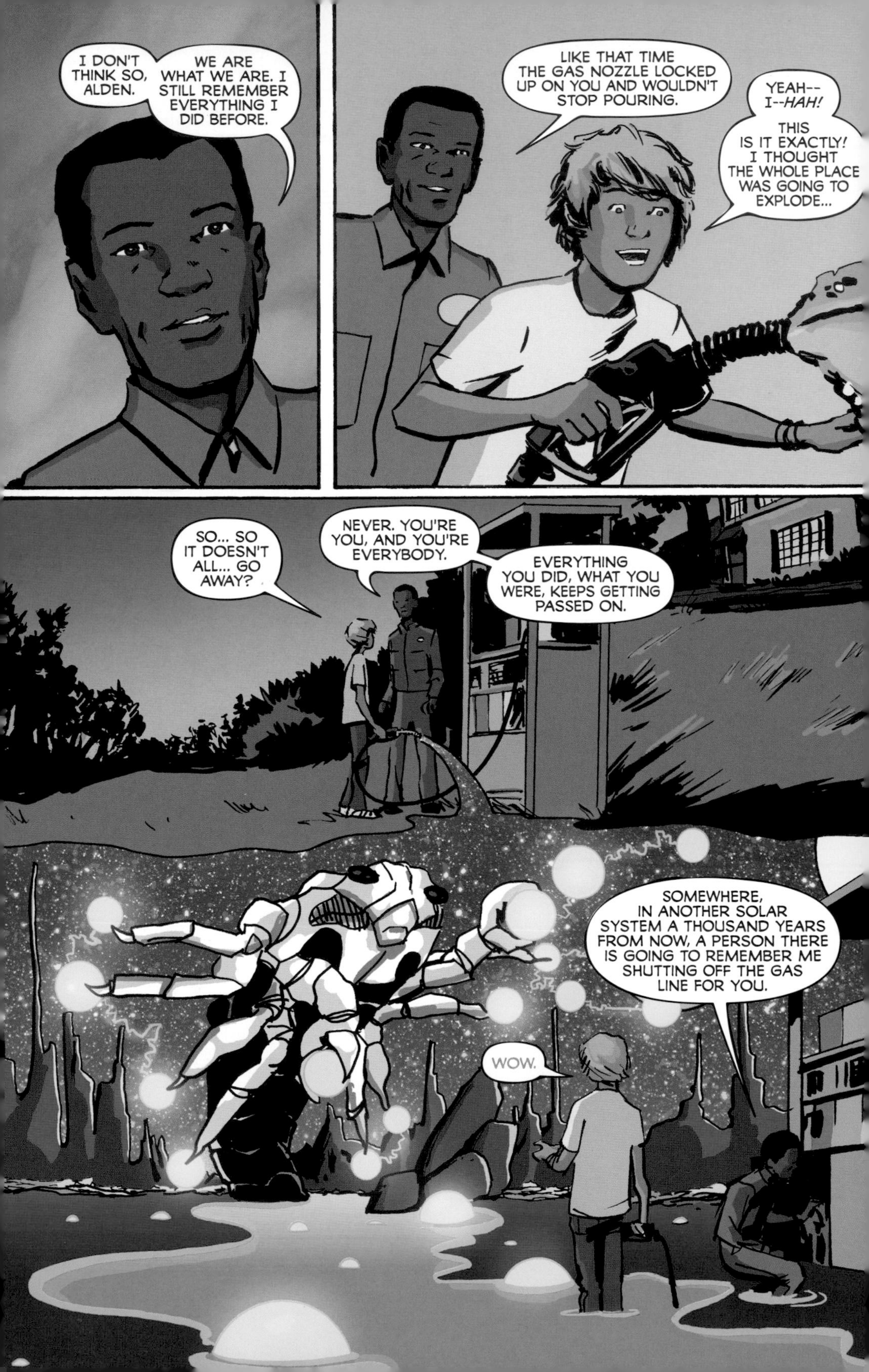
I DON'T THINK SO, ALDEN.
WE ARE WHAT WE ARE. I STILL REMEMBER EVERYTHING I DID BEFORE.
LIKE THAT TIME THE GAS NOZZLE LOCKED UP ON YOU AND WOULDN'T STOP POURING.
YEAH-- I--*HAH!*
THIS IS IT EXACTLY! I THOUGHT THE WHOLE PLACE WAS GOING TO EXPLODE...
SO... SO IT DOESN'T ALL... GO AWAY?
NEVER. YOU'RE YOU, AND YOU'RE EVERYBODY.
EVERYTHING YOU DID, WHAT YOU WERE, KEEPS GETTING PASSED ON.
SOMEWHERE, IN ANOTHER SOLAR SYSTEM A THOUSAND YEARS FROM NOW, A PERSON THERE IS GOING TO REMEMBER ME SHUTTING OFF THE GAS LINE FOR YOU.
WOW.

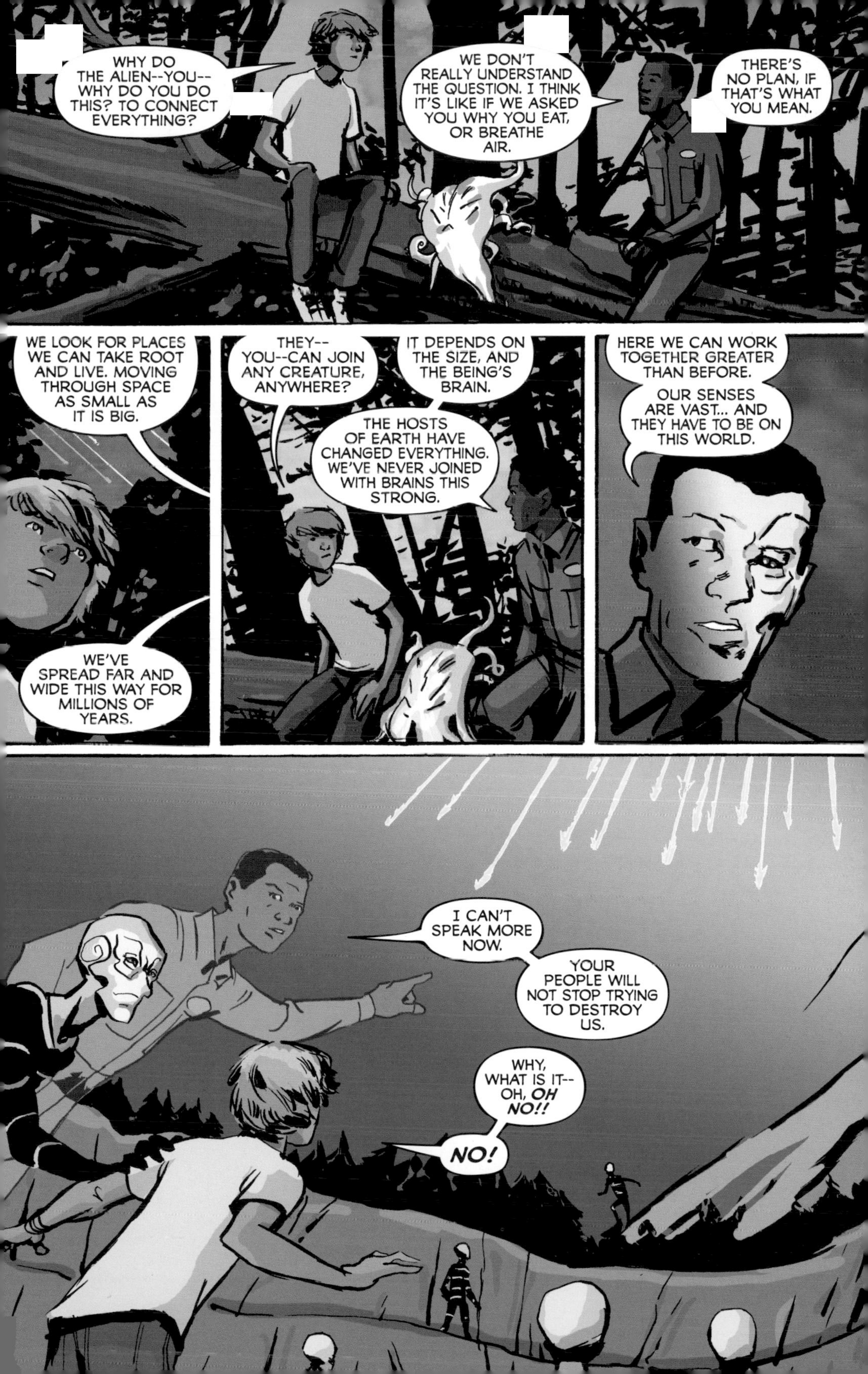
WHY DO THE ALIEN--YOU-- WHY DO YOU DO THIS? TO CONNECT EVERYTHING?
WE DON'T REALLY UNDERSTAND THE QUESTION. I THINK IT'S LIKE IF WE ASKED YOU WHY YOU EAT, OR BREATHE AIR.
THERE'S NO PLAN, IF THAT'S WHAT YOU MEAN.
WE LOOK FOR PLACES WE CAN TAKE ROOT AND LIVE. MOVING THROUGH SPACE AS SMALL AS IT IS BIG.
WE'VE SPREAD FAR AND WIDE THIS WAY FOR MILLIONS OF YEARS.
THEY-- YOU--CAN JOIN ANY CREATURE, ANYWHERE?
IT DEPENDS ON THE SIZE, AND THE BEING'S BRAIN.
THE HOSTS OF EARTH HAVE CHANGED EVERYTHING. WE'VE NEVER JOINED WITH BRAINS THIS STRONG.
HERE WE CAN WORK TOGETHER GREATER THAN BEFORE.
OUR SENSES ARE VAST... AND THEY HAVE TO BE ON THIS WORLD.
I CAN'T SPEAK MORE NOW.
YOUR PEOPLE WILL NOT STOP TRYING TO DESTROY US.
WHY, WHAT IS IT-- OH, ***OH NO!!***
NO!

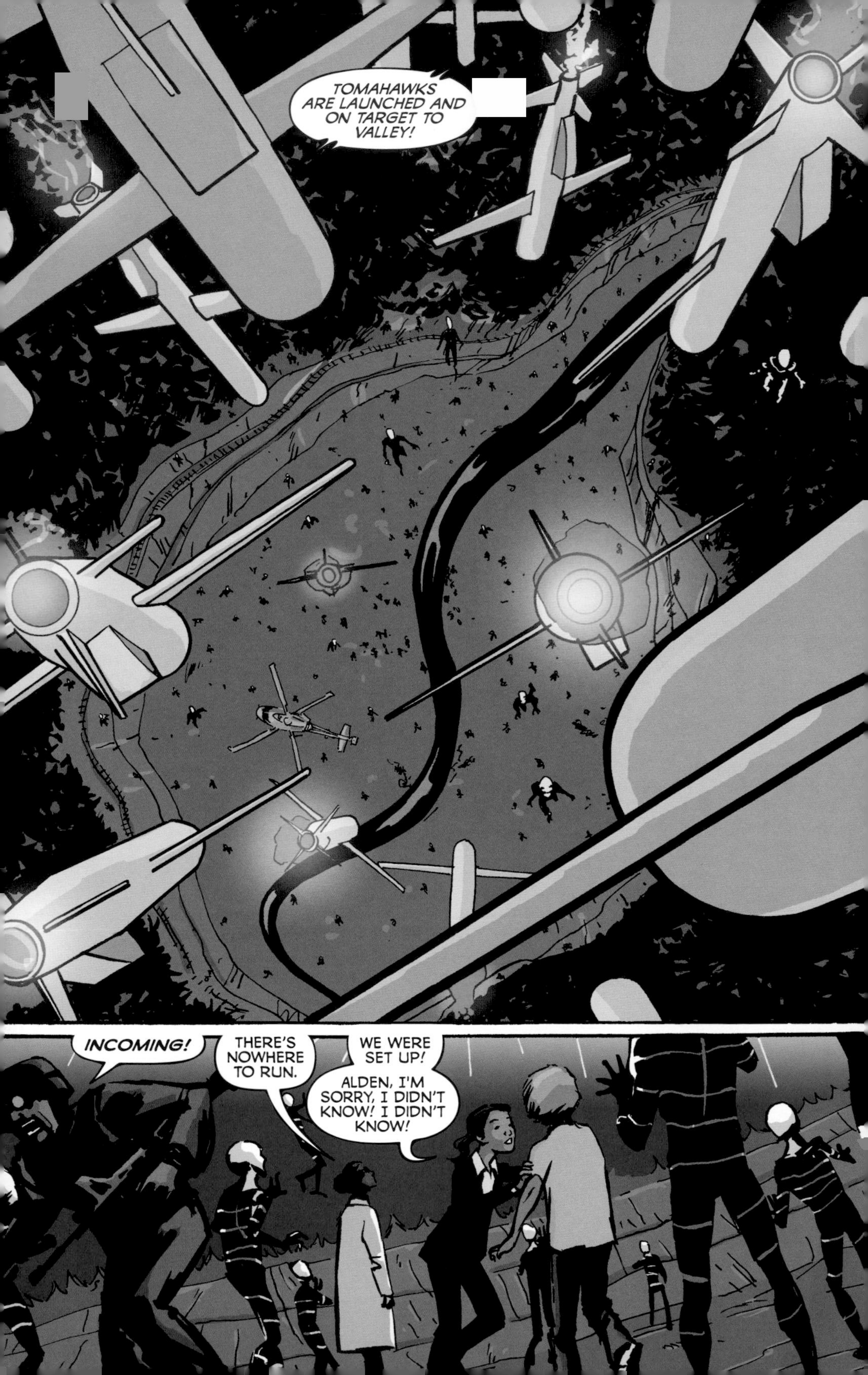
TOMAHAWKS ARE LAUNCHED AND ON TARGET TO VALLEY!
INCOMING!
THERE'S NOWHERE TO RUN.
WE WERE SET UP!
ALDEN, I'M SORRY, I DIDN'T KNOW! I DIDN'T KNOW!

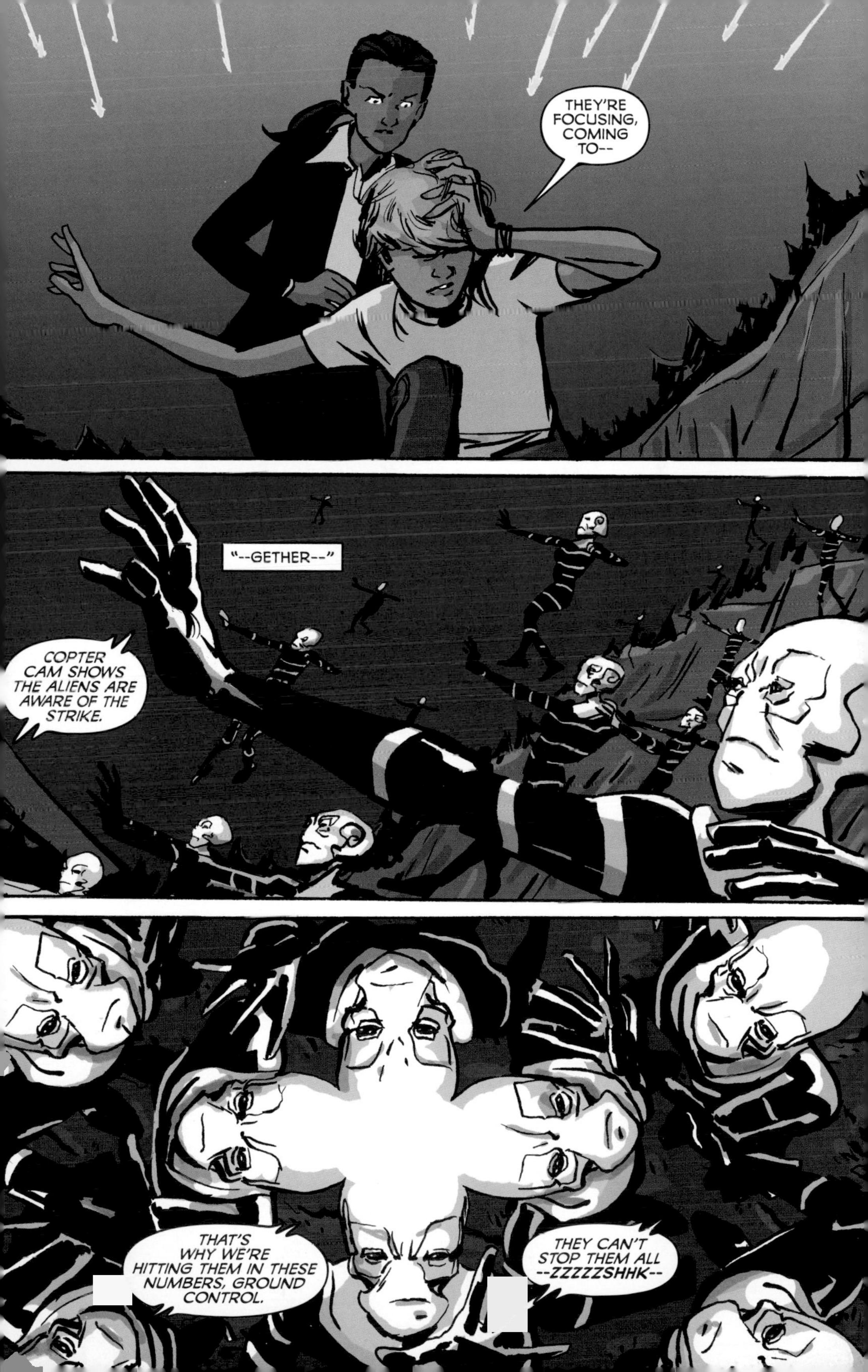
THEY'RE FOCUSING, COMING TO--
"--GETHER--"
COPTER CAM SHOWS THE ALIENS ARE AWARE OF THE STRIKE.
THAT'S WHY WE'RE HITTING THEM IN THESE NUMBERS, GROUND CONTROL.
THEY CAN'T STOP THEM ALL --ZZZZZSHHK--

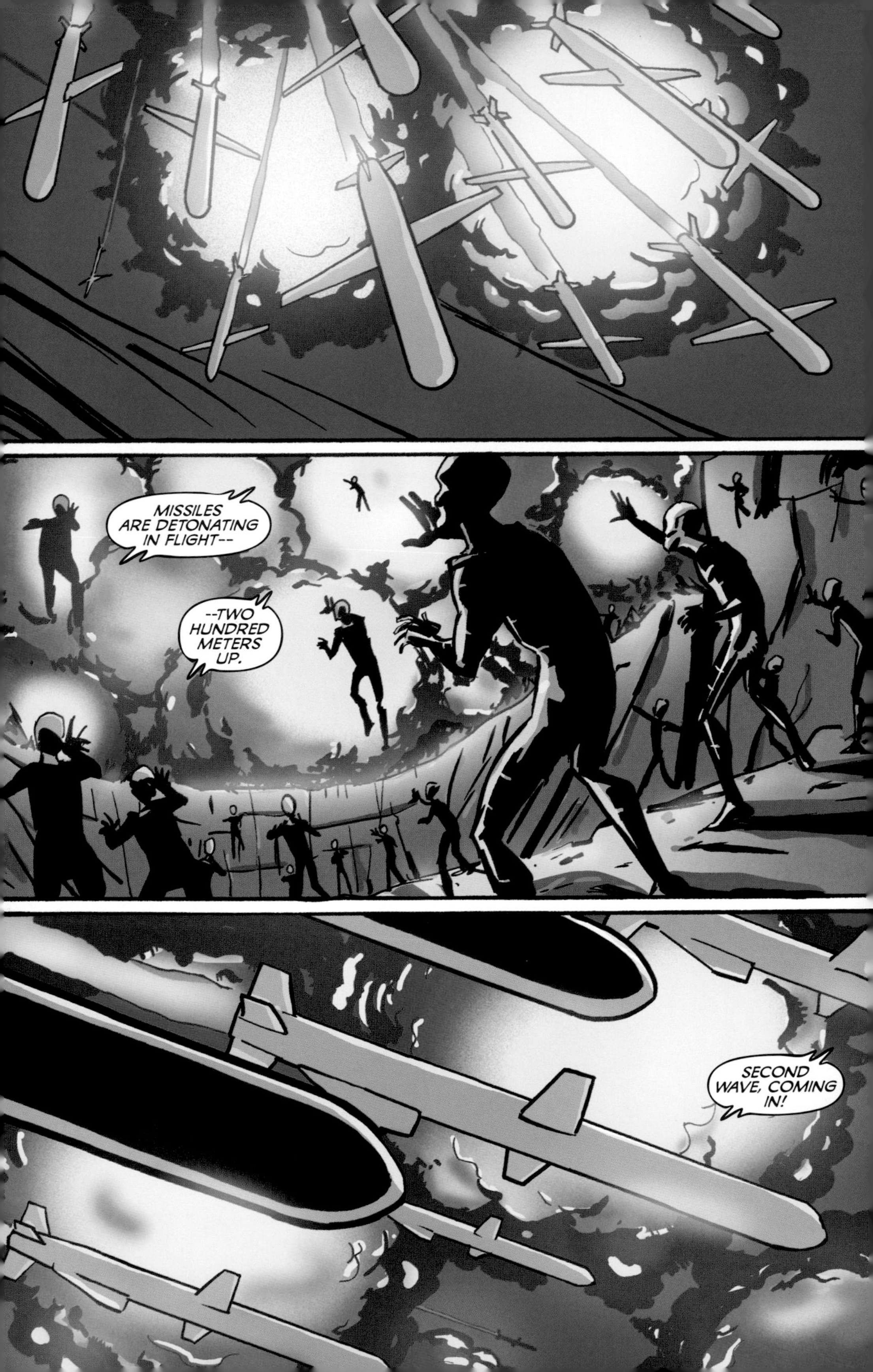
MISSILES ARE DETONATING IN FLIGHT--
--TWO HUNDRED METERS UP.
SECOND WAVE, COMING IN!

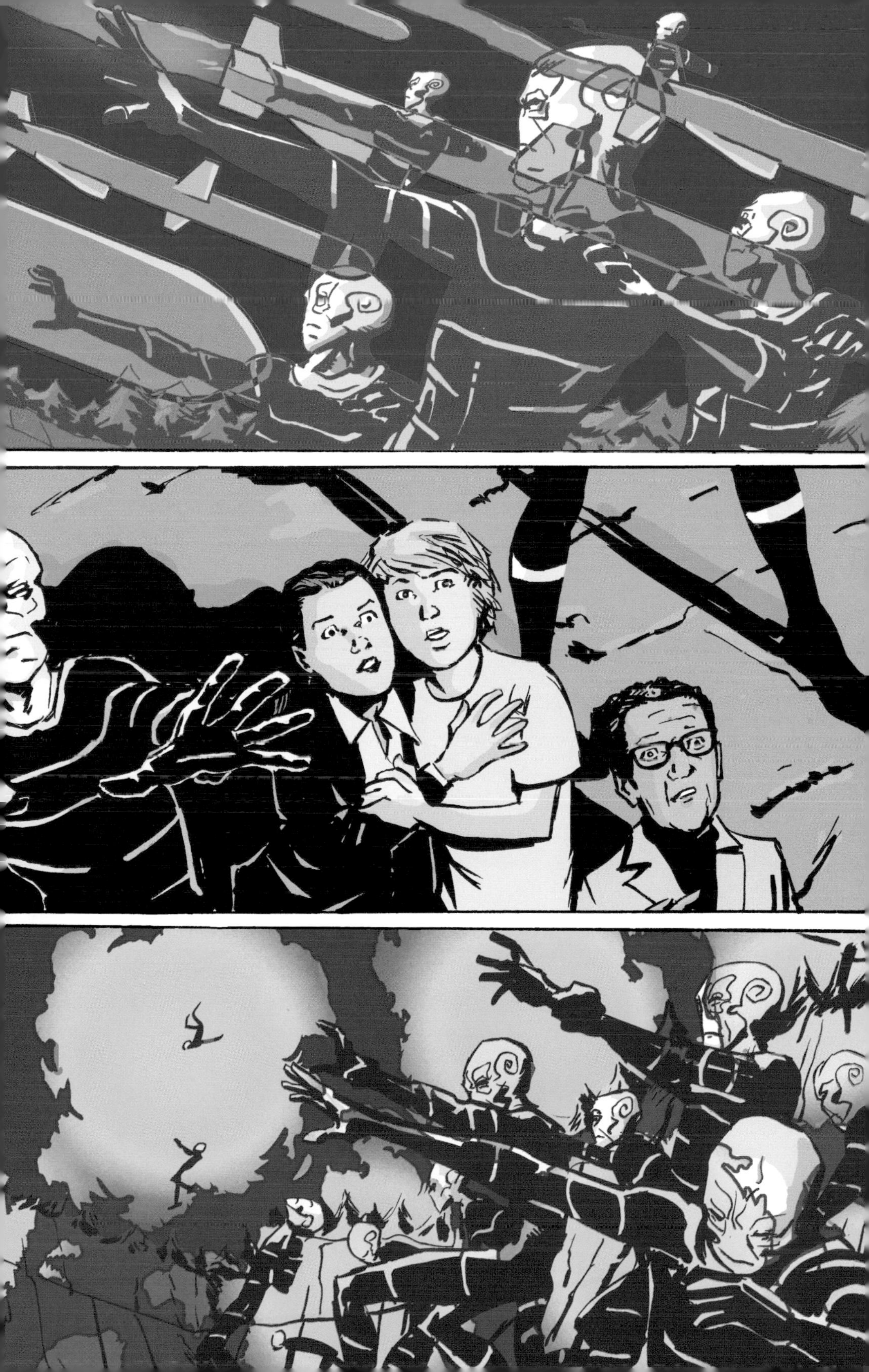

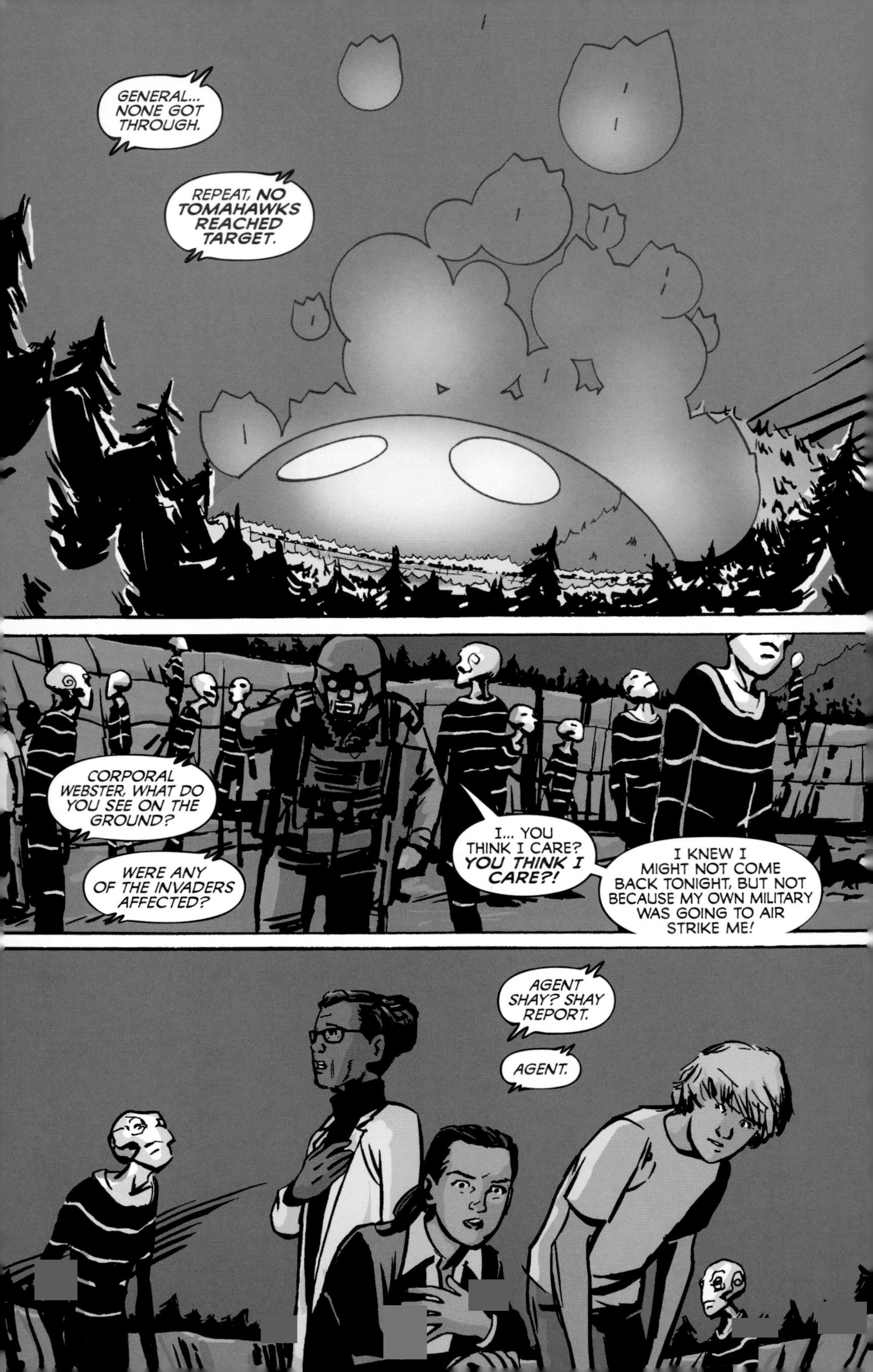
GENERAL... NONE GOT THROUGH.
REPEAT, NO TOMAHAWKS REACHED TARGET.
CORPORAL WEBSTER, WHAT DO YOU SEE ON THE GROUND?
WERE ANY OF THE INVADERS AFFECTED?
I... YOU THINK I CARE? YOU THINK I CARE?!
I KNEW I MIGHT NOT COME BACK TONIGHT, BUT NOT BECAUSE MY OWN MILITARY WAS GOING TO AIR STRIKE ME!
AGENT SHAY? SHAY REPORT.
AGENT.

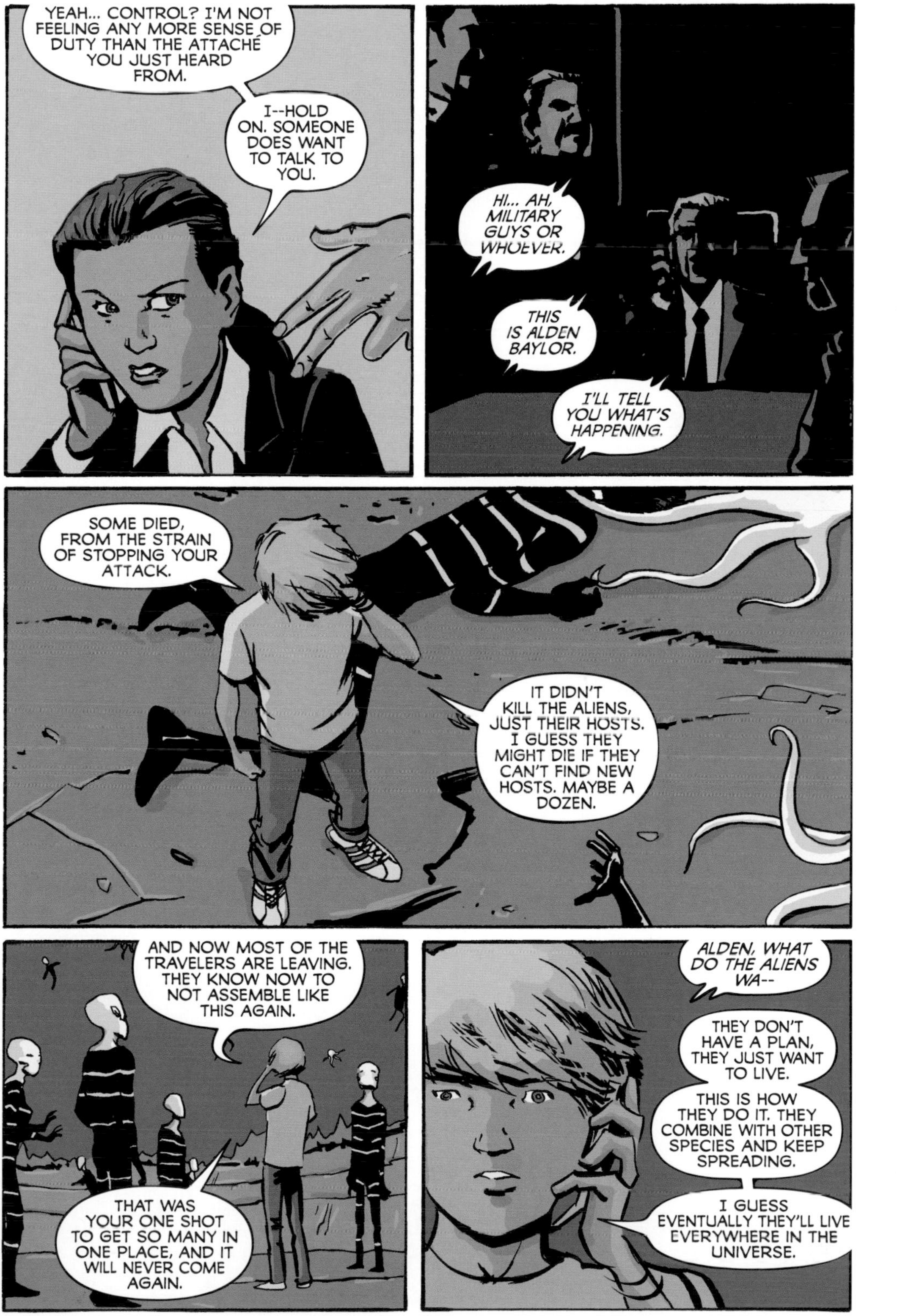
YEAH... CONTROL? I'M NOT FEELING ANY MORE SENSE OF DUTY THAN THE ATTACHÉ YOU JUST HEARD FROM.
I--HOLD ON. SOMEONE DOES WANT TO TALK TO YOU.
HI... AH, MILITARY GUYS OR WHOEVER.
THIS IS ALDEN BAYLOR.
I'LL TELL YOU WHAT'S HAPPENING.
SOME DIED, FROM THE STRAIN OF STOPPING YOUR ATTACK.
IT DIDN'T KILL THE ALIENS, JUST THEIR HOSTS. I GUESS THEY MIGHT DIE IF THEY CAN'T FIND NEW HOSTS. MAYBE A DOZEN.
AND NOW MOST OF THE TRAVELERS ARE LEAVING. THEY KNOW NOW TO NOT ASSEMBLE LIKE THIS AGAIN.
THAT WAS YOUR ONE SHOT TO GET SO MANY IN ONE PLACE, AND IT WILL NEVER COME AGAIN.
ALDEN, WHAT DO THE ALIENS WA--
THEY DON'T HAVE A PLAN, THEY JUST WANT TO LIVE.
THIS IS HOW THEY DO IT. THEY COMBINE WITH OTHER SPECIES AND KEEP SPREADING.
I GUESS EVENTUALLY THEY'LL LIVE EVERYWHERE IN THE UNIVERSE.

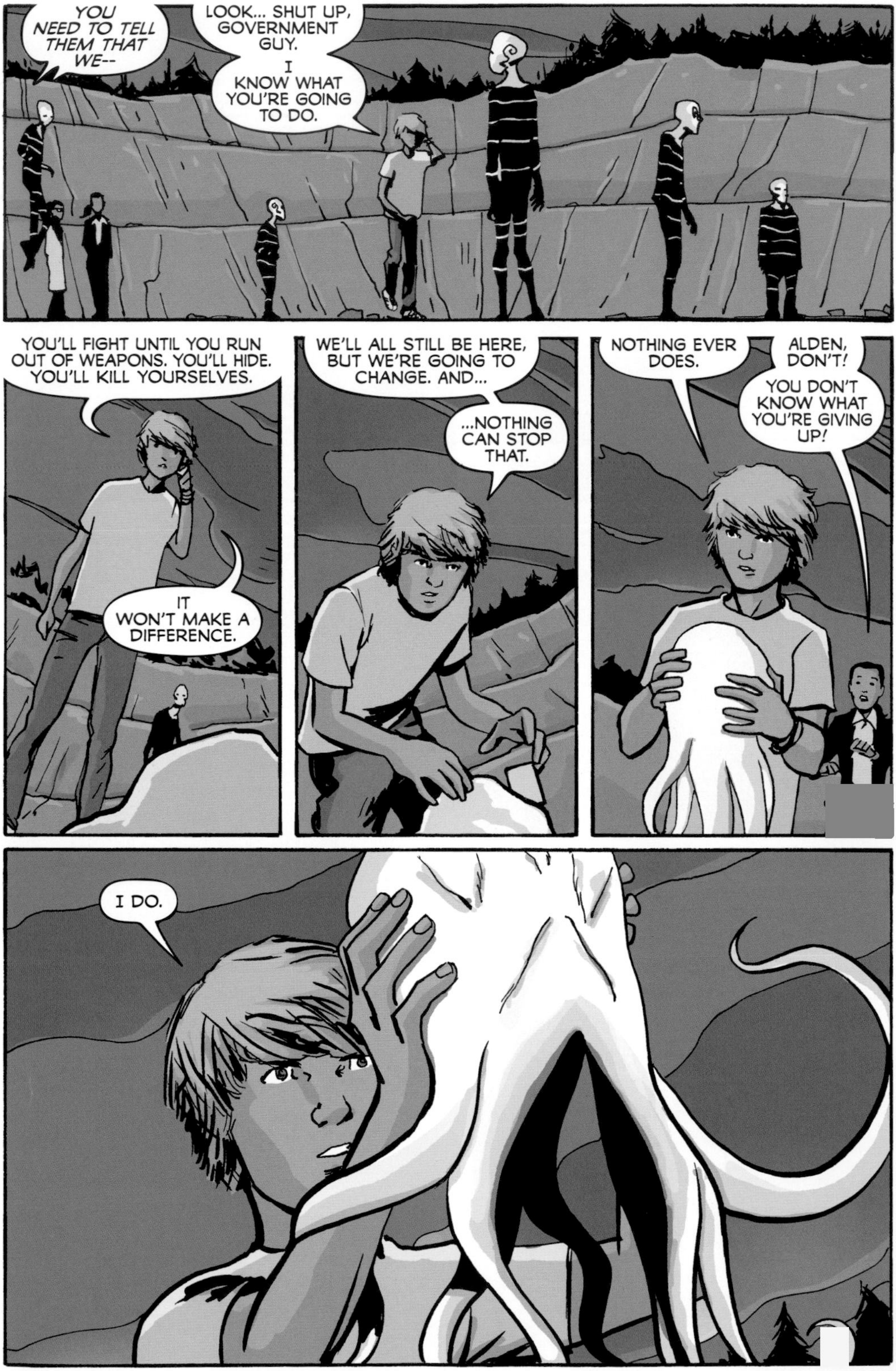
YOU NEED TO TELL THEM THAT WE--
LOOK... SHUT UP, GOVERNMENT GUY.
I KNOW WHAT YOU'RE GOING TO DO.
YOU'LL FIGHT UNTIL YOU RUN OUT OF WEAPONS. YOU'LL HIDE. YOU'LL KILL YOURSELVES.
IT WON'T MAKE A DIFFERENCE.
WE'LL ALL STILL BE HERE, BUT WE'RE GOING TO CHANGE. AND...
...NOTHING CAN STOP THAT.
NOTHING EVER DOES.
ALDEN, DON'T!
YOU DON'T KNOW WHAT YOU'RE GIVING UP!
I DO.

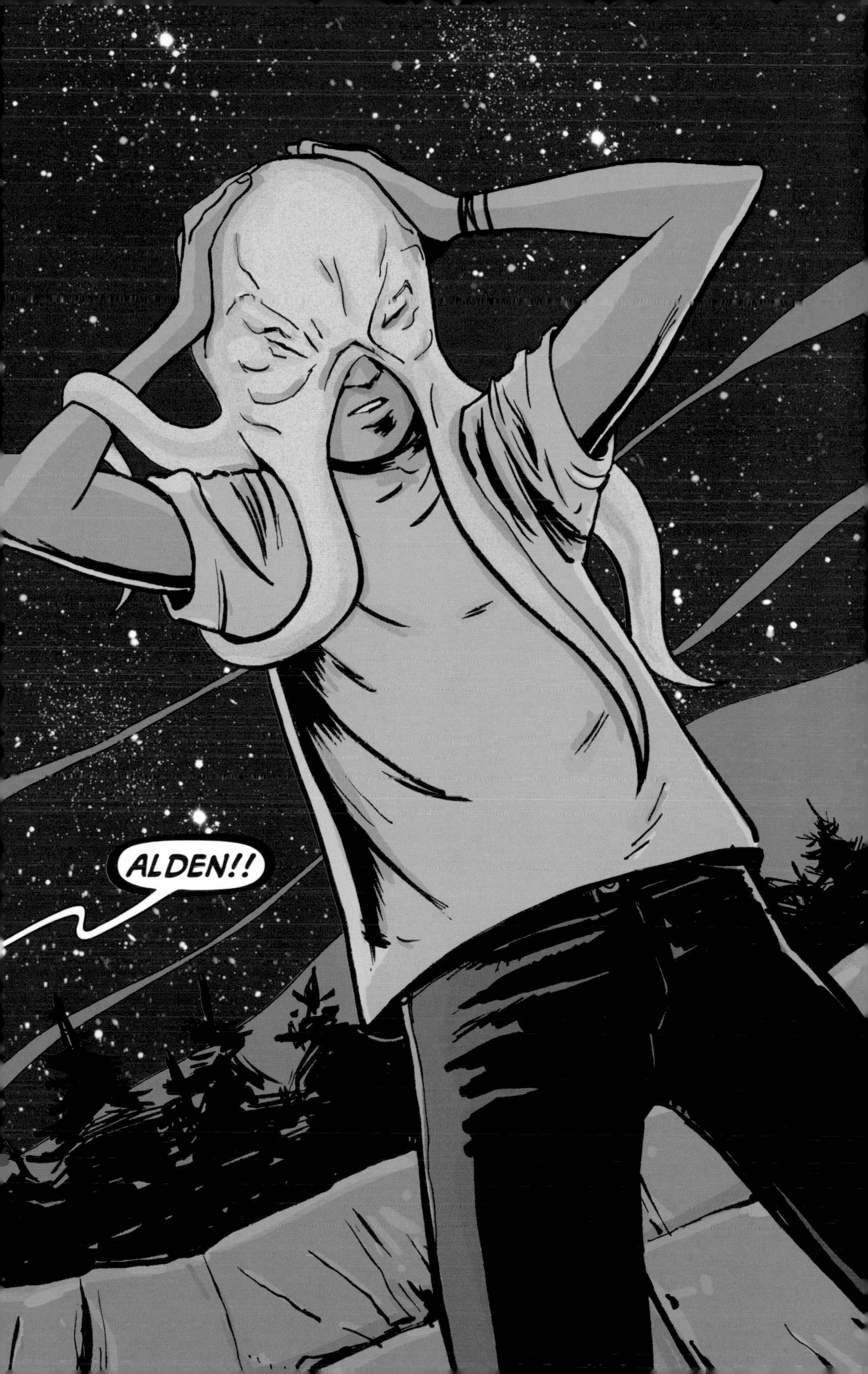
ALDEN!!

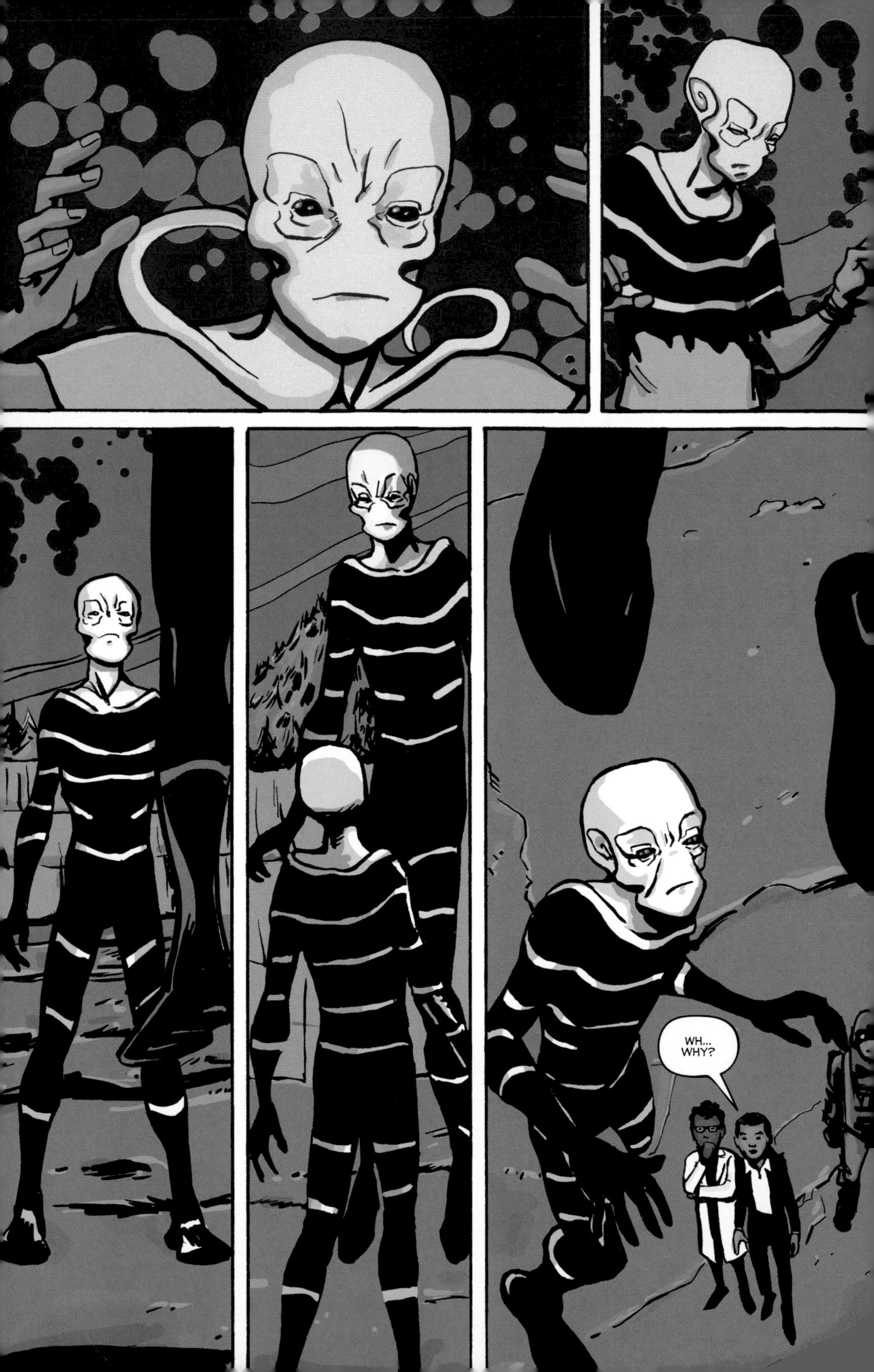
WH... WHY?

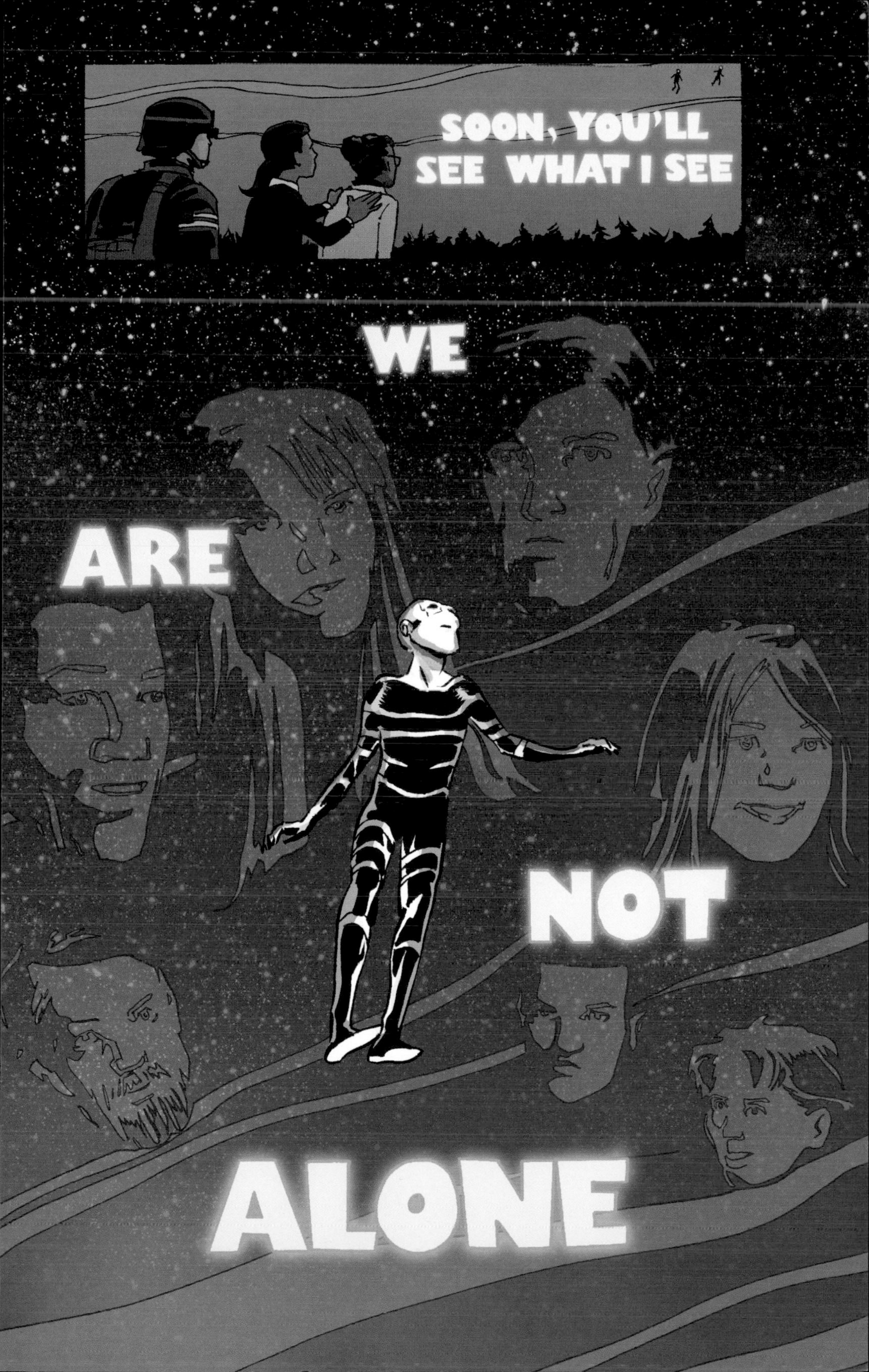
SOON, YOU'LL SEE WHAT I SEE
WE
ARE
NOT
ALONE

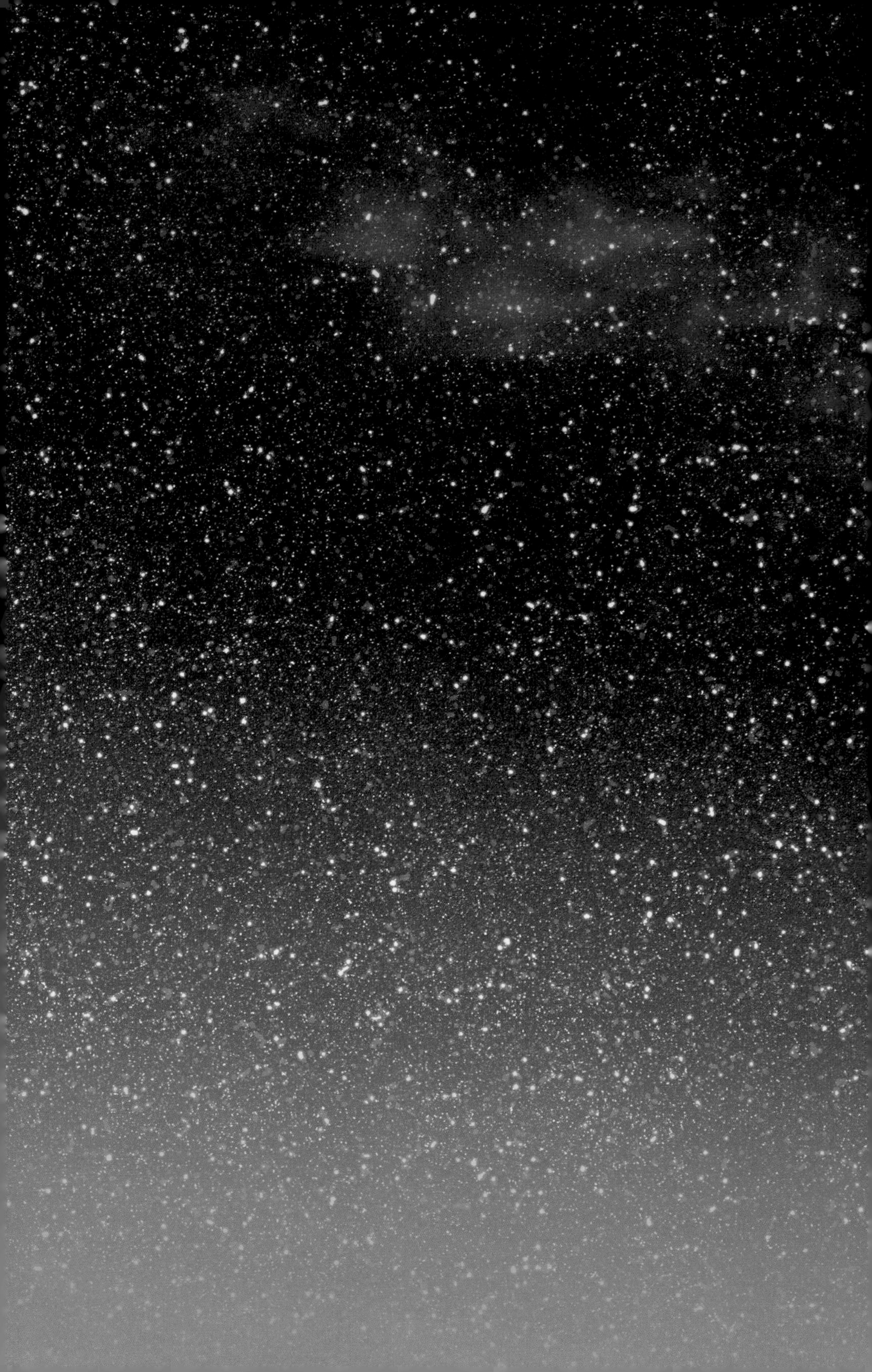

JEFF PARKER

JEFF PARKER HAS WRITTEN THE ADVENTURES OF *AQUAMAN*, *BATMAN, THE HULK* AND *THE X-MEN* AS WELL AS HIS OWN CREATIONS LIKE *UNDERGROUND, THE INTERMAN*, AND *MYSTERIUS THE UNFATHOMABLE*. WITH WIFE JILL AND ALIEN KIDS ALLIE AND STEPHEN, HE LIVES IN PORTLAND, OREGON AND CAN BE FOUND ONLINE AS @JEFFPARKER AT TWITTER AND HIS HOME SITE PARKERSPACE.COM.

SANDY JARRELL

SANDY JARRELL IS A COMIC ARTIST WHOSE WORK INCLUDES
BATMAN '66, UNFAIR (MONKEYBRAIN) AND ISSUE 39 OF *WASTELAND*
FOR ONI PRESS. HE LIVES IN CARY, NORTH CAROLINA WITH HIS
WIFE, TWO KIDS AND MICRO-TERRIER. HE'S ON THE INTERNET AT
SANDYJARRELL.COM AND ON TWITTER AT @SANDY_JARRELL.

KEVIN VOLO

KEVIN VOLO IS A FREELANCE COLORIST WHO HAS WORKED ON SEVERAL INDEPENDENT TITLES SUCH AS BIG DOG INC'S *REX ZOMBIE KILLER*, ZENESCOPE'S *2013 HALLOWEEN ISSUE*, AND APE ENTERTAINMENT'S *ATHENA VOLTAIRE*. HE HAS WORKED AS PART OF THE HI-FI COLOR TEAM ON NUMEROUS DC TITLES SUCH AS *ACTION COMICS*, *JSA*, *NIGHTWING*, *BOOSTER GOLD*, *TEEN TITANS*, AND *FIRESTORM*. HE IS ALSO THE WRITER AND COLORIST FOR HIS OWN SUCCESSFULLY FUNDED KICKSTARTER WEBCOMIC *MAX & THORNE*, ON WHICH HE COLLABORATES WITH HIS SON MAX AND ARTIST DAFU YU. YOU CAN VIEW KEVIN'S WORK AT ENIGMAMEDIAGROUP.COM AND LEARN MORE ABOUT MAX & THORNE AT MAXANDTHORNE.COM AND @KEVINVOLO.

DOWN SET. FIGHT!

DOWN, SET, FIGHT!

By Chad Bowers, Chris Sims, and Scott Kowalchuk

152 PAGES ▪ SOFTCOVER ▪ FULL COLOR

ISBN 978-1-62010-116-2

SCOTT PILGRIM
1
SCOTT PILGRIM'S PRECIOUS LITTLE LIFE
BY BRYAN LEE O'MALLEY
COLOR EDITION

SCOTT PILGRIM HARDCOVER, VOL. 1: PRECIOUS LITTLE LIFE

By Bryan Lee O'Malley

192 PAGES ▪ HARDCOVER ▪ FULL COLOR

ISBN 978-1-62010-000-4

WASTELAND

WASTELAND: THE APOCALYPTIC EDITION, VOL. 1

By Antony Johnston & Christopher Mitten

384 PAGES ▪ HARDCOVER ▪ BLACK & WHITE

ISBN 978-1-934964-19-4

THE SIXTH GUN
BUNN
HURTT

THE SIXTH GUN, VOL. 1: COLD DEAD FINGERS

By Cullen Bunn & Brian Hurtt

176 PAGES ▪ SOFTCOVER ▪ FULL COLOR

ISBN 978-1-934964-60-6

CAPOTE

CAPOTE IN KANSAS HARDCOVER

By Ande Parks & Chris Samnee

160 PAGES ▪ HARDCOVER ▪ BLACK & WHITE

ISBN 978-1-934964-87-3

MEGAGOGO
WOOK JIN CLARK

MEGAGOGO, VOL. 1

By Wook-Jin Clark

176 PAGES ▪ SOFTCOVER ▪ BLACK & WHITE

ISBN 978-1-62010-117-9

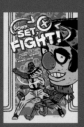

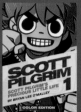

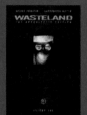

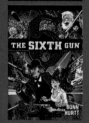

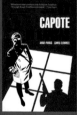

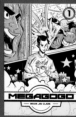

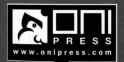